Open Source Software

Open Source Software
Implementation and Management

Paul Kavanagh

ELSEVIER
DIGITAL
PRESS

AMSTERDAM • BOSTON • HEIDELBERG • LONDON
NEW YORK • OXFORD • PARIS • SAN DIEGO•
SAN FRANCISCO • SINGAPORE • SYDNEY • TOKYO

Elsevier Digital Press
200 Wheeler Road, Burlington, MA 01803, USA
Linacre House, Jordan Hill, Oxford OX2 8DP, UK

∞ Recognizing the importance of preserving what has been written, Elsevier prints its books on acid-free paper whenever possible.

Library of Congress Cataloging-in-Publication Data
Application submitted.

ISBN: 1-55558-320-2

British Library Cataloguing-in-Publication Data
A catalogue record for this book is available from the British Library.

For information on all Digital Press publications
visit our Web site at www.digitalpress.com and www.bh.com/digitalpress

04 05 06 07 08 09 10 9 8 7 6 5 4 3 2 1

Printed in the United States of America

To John, Jessica, Danny, and Allison.

Contents

4   Five Immediate Open Source Opportunities   67

5   Five More Open Source Opportunities   99

Preface

Open source software is now under serious consideration in many organizations. The success of several open source products, particularly Apache and Linux, in the enterprise has come surprisingly quickly, given that they were not commercially available ten years ago. It is important for managers responsible for adopting technology to be fully aware of the issues that open source represents to their organizations.

A set of new technologies is nothing new to the information technology professional, of course. There are always new technologies and business structures, and the steps that we take to evaluate and adopt them are not so different. But each new set of innovations can also bring new kinds of challenges. Open source offers, in addition to a very rich set of technologies with long histories, a set of new ways to look at certain problems. Issues that are new now include:

- A variety of new licensing options, and claims from some quarters that some of these introduce new business risks

- Opportunities to deal with the loosely structured community that creates open source, from selecting distributions and buying products to hiring and retaining staff

- The possibility that open source software is built and maintained in a different way, and the implications this has for our organizations

The biggest challenge we all face at this time is the difficult climate our industry is in. This is a very tight time for spending, and every technology decision needs to be justified by carefully analyzing costs and risks. Fortunately, open source may be able to help us here, and this book will stick closely to the areas where we can achieve a clear and reasonably rapid return on investment.

Intended Audience for This Book

This book is written for professional managers and implementers of information technology, who are not currently experts in open source software, but who will, over the next year or so, evaluate it and then, in many cases, adopt the technologies, tools, and practices for themselves and their teams.

The book is aimed, in a sense, at generalists. That is partly because most open source software is a set of disruptive technologies rather than in direct line with what is in place. When a set of technologies is mature, we often react to these technologies in specialized, rigid ways. As a new set of technologies is introduced, they can often combine differently. The Web, for instance, changed the boundaries of what many people do. Also, with new ideas, it is often necessary to do everything from building the business case to doing hands-on experimentation. With each component, we will look at the business case, at the technology from an overview, and at the way it works in practice to install and use.

This is a self-teaching guide to the issues faced in transitioning to this new set of technologies. The issues range from business and social concerns through technology and architecture to cookbook-style details. The book should:

- Convince you that there are roles for open source software in your organization

- Place open source development in the context of software history

- Enumerate the various scenarios involving open source that are more (or less) appropriate for most organizations over the next couple of years

- Give you enough examples and successful references for the constituent parts so you feel comfortable entering a process of selecting and using them

- Contrast and compare open source products among themselves and with products for the Windows systems and others that are most widely used today so you know what they are for and which ones you'll need

- Guide the process of getting an open source lab off the ground quickly and without errors and wasted time to the point where you can run it yourself.

This book is aimed at the group known to technology marketers as the "early majority." These are not the very first people to adopt technology, who often do it for its own sake. It is the group of people who, in their professional life, take new ideas in technology and practice and have the vision and practical leadership to put them in widespread business use in their organizations.

The emphasis of the book is on developing new uses for systems using open source software rather than just considering the migration of existing systems. In my experience, it is difficult to cost justify migrations and to achieve customer satisfaction. Migration and interoperability always play a part in system introduction and are thoroughly covered, but only as a tactical element.

How This Book Is Structured

First, given the independent history of the open source community, it is useful to deal with the people, organizations, and programs that have brought us to this point; however, we will do that briefly, because there are many good sources of this information available.

Next, we cover the question of whether open source systems are ready for use in any circumstance, particularly in large conventional organizations (including commercial businesses and government organizations). We will look at the advantages open source has offered to others and can offer to you, as well as the challenges you will likely face in attempting to adopt it and introduce it in your organization.

After this, the book looks at the systems that can be implemented now from the perspective of a business decision maker. My emphasis is the systems that will work and deliver value quickly, the measures used to determine that, and the road maps for deployment. We separate the systems, where open source is already a preferred choice that will work in almost every organization, from those where a careful evaluation must be made or where there is more work to be done before a pragmatic decision would select open source.

The next major part of the book reviews the technology components of open source software, including strengths, weaknesses, and migration and interoperability issues, including:

- The Linux operating system, the BSD alternative, and their variations and distributions
- How open source systems have actually been developed; the methods and languages used, and lessons we can learn from them
- Server applications, including infrastructure, Web, database, and communication servers
- Desktop applications, including desktops, browsers, office suites, and a variety of professional and personal applications

Next, we cover the methods for managing open source in the organization, including best practices for management of infrastructure, development, costs, risks, and licensing. There are sections on how to introduce open source to the organization, the specific hands-on details of setting up an open source lab, pitfalls to avoid as a new user of these technologies, and best practices and tricks for interoperability. The business scenarios are reviewed using simple spreadsheet models to assess costs, benefits, and risks, so you can use them as a basis for analyzing your own situation.

Finally, there are chapters on licensing and on essential resources for follow-up, including books and Web sites. In the open source community, the information is always out there; the trick is to navigate to it efficiently.

I've attempted to keep the style and language used in this book simple. Each chapter is quite long and contains complete treatment of a subject, but is structured into segments so that useful information can be gained in a short sitting. There is some theory, but every theoretical point is illustrated with real-life examples.

Acknowledgements

I would like to thank the Florida Linux Users Group, for inspiring me initially and then providing the support of a diverse group of users and experts working together. In particular, thanks to Adam Glass who put the group together and keeps it happening.

Kwan Lowe was technical reviewer. He reviewed this patiently and with humor and intelligence. Alan Rose patiently kept this on track, as he's done before. Tim Donar typeset the book, quietly fixing all kinds of errors.

Several people, notably Eduardo Dardet and Carolina Oria, contributed ideas in discussion on the content and approach of this book. I use ideas here that I learned from the three great managers I had at Microsoft; Joe Menchaca, Howard Kilman, and Marty Paradise. Much material has sprung from conversations with a variety of technical colleagues at Microsoft, but I'll not list their names; hopefully, they know who I mean.

Of course, I am solely responsible for all of the errors, omissions, and biases in this. Let me know of any, and I'll post them on my web site.

Open Source Software: Definitions and History

If you are going to become an advocate for open source software, there are some definitions, frequently asked questions, and historic issues that will be raised repeatedly. We will cover them in this chapter.

1.1   Definition of Terms

Open source software is software that must be distributed with source code included or easily available, such as by free download from the Internet. The source code should be in the same form that a programmer would actually use to maintain it—not, for instance, a generated, obfuscated, or intermediate code form. The license of this software will not restrict others from distributing the code or modifications and derived works under the same terms. It will not discriminate against people or fields of endeavor. Sample licenses are included in an appendix.

The Open Source Definition is included in Appendix B. The Open Source Definition (OSD) was originally written by Bruce Perens for Debian Linux and was completed in 1997. It is an established definition of open source that is simple without being too simple, and it includes several licenses that are acceptable.

Some people call software like this, distributed under licenses such as the GPL, Apache, or Mozilla licenses, "Open Source Software." Others call it "Free Software." Yet others, particularly in Europe, call it "Free/Libre or Open Source Software" (FLOSS). Capitalization of these terms varies. There are other expressions in use also, but the most widely used term seems to be open source. In this book, we will refer to software that meets the Open Source Definition as "open source." This is a simple expression that avoids capitalization and acronyms such as "OSS," both of which are annoying to read repeatedly.

The alternatives to open source can be called proprietary software, commercial software, or, alternatively, nonopen, nonfree, or closed software. These may have slightly different meanings, since there can be different ways of failing to meet the tests of open source. Some of these terms may strike a reader as derogatory, although that is not intended, probably because in our society "freedom" and "openness" sound more attractive than their opposites. For our purposes, it will be helpful to have a term for these alternatives. We will refer to software that does not completely meet the OSD as "closed code." In this use we are following Lawrence Lessig in his book, *The Future of Ideas*. If a piece of software (a product) combines open and closed elements, such as Apple OS X, it will be defined as closed. So any software product, as licensed, will be defined as either open or closed.

There is a third term that we will use in two special cases. Some software is offered under different licenses. It may be offered to some groups as open source and to others as closed. Note that to meet the terms of the OSD (to be considered open source), this must be at the user's discretion. This is a hybrid licensing model.

We can also apply the term *hybrid* when looking at a group of products. If a group of products is purchased or installed together, some of which are open source and some closed code, we will call the result a hybrid system. An example would be IBM WebSphere, which includes Apache (open source) and some other products that are closed code.

First, we will deal with a few frequently asked questions.

1.1.1   What Is Free Software?

Many people prefer the term *free software* to *open source software*. The term *free software* dates from 1984, when the idea and arguments for it were first published by Richard Stallman. The idea is not that software should be free "as in beer," or available at no charge, but that it should be free "as in speech," so you can review it and change it as you need to. The position of the Free Software Foundation is simply and well stated, including criticism of the open source position, at the Free Software Web site, http://www.gnu.org/.

The term *open source* dates from 1997, when a group of people, including Eric Raymond, Tim O'Reilly, and Bruce Perens, decided that the term *free software* and some of the arguments employed in support of it were making the idea less attractive to many businesses. They decided, as a marketing decision, to emphasize technical and practical advantages of open source software rather than arguments from principle. Those positions are stated by Eric Raymond and others at the open source Web site http://www.opensource.org.

Everyone should probably read these documents at some point. While they refer, with a few minor exceptions, to the same licenses and the same software products, some people are more motivated by the "free software" aspect and others less so. This book is intended for the pragmatic manager, who will establish the value of a particular open source product by comparing it with competitive products on a case-by-case basis using traditional measures, including price, functionality, reliability, support, and documentation. Open source code may in fact improve certain measures of quality, such as the ability to freely customize a product, to review the code to determine how some function is implemented, or to support custom extensions. Open source products also appear to have lower prices in many cases. If so, these products will do well in our evaluation on those measures.

1.1.2   What Are Good Examples of Open Source?

Flagship products of open source software include:

- The Apache Web server, with a share of 65 percent of installed worldwide Web servers and still growing
- The Linux operating system, used on millions of servers, which demonstrates that no system is too large and complex to be developed as open source
- The GNU C/C++ language suite, used to build Linux and Apache and thousands of programs on almost every operating system

These programs are huge, have been used by millions of people over many years, and have developed a reputation for reliability and customer satisfaction. There are thousands of other examples. Some are less well known than Apache and Linux and have even more users, such as the ubiquitous Internet BIND and Sendmail programs. Others are not so big or well known and may have a few thousand or a few hundred users. A good place to see a sample of open source projects is SourceForge (http://sourceforge.net).

1.1.3   Is It Necessary to Adopt Open Source Wholesale?

It is possible to assemble a complete "platform" from open source software, and many of the most popular open source programs work well together.

Some small startup companies have done this. For most people, open source solutions will be adopted one product at a time. Most adopters will not be able to, or desire to, discard all closed code software at this time, and there is no reason they should need to. Many new solutions, such as IBM WebSphere, contain a mixture of open software and closed code.

It is possible to run open source products on existing Windows installations, or to migrate closed code programs you already have to run on Linux.

1.1.4   Does "Open Source" Mean Linux?

It is possible to adopt open source without using Linux at all. Many developers, for example, may use open source on Windows. On servers, for example, Apache is an open source Web server that runs on Windows and UNIX servers and IBM mainframes as well as Linux.

On workstations, OpenOffice rivals Microsoft Office in functionality and can be installed from CD or the Internet in less than five minutes for no cost on Windows desktops. The Mozilla open source browser can be chosen, for instance, to standardize on a single browser for Windows and the Mac.

We will look at some scenarios for Linux and some for other open source products.

1.1.5   Does Open Source Require Different Business Methods?

It is not necessary to adopt an open source approach to development or distribution in order to use open source software, and most organizations do not. Many companies develop closed code software products that run on open source software and sell them for a profit; this includes almost every large software company today—IBM, HP, Oracle, SAP, and Apple. Other companies develop applications that run on open source for their own business purposes—for instance, Google, Amazon, or eBay—without feeling in any way restricted by open source licensing or development models.

It is never a problem to develop an application for your own use in an organization, to sell or distribute an application written in an open source language, or to run on an open source platform. Nor is it a problem to distribute the open source software alongside yours.

If you change or extend the open source software and redistribute it, you may have responsibilities under the license. In that situation, it is necessary to look carefully at the license and choose one that works for your business model.

1.1.6   Will All Systems Be Open Source One Day?

Given current installed systems and sales trends, we can be certain that over the next few years open source and closed code software will coexist. In the long run, there is reason to expect some balance. There are advantages to open source but also limits.

First, both commercial and government organizations have legitimate reasons for secrets. Organizations such as the CIA and Merrill Lynch, both of which have deployed open source quite widely, are never going to open up all their code for public scrutiny.

Second, some classes of applications appear to be more likely to fit the open source model than others. There is very little market share for open source in commercial ERP and CRM systems or in large commercial databases. This may change, and the development of open source for these enterprise systems may be a matter of time, but it would certainly take many years for that to happen. Alternatively, we may discover rules of thumb that limit the open source model to certain areas only and find that some complex business areas never really become open source.

Third, there could be a trend back toward closed code applications. Some people argue that a new wave of innovation might demonstrate the added value that closed code companies can offer. Others say that changes in the legal climate, such as patent law, might be introduced that would tilt the balance in favor of closed code systems again.

1.1.7   Is Open Source a Fad That Will Go Away?

The information technology business has seen its share of fads. But this seems more like a trend of the kind we see in other industries as they mature. Mature products such as office suites often become commodities. Mature services often become organized to more closely reflect where the real costs lie—in this case, in service and support rather than the original code.

Already, the majority of organizations have some role for programs such as Linux, Apache, and Perl. It is likely that at some point most organizations will have some open source widely deployed. So far, we are seeing open source software improve, if anything, more rapidly than closed code software. The open source cost advantage may narrow if closed code prices come down, but it is going to continue to exist.

1.2　A Brief History of Software

In this section, we will look at the closely entwined histories of open source software, UNIX-like operating systems, Linux, the Internet, and the World Wide Web.

1.2.1　Early Years

In the 1950s, the first modern business computers were introduced, based on work done during World War II. These were practically one-of-a-kind machines, running custom programs written in binary code, later assembler language. They were extremely expensive and it was thought by some (such as a famous IBM market estimate) that only a few might ever exist.

In the 1960s, commercial mainframes were introduced by several companies. These were custom programmed for applications, usually in COBOL or FORTRAN. System software (e.g., the important programs such as CICS, IMS, programming languages, sort, and other utilities) was developed in assembler language. A major success of the System/360, introduced by IBM in 1964, was that for the first time, the same assembly language ran on all the related systems, so that system software could run on a family of computers.

Prior to the 1970s, software was, essentially by default, "open" or "free." It had grown out of the scientific research community, where information was generally shared, and nobody had thought of an alternative. Software was developed by vendors, or by user companies, to meet a particular user problem, and was then freely distributed by user groups or computer vendors to other users who might have the same problem. Since software only ran on systems from a single vendor, a good software product could help to sell the platform.

1.2.2　Software Companies

The first software companies had started in the late 1960s, enabled by the System/360 platform, an ongoing legal action against IBM for "bundling" products, and by the falling prices of the systems. In 1970, IBM unbundled its software, except for operating systems, and settled a lawsuit with ADR, one of the first independent software vendors. At this time, several independent software companies became successful businesses following a closed code model. Some provided development tools and databases such as SyncSort, Mark IV, Cullinet, and Total. Others developed application software for automation of accounting and manufacturing and to support some vertical industries, such as banking and insurance.

Software companies originally focused on mainframes, but by the 1970s minicomputers such as the DEC PDP-11 and then the VAX were in general use. Because smaller mainframes and minicomputers were less expensive, there were more of them and more of their customers were likely to acquire software packages rather than perform expensive custom development. Relational databases such as Oracle, Ingres, and Informix were big sellers on minicomputers.

In the 1970s, the new idea of closed source software companies was heavily proselytized. In 1976 the "Open Letter to Hobbyists" written by Microsoft's Bill Gates stated that "software is not a public good . . . but private property." In the late 1970s, men like Gates, Larry Ellison of Oracle, John Cullinane of Cullinet, and Martin Goetz of ADR were arguing for the importance of a strong software industry with closed code products, separate from the hardware industry. Cullinet and ADR were later acquired by Computer Associates. It is not a coincidence that Microsoft, Oracle, and Computer Associates were able to build on this early start to become and remain the largest companies in the software business.

1.2.3   UNIX

At the beginning of the minicomputer period, the C programming language and UNIX operating system were developed together at AT&T and distributed through noncommercial channels.

The history of UNIX code dates back to 1969, when it was first developed. It is a long history and an involved one, since the code has had several corporate owners and has forked and even been reunited on more than one occasion. Fortunately, most of the people who have been involved with UNIX throughout that history, including the original authors, Ken Thompson and Dennie Ritchie, are still available. So the history and the code are well documented and understood. Those of us who do not understand every line and its derivation can be confident that there are people who do and can prove it. Unfortunately, this has been necessary from time to time. UNIX and its derivatives are too valuable not to be fought over, and there have been several legal actions conducted on the subject of ownership of UNIX trademarks and copyrights.

UNIX was written in C and constructed as a set of small programs that worked well together. By 1974, the UNIX system, including the C language and tools, had been ported to several platforms. AT&T was not at the time in the computer business, and versions of UNIX were distributed freely, particularly thoughout the academic and scientific communities, until Version 7 in 1978. AT&T stopped publishing UNIX source code in 1976, and after 1978 the distributions of UNIX from Bell Labs ceased.

In the 1980s, AT&T began to sell UNIX itself, first System III and then System V, both directly and by licensing it to different vendors. The cost of source licenses, which had been nominal, started to go up, so that by 1982, for example, an AT&T source license was $100,000. This fee would be spread across that vendor's customers, which numbered a few hundred or less, so UNIX was typically several hundred dollars for an end user. UNIX did begin to be adopted in business, first on smaller systems but ultimately on midrange and the very largest systems.

By the end of the 1980s, every hardware vendor in the world was offering a UNIX version. Unfortunately, different manufacturers competed by attempting to "embrace and extend" the code base, so it was fragmented and incompatible, and "porting" of an application between UNIX variants usually turned out to be too expensive to be worth undertaking.

Earlier versions of UNIX have been placed in the public domain and are often used in teaching operating system principles.

1.2.4   BSD

The University of California at Berkeley had the UNIX Version 4 code in 1974. By 1975, Berkeley engineers, including Bill Joy, were adding tools and kernel improvements, and in 1977 a "Berkeley Software Distribution" (BSD) was put together. This was to be the first of a series of distributions issued at approximately annual intervals and licensed to about 500 machines by 1980.

From 1980 through 1995, BSD releases numbered 4.x were handled by the Computer Systems Research Group of UC Berkeley (CSRG). In a sense, responsibility for distribution of the UNIX operating system passed to Berkeley at this time, funded by the Defense Advanced Research Projects Agency (DARPA), but each recipient had to get its own source license from AT&T.

In 1989, the networking code was released separately as Networking Release 1 under the very unrestricted Berkeley license. It was now clear that the original Bell Labs code could be replaced and BSD "freed" from the need for an AT&T license. A large volunteer development effort replaced most of the utilities, and in June 1991, Networking Release 2 shipped—only six kernel files short. Later that year, William and Lynne Jolitz replaced the last six files. 386/BSD was released for the Intel 386, replacing the Bell Labs code and eliminating the need for a UNIX source license. In 1992, 386/BSD was offered for sale by BSDI for $995 under a license that allowed onward distribution. Three versions of BSD forked from this original code base: NetBSD, OpenBSD, and FreeBSD. FreeBSD is the largest BSD distribution, aimed at PC hardware and a mass market user base similar to Linux.

During 1992, UNIX System Labs (USL), an AT&T organization created to hold the UNIX copyrights, sued Berkeley over its use of UNIX code. After USL was transferred from AT&T to Novell in 1993, a settlement was reached leaving an unencumbered BSD system, which was released as 4.4BSD-Lite in 1994 and reincorporated into the three BSD forks. So BSD had been available as a complete free operating system since 1991, but this was clouded by a lawsuit until 1994.

Berkeley licensing allows others to use the code freely as long as copyright is attributed, and the code has been freely used. BSD networking code, including the TCP/IP stack, was incorporated into almost every modern system, including Microsoft Windows, and is the practical basis for the Internet as it exists today. BSD was the basis for SunOS (later Solaris), although later Sun merged in System V. BSD code is also extensively used in other UNIX variants, such as AIX. Mac OS X is based on Darwin, which in turn is based on FreeBSD, with the Apple GUI Aqua and applications on top. Approximately half the utilities in Linux are derived from the BSD effort.

1.2.5 GNU and FSF

In 1984, an important chapter in free software began with GNU. GNU is derived from the acronym "GNU's Not UNIX," which is recursive (on the G). GNU was begun by Richard Stallman as a project to develop a complete operating system that was modeled on UNIX functionality and philosophy but that used no code from UNIX in order not to be encumbered by the corporate ownership of UNIX. GNU was modeled on UNIX for several reasons:

- UNIX was arguably the best available operating system to emulate in some respects (for an amusing discussion of this, see Richard Gabriel's paper, "The Rise of 'Worse Is Better'").

- UNIX tool implementation was well known to Stallman and the GNU community, so similar tools could be developed more rapidly.

- By modeling the OS APIs and binary formats on UNIX, parts of GNU that were developed could be used on UNIX before the whole thing was complete.

This project developed the essential utilities (including editor, compilers, debugger, make, source control) of the UNIX system as a completely independent code base. These tools turned out to be reliable and high performance and were available on many systems, including basically all versions of UNIX. The GNU project produced many useful tools over the years, but was less successful in producing a kernel.

By 1990, GNU was essentially a complete and very useful operating system without a production-ready kernel. This is more useful than it sounds, because the GNU design philosophy was successful, so that the GNU tools could be run on any UNIX system, and every computer company sold UNIX systems.

The GNU Public License was released in 1989. In a more philosophical vein, the GNU project is also the Free Software Foundation (FSF), whose goal is a world where programmers can share their work freely without commercial interference. GNU and FSF clearly began as the work of one man, Richard Stallman. They have developed in several directions and come to include a community with a shared vision, a large suite of programs and projects, a very specific and original licensing idea, and a foundation to keep this all together.

Work continues today on the GNU kernel, Hurd, which is available for testing purposes, and on many essential pieces of software. GNU, with the Free Software Foundation, is at the very least two things: a founding spirit and, together with BSD and the Linux kernel, one of three essential pieces that together have created Linux.

1.2.6 Linux

In 1991, a Helsinki University student named Linus Torvalds began developing a free UNIX kernel for Intel-based PC systems. It was initially based on Andrew Tanenbaum's Minix system, which was a teaching system based on early UNIX source code and published as a book.

From early on, Linus began using the "hacker" model of software development, at this time unchristened, and this was surprisingly successful. The Linux kernel was built with GCC and GNU utilities and relies on GCC for

Figure 1.1
Linux family tree.

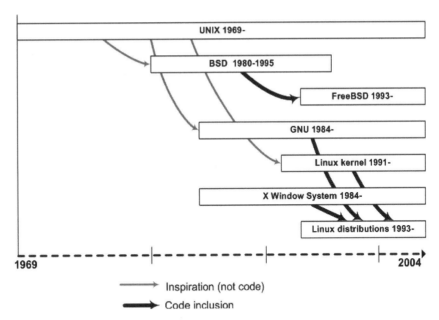

its portability. As early as 1992, by combining Linux with GNU, a complete operating system was available.

By 1993, Linux was functionally competitive for some purposes with some of the available commercial UNIX systems, which cost hundreds of dollars, and it was being commercially distributed on CD-ROM by Red Hat among others.

Figure 1.1 shows the relationship between Linux and other systems that have contributed. The dotted line represents inspiration. The UNIX system inspired the development of GNU and BSD, which are both obviously UNIX like, although for different reasons ultimately neither has any UNIX code. The solid line represents code contribution. Both GNU and BSD have contributed code to the system we now know as Linux.

1.2.7 The Personal Computer

In the 1980s, the personal computer (PC) was introduced to business. Intel had introduced the first microprocessor in 1971, and personal computers such as the Apple II and various CP/M models were available in the late 1970s, but the IBM introduction in September 1981 of a PC powered by Microsoft's operating system MS-DOS opened the floodgates in corporate systems. The applications that drove heavy adoption ("killer apps") were, in order of importance:

- Spreadsheets (VisiCalc, then Lotus 1-2-3)

- Other office programs, including word processors, presentation, publishing, and small database programs such as WordStar, PFS, and dBASE II

- End-user programming using BASIC

Client/Server Systems

What PCs originally lacked was access to data. Users would put mainframe reports on their desks and retype the numbers into spreadsheets. By the late 1980s, networks were used to couple the user interface and scalable processing benefits of the PC with centralized data, usually managed in a relational database. Office tools allowed end-user access to browse these databases, but more complex applications had to be custom developed.

There was a proliferation of graphical user interface (GUI) tools for application development, the leaders being Visual BASIC and Power-Builder. These promised an easy-to-use interface and the ability to scale through applying lots of front-end hardware.

Unfortunately, client/server development tools had several problems. They were a big step back in development productivity from the simplicity of the terminal-based "4GLs" on mainframes and minicomputers. The management of these systems, with logic distributed across all the participating computers, was difficult. Neither the ease of use nor scalability worked out as promised. They were also all proprietary and platform specific.

What was needed was a new development paradigm that would simplify the creation and distribution of forms-based graphical networked applications. This had to wait for the invention of the World Wide Web.

1.2.8   The Internet

The Internet is surprisingly old. The first ARPANET paper was published at an ACM conference in 1967. By 1969, there were Internet nodes at UCLA and Stanford. By 1972, the file transfer protocol (FTP) and Internet mail addressing had been invented and the system was publicly demonstrated in Paris.

The open source mail routing program Sendmail was originally written by Eric Allman at Berkeley in 1975. It is probably the oldest open source product still in widespread use, since it predates BSD and GNU efforts by years. I believe it is still today the most widely used program for transport of mail.

The Internet switched to the full TCP/IP protocol in 1981. At that time, Berkeley Internet Name Domain (BIND), the open source program that implements DNS and maps names such as "news.google.com" to Internet addresses such as "10.1.203.45," was written. This program runs on 95 percent of Internet name servers and all the root DNS servers. Those servers have been accessed by every transaction between machines on the Internet from 1981 through today, so it is probably the most widely used program on the Internet.

From 1981 through the 1990s, the Internet, as measured by connected systems, users, and information transfer, was approximately doubling every year. That rate of growth would only be sustainable if almost everyone in the Western world started to use it. It looked like the limit on growth would be the difficulty of use, since the main applications were mail, file transfer, and remote terminal use (Telnet), and they all required technical skills and needs. Then the World Wide Web was invented.

1.2.9 The World Wide Web

Around 1991, HTML and the World Wide Web were invented at CERN, the European Center for Nuclear Research, and at the time the largest Internet site in Europe, by Tim Berners-Lee. It spread very quickly. In 1993, the Mosaic browser was developed at the National Center for Supercomputing Applications (NCSA) in Illinois. Work on the Apache server began in 1995, based on prior work on the NCSA Web server.

The Web server and browser solved the problem of ease of use for Internet users, as well as the problem of a simple model for GUI network development and deployment. It has turned out to be the most important new development in the history of computer software. We may not yet understand all of its implications.

Berners-Lee might have licensed the Web idea using the GPL, which would have ensured it was open source, but he put it in the public domain. This meant that open source and closed code developers are free to use the ideas and code. For a while, it was not clear whether the Web would take a closed code direction. Netscape had acquired much of the NCSA development team and planned to sell closed code browsers and servers. Microsoft licensed the original Web code and planned to distribute closed code Web browsers and servers with custom extensions with Windows. If the protocols were extended by competing closed code companies, there might in effect be not one but several competing proprietary Webs by now, as there are competing incompatible versions of instant messenger software.

In the mid-1990s, the question of whether the Web would be open source or closed code was effectively decided by the votes of companies and individuals who chose Apache or competing Web servers; Netscape, Mosaic, or competing Web browsers; by the tools and standards that were supported; and by the World Wide Web Consortium (W3C). If server administrators had supported Netscape or Microsoft proprietary extensions (as some did), and if browser users had been content to load different browsers to get to those sites, the Web could have become proprietary. The direction that was taken was open, and this was effectively sealed in 1998 when IBM announced support for the Apache Web server, and the Mozilla (formerly Netscape) browser was open sourced.

1.3   Summary

The Internet is clearly the "killer application" of open source, as the spreadsheet had been for the personal computer. The Internet has projected open source software into widespread use.

While most of the important Internet software is open source, this "virtuous cycle" extends both ways. Open source development has been enabled from the beginning by the cooperative technologies of the Internet. Initially, developers at Berkeley used the Berkeley campus TCP/IP network to build and the new Internet to distribute BSD. Later, Usenet was used to support collaborative development of GNU tools and put developers in touch with Linus Torvalds through the comp.os.minix newsgroup. Today, the Internet supports collaborative development such as CVS, continuous update of packages using tools such as Debian apt-get, social software such as Slashdot, and collaborative instruments like SourceForge.

The economist Bradford DeLong has a framework for the economic analysis of technological revolutions. The four key questions to monitor for a revolution are:

1.   What goods and services become extraordinarily cheap as a result?

2.   What jobs and skills become key bottlenecks and thus become remarkably valuable and well paid?

3.   What risks blindside the society as the technology spreads?

4.   What risks do people guard against that turn out not to be risks at all?

This immediately reveals a couple of important points. First, the framework is all questions. It is very difficult to determine the answers to questions such as these posed for several years in the future. Second, half the questions are about how we are likely to get the predictions that we do make wrong.

It appears that certain essential code is becoming extraordinarily cheap. It seems that this will include operating systems, Web and database servers, office tools, Web browsers, and much personal and professional workstation software.

At this stage, it seems that the development and pricing of large-scale complex applications such as ERP and CRM will not be affected much, at least on the same timescale.

Jobs and skills involving integration, custom extension, deployment, and training of these systems do not appear likely to become more efficient or markedly less well paid. There may be some pressure on the pricing and packaging of these services from some of the new customers that the low prices have made possible. On the other hand, some of these skills will be bottlenecks to the introduction of systems with large payoffs and will become valuable, at least for a time. Perhaps one group of winners will be companies that figure out how to support larger numbers of users with tools that scale and are appropriately priced using some combination of technology and community organization. That still has to be decided.

It is possible that the lower prices of core software will lead to an explosion in demand for other, more specialized software and services based on top of this layer. This has been the pattern of the computer industry for many years, particularly in hardware, where falling prices have driven expanded markets. It is also the pattern in system assembly businesses such as automobiles and aircraft. Over time, the value of the airframe in an aircraft or the body in a car declines relative to the value of other systems, and to the total.

Figure 1.2, based on a comment by venture capitalist and former Oracle CEO Ray Lane, illustrates this. The software product industry was about a $200B business in 2001, and the diagram shows the approximate composition of the business. At that time, people thought it would grow to $400B by 2010. The collapse of the "Internet bubble," the rise of open source software, and movement of some production offshore mean the business may be about $200B in 2010. But components lower in the stack, such as operating systems, will get a smaller share of the revenue. This can be seen as caused by or as causing the adoption of open source in these components.

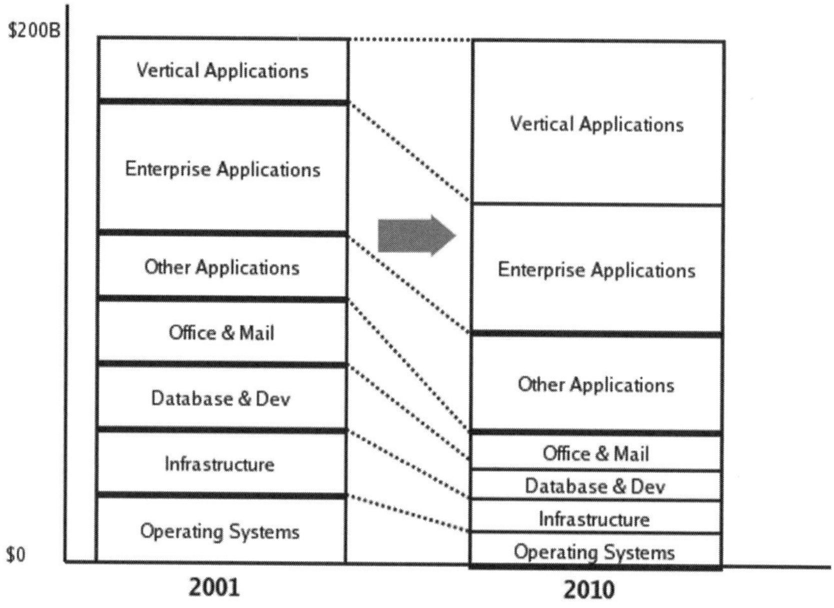

Figure 1.2
Value moves up the stack.

As some of the basic components become less expensive, more of the value will be higher up the stack and the revenue will reflect that.

One set of risks we probably do not need to be concerned about is the various claims that open source is somehow a parasite on the innovation of private enterprise—so that if closed code companies were to fail, eventually there would be no more software research and we'd all be worse off. This worry begins by misunderstanding where research has been done. Large-scale R&D has been funded mostly by two groups. Large private labs have done basic research without plans for direct return. Examples include Bell Labs developing the transistor and UNIX; Xerox developing the GUI, Ethernet, and laser printing; and IBM developing SQL. The government has funded much work, looking for a direct return but also making the results public. Examples include the Internet, Berkeley developing BSD, and NASA developing databases and project management. Small-scale work, such as developing programs and algorithms, has been done by academics and small companies hoping to profit from their investments. There is no reason any of this should change. Nobody is advocating that ALL research and ALL programs should be placed in the public domain.

Claims that closed code companies are essential to the software economy generally come from these very companies and are self-serving. This is not a realistic concern for customers; if open source developers can produce sufficient innovative new applications without needing to be paid a lot of licensing fees, we should be very happy. Where they cannot, the closed code industry would be happy to fill the gap.

Some worry that without software companies to pay programmers, there would not be many open source programmers around to work for free. But most software companies are in areas where open source has no great presence. The great majority of programmers, including open source contributors, work in organizations on custom software or integration used in house, not at software product companies on product development. So whatever happens to software product companies will not have much of a general effect on programmer employment or open source production.

2

Where Open Source Is Successful

This is a game of picking winners, so we begin this chapter with a definition of the playing field. Then we will look at the areas where open source is succeeding and then the areas where open source has advantages and disadvantages, real or apparent.

2.1 Analytical Framework

This section looks at how technology is adopted, when, and by which organizations. Important issues are disruptive innovation, lock-in, and the type of adoptions.

2.1.1 Disruptive Innovations

In Clayton Christiansen's book, *The Innovator's Dilemma*, the argument is made that businesses are threatened by "disruptive innovations," which are new approaches that come up from under their radar. Ironically, the businesses that pay the closest attention to the needs of their best customers and sales channels are the most vulnerable to such threats, because the needs of those customers and channels are not well satisfied by the innovation in its early stages.

Familiar examples of disruptive technologies include the personal computer, which is an obvious success, and the electric vehicle, which has great potential but has not yet really broken out. A large part of Christiansen's book focuses on the history of specific products, such as steam shovels and disk drives, that offer detailed examples of successive cycles of disruption. The disk drive story, for instance, is mostly one of smaller and less capable drives finding new functions, solving new sorts of problems, and then growing up to replace the larger, previous generation.

Figure 2.1
*Successive
disruptive
technologies.*

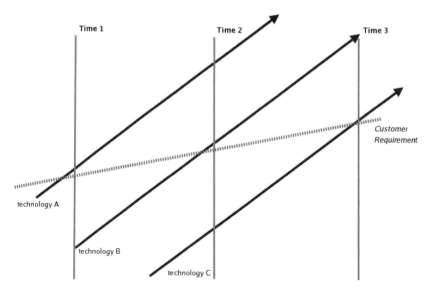

Disruptive innovations often take the form of being "good enough" as opposed to "better," at least as the incumbents see it. When a disruptive product is compared with existing choices, there may be severe current limitations in some uses, but the new product is much simpler and cheaper in a way that is important to some customers. This type of activity happens in industries where products are improving faster than customer needs. This is very common in technology.

In Figure 2.1, we see three technologies, A, B, and C, whose performance (on the Y axis) is compared over time (on the X axis). For the sake of argument, let them be three sizes of disk drive, such as 3.5, 2.5, and 1.8 inches. The performance measure is capacity (GB). The newer products will be smaller in size and price.

At any point of measurement, such as Time 1, 2, or 3, A is always better in performance than B and B is better than C. A possible customer requirement is drawn with the dashed line. The customer need grows, but more slowly than the competing technologies improve. As a result, while initially only A will satisfy this customer, by Time 2 A or B will suffice, and by Time 3 C will also be sufficient for this customer. Although A and B have continued to improve in performance through the period, this does not help them. The customer may switch to B and then to C if circumstances are right.

If certain assumptions hold, we can expect that the customer will switch when the newer technology crosses the dotted line representing the customer's need. The two important assumptions in this model are:

- The new technologies must have some advantage in another dimension, often that they are significantly less expensive or less difficult to use than the old.
- The switching costs must be fairly low, as they are when substituting a part in product design.

With disk drives, the new drive is lighter and cheaper and switching costs are low. In this case, Figure 2.1 suggests that the customer represented by the dotted line will switch from A to B at T2 and from B to C at T3.

There are simplifications in this graph. The technology lines are parallel, meaning that the technologies are improving at the same rate. Often, the new technology starts to improve at a better rate than the old. Also, the customer requirement is generally not a single line but a distribution.

Also, note that today's disruptive innovation becomes tomorrow's incumbent, where it may be attacked later.

Open Source as Disruptive Innovation

Much open source software qualifies as this sort of "disruptive innovation" at this stage. Open source systems are usually less expensive than the alternative and often easier to use. In some cases, open source systems are a little more difficult to use, but this appears to be related to their immaturity and novelty rather than anything fundamental.

Often today, although not always, open source is following a closed code technology, catching up in performance or scale while offering lower price and other advantages. Performance and price/performance in the computer industry are always improving faster than the typical customer can absorb, but this is particularly true in the recessionary atmosphere of today. In other words, the customer is prepared to see many systems as "good enough."

Lock-In

From the customer's view, Figure 2.1 represents "commodification." The customer has limited new needs and is ready to substitute less expensive products as they improve. Improvements above the line are incorrect attempts by vendors to avoid this commodity trap.

In a commodity explanation, as a solution becomes mature it becomes more difficult to differentiate by innovation, and eventually all suppliers tend to the same low margins over cost of goods. In software, with distribution costs close to zero, the product price will tend to zero and the only money to be made will be in service and training.

We have seen software become better and less expensive over time, but we have certainly not seen it tending toward zero in margin or price. This possibility has been resisted up to now by something variously called "network effects" or "increasing returns," but which we will call "lock-in." If there is an advantage to using the same product as other people, a market may go "winner takes all"; the winning product can then charge a substantial premium because possible switching to new technology can be made more difficult by locking in customers to existing patterns of use or interfaces.

The desktop operating system and office suite markets are cases where vendors control and network effects predominate; another clear case of this is instant messaging. It is very difficult to switch off these systems. The Web browser market is largely a commodity/standards market, and the Web server market even more so. Although vendors such as Netscape and Microsoft resisted this, you can change browsers or even Web servers easily. Mail by itself is a commodity market, but typical vendor extensions such as calendaring and forms management are not. Database is a commodity at the API level, such as using ODBC or JDBC, but the vendors have done as much as possible to resist this by introducing attractive proprietary extensions.

Vendors will be looking to increase differentiation and encourage most customers to become locked in to a single product. Customers will be well advised to look for standards, either legislated or de facto, allowing them to "pick and choose" and switch easily.

The effect of switching costs in Figure 2.1 is to lower the line of the new technology by the amount of the costs. This makes it harder to adopt the new technology against the old, as it appears effectively worse when those costs are considered. If switching costs are high, the new technology will have to be deployed into new uses until it is much better than the old, which could take years. The switching costs, although one time, create a situation where the vendor can earn a premium indefinitely. In Figure 2.2, the switching cost lowers the line of the new product, delaying its adoption.

In the open source case, switching costs are low when the technology is deployed in the background and high when deployed in the foreground, particularly on existing desktops. The difference in switching costs is the

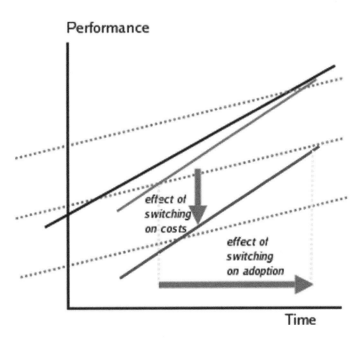

Figure 2.2
Effect of switching costs on adoption.

main reason why open source share is as high as 70 percent in many server and appliance functions, and only about 3 percent in desktops.

Many customers will look on avoiding vendor lock-in as a legitimate goal that may be worth putting a price on. The city of Munich, Germany, for instance, did not plan to save money in its much publicized migration to open source within the time frame of the migration. It expects to gain financially when it escapes vendor lock-in later.

2.1.2 The Technology Adoption Curve

In Geoffrey Moore's book, *Crossing the Chasm* (Harper 1991; re-released 2002), he showed the established Technology Adoption Life Cycle, which highlights transitions between classes of purchasers. A version of this is shown in Figure 2.3. Moore commented on the most difficult transition to make, which is the one from "early adopters" to "early majority." Briefly, the early adopters are lovers of the technology and are often easily sold, accepting all kinds of problems and possibly buying without adequate cost justification—for instance, for evaluations. The early majority can also be visionary, but in a pragmatic way. They are people who see the benefits they and their organizations can derive by employing the technology early.

The challenge of technology sales is "crossing the chasm" from the early adopters to the early majority, since this involves something very different

Figure 2.3
*Technology
adoption curve.*

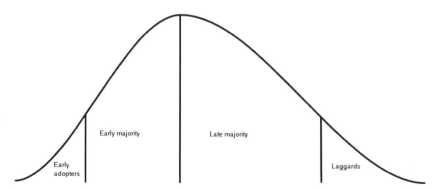

from increasing the volume of sales. It is a qualitative difference between two very different types of customers. The histories in this chapter contain a mixture of early adopters and the beginning of the early majority. The open source community has more than its share of early adopters: people who love the idea of free software and a community sharing code, and people who love the particular quirks of these technologies, such as the UNIX-like operating system, little languages, command-line interfaces, and so on.

Some open source technology, such as Apache and Linux servers, has moved beyond the early adopter group now. Others, such as the Linux desktop, are still there. The purpose of this book is to look at the technologies that are in a position to be deployed by the early majority. In this area, the important questions are on the value the deployment will bring to the business: money saved, opportunities created.

Systems integrators such as IBM, HP, and Sun are important early adopters. They have chosen to deploy open source widely in their own organizations. All of these have announced a complete switch to Linux desktops. When looking at this group, there is little to be gained by asking why they did it. These companies know that by planting early successes they will create the references that early majority customers look for. The important questions are: How successful have they been, and what lessons have they learned? They may have faced challenges we would have preferred to avoid.

When a technology "crosses the chasm" and becomes a success, the rate of adoption increases and then remains high until the market is saturated. This often takes the shape of the S-curve in Figure 2.4, which plots percentage of adoption against time. This shows the impact of the early adopter to late majority transition as the opportunity it represents. Between T1 and T2 in Figure 2.4, a product that has taken years to reach 25 percent market

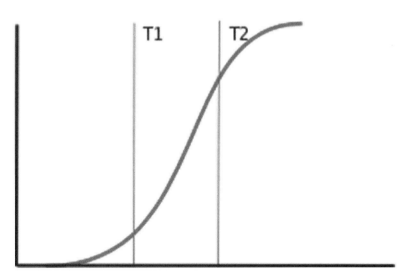

Figure 2.4
Classic technology
S-curve.

share can suddenly go to 50 percent or 75 percent in a short time. We have seen this with TVs, PCs, VCRs, and cell phones, for example.

Because people have a tendency to assume linear change, the shape of this curve continually catches us by surprise. One popular saying that captures this curve is: Things change much less in two years than you expect, but much more in ten. In Figure 2.4, Linux desktops are on the left, Linux servers in the center, and Apache on the right. Linux servers would appear to be on the rising segment of the curve now.

2.1.3 The Open Source Stack

It is possible to get open source products for all the elements of an organization's computer network. Most people will be using a mixture of open source and closed code, of course. Figure 2.5 is an abstract diagram that shows the layers of typical software on a server and a desktop system. Not all systems have all of these functions, of course, but most business systems will support these functions across the organization in a similar manner.

Typically, of course, there will be many of these, and there will be a more heterogeneous set of systems than this shows. Later, we will elaborate on this diagram, where appropriate, to include other functions such as systems management.

The intent of Figure 2.5 is to show at a glance how an open source architecture might look if deployed fully. Packaged and custom applications

Figure 2.5
*Typical open code
stack.*

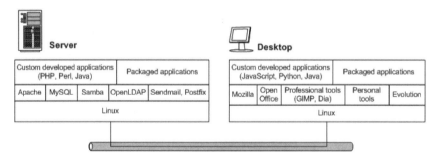

might include ERP or CRM, line of business applications such as POS or call center, or more specific applications.

Open source software usually offers more choices than closed code, so there are alternatives available for most of the boxes shown. We will discuss these in more detail later.

On the server, you could use FreeBSD, UNIX, and/or Windows in addition to Linux. You could use PostgreSQL or Oracle instead of MySQL. Mail servers include Postfix and Sendmail, with other servers providing specialized functions such as Web mail access.

On the client, you could support Windows and/or Mac OS X in addition to Linux. You could use other browsers in addition to or instead of Mozilla, such as Internet Explorer, Konqueror/Safari, Epiphany, or Opera. Most organizations would add some more professional tools, and individuals might add preferred applications.

The development tool choices are just suggestions from many available choices. PHP and Perl are the most common choices on Linux servers. Python and JavaScript are common on Linux and Apple clients, as well as for Web applications, because they are supported by Mozilla. Of course, you could certainly choose C++ in either case or develop applications in Java rather than an open source language.

2.1.4   Adoption of Specific Open Source Technologies

We can now apply the previous disruptive innovation diagram to some specific examples, which are:

- Database servers
- Web servers
- Operating systems
- Office suites

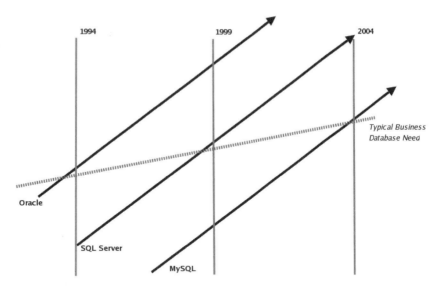

Figure 2.6
Successive business databases, 1994–2004.

Database Servers

Figure 2.6 shows the market for the database servers Oracle, SQL Server, and MySQL from 1994 through 2004. This is, of course, a conceptual diagram to illustrate the trend. Actual numbers depend first on the customer requirement, which would have to be calculated for a specific customer, and then on database benchmarks, which would have to be derived from the requirement. MySQL follows the classic disruptive curve in this situation. While Oracle continues to improve over time and to outperform the competition, it can be replaced for this customer requirement by SQL Server in 1999 and SQL Server can be replaced by MySQL in 2004.

Web Servers

The World Wide Web is an astonishing case of disruptive technology, and Apache is the leading instance. Apache grew out of the first Web server (since it is based on the original NCSA server), so unlike many other open source products it never had to compete with closed code from a position of weakness. It began as, and has remained, the market leader.

This is not simply a case of a new technology being cheaper and simpler, although it is. In addition to making it easier and less expensive to develop applications, the Web server went further and made a new class of application possible that reached orders of magnitude more people than prior systems ever had.

Even though the Web is one of the most successful new paradigms in history, there were still migration difficulties in early deployment. Applications that had been deployed on client/server systems or dedicated terminals could not be migrated to the Web without dumping existing investments, and had to be either kept or discarded wholesale. For the class of users who were attracted to client/server applications and therefore had control of their desktops in house, the Web interface was weak (slow and difficult to control precisely) and a poor use of their existing investments in powerful standardized client systems.

Operating Systems

Linux was clearly a case of "good enough" but simpler and cheaper when introduced to commercial businesses around 1994. Most early Linux customers were looking for a UNIX-like system that was inexpensive and ran on inexpensive Intel-based hardware. At that time, it was not likely to be adopted by existing UNIX customers as an upgrade to their existing systems.

By 2000, Linux had overtaken the largest-selling, lowest-functionality UNIX system, Santa Crux Operation. Large SCO customers were ripping and replacing their systems with Linux, and the company abandoned the UNIX server business to pursue other businesses as Tarantella.

In 2004, it seems that large Linux servers can compete for new business installations with large UNIX servers for everything but a few specialized niches. Linux is a serious competitor to UNIX even in supercomputers and other high-performance niches. Although there will be several years of coexistence, IBM and HP agree that within a few years Linux will entirely replace their proprietary UNIX systems.

In Figure 2.7 there are a couple of new wrinkles compared with the previous figures. First, the business needs vary more than for the database model and are expressed by a pair of lines. Second, the technology lines are not parallel but converge in three or four years from now. Operating systems can adopt each other's improvements in leveraging hardware using SMP and clusters. As a result, Windows has been catching up to UNIX, and Linux to Windows and UNIX. In this area, Linux is well beyond "good enough" and is simply the best choice at any price.

Office Suites

OpenOffice is a great example of a product that is "good enough." It is not much different in functionality or look and feel from Microsoft Office. If you have used neither before, you will most likely find them similar to learn and use, with more features than you need. Most of us don't use all of any office suite, so it has more than we need.

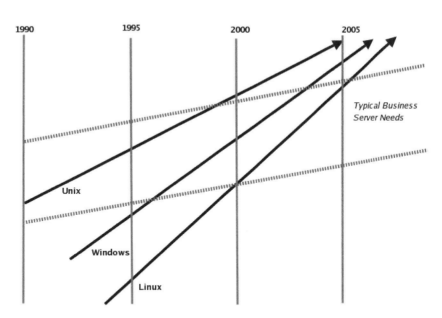

Figure 2.7
Server operating systems, 1990–2005.

The "disruptive innovation" diagram for Office Suites looks attractive for OpenOffice. It meets most customer needs and is certainly very much less expensive than Microsoft Office. If you have 10,000 users, you will pay millions of dollars for Microsoft Office and almost nothing for OpenOffice. Unfortunately for Open Office, the switching costs are so high that it is usually difficult to justify migration for existing Office users. This is why computer vendors are targeting new deployments, such as the Asian market, for Open Office.

2.2 Open Source Is in Widespread Successful Use

The Linux and FreeBSD operating systems, the GNU compiler suite, and the Apache Web server are massive software systems used all over the world. They are large and sophisticated and compete with the largest closed code systems, such as Windows. Here are some of the key "bullet points" on open source use.

2.2.1 Open Source Is the Heart of the Internet

There would be no Internet without open source. Open source software has been in use on critical parts of the Internet, including mail routing, domain name assignment, and key components of the TCP/IP network stack, for well over 20 years, exhibiting great reliability and capacity for growth and change. All of this code at the heart of the Internet is open source software:

- TCP/IP, the core protocol code of the Internet, is distributed under a Berkeley open source license and included in Windows and IBM mainframes as well as UNIX and Linux.

- BSD, the original free UNIX distribution, includes many Internet utilities, such as implementations of remote terminal, file copy, and the Internet programming API (Berkeley sockets).

- Sendmail was written as open source in 1975 and is still the most used mail server program.

- BIND, the program that maps server names to IP addresses, has been an essential component of the Internet since 1981.

- Apache is the most used Web server, with 67 percent share (Netcraft).

- Linux is the operating system used by most Apache servers.

- Mozilla, the browser that was formerly Netscape, is the #2 browser in use (after Internet Explorer).

2.2.2   Linux Is Shipping a Lot

Linux is the #2 shipping server worldwide (after Windows). In 2002, Windows shipped 2,533,671 servers and Linux 485,679 (IDC), so Linux shipped at about 20 percent of the Windows rate. The server growth rate was 35 percent for Linux and 14 percent for Windows (also IDC). In 4Q 2003, Linux server unit shipments were 250,000, which is a 63 percent growth over 4Q 2002 (IDC).

In 2003, Linux overtook the Mac for client operating system sales to become the #2 desktop operating system after Windows (IDC).

In 2004, the following events are expected:

- The majority of CIOs expect to deploy Linux in 2004–2005 (*CIO Magazine* 2003).

- There will be approximately 25 million Linux systems in use (IDC).

- IDC projects Linux as 25 percent of new OS for servers, with Windows as 50 percent.

- Linux is projected (from IDC 2002/2003 numbers and CAGR) to be at 1 million annual run rate going into 2004.

- Linux will outship all UNIX systems combined, and the Mac in unit sales, to become the #2 OS (also projection from IDC).

By 2005/2006 Giga predicts "with high probability" that Linux will overtake Windows to become the leading operating system on new server shipments.

Linux will rapidly mature and gain momentum as an ISV reference platform, moving beyond high-volume Web, technical computing, and appliance server environments into mainstream application and DBMS server roles by 2004/2005. (Meta Group 2003.)

One warning: Most of the numbers given previously are unit shipments. Linux sales percentages in dollar numbers are always much lower than unit shipments, because Linux costs less. UNIX server sales for 2003 by dollar volume were still larger than Windows and Linux combined, although 2003 is probably the last year where this will be the case.

2.2.3   Open Source Appliances Are Everywhere

Appliances based on Linux and open source tools have been widely deployed in corporate networks, small businesses, and homes for several years with proven reliability. Corporate appliances for caching, proxy, firewall, and security running on Linux are sold by IBM, HP, Dell, and Sun.

There are a variety of small appliances making their way into the home today. They typically include a small computer and disk drive, often with an LCD display or TV output, sometimes controlled from another system over a network using a Web browser. These systems can cost from under $50 for a simple firewall/router to a few hundred dollars for a fairly full business system such as the Sun Cobalt Web and file servers. These systems need a very reliable OS that can be configured to do only what they need, and at a low price. The operating system used is not usually advertised, since the buyer does not care, although it is generally not a secret that it uses Linux. Examples of these consumer, home office, and small business devices include the following, all based on Linux:

- TiVo television recorders

- Mirra network-attached disk drives

- Linksys (Cisco) and Netgear home router, firewall, and wi-fi appliances

- Cobalt (Sun) Web and mail server appliances

- Pogo database (MySQL) appliances

- Zaurus (Sharp) PDAs

Other Linux appliances include Snapgear and Guardian. There are numerous Linux-based MP3 players, video players, PDAs, and cell phones. It is difficult to get accurate statistics, but it does appear that Linux is the main player in this category of new appliances, aside from the established markets of PDAs and cell phones.

In the case of the more mature category of devices making up the PDA, PalmOS and Windows CE are the leaders. However, the Sharp Zaurus series is a strong Linux-based contender, and recent moves among consumer electronic manufacturers suggest that there will be movement toward Linux in the future.

Microsoft offers both Embedded Windows 2000 and Windows CE, both evangelizing vendors and making its own systems, but does not appear to have much share except in PDAs and when selling its own brands. For example, the Linux-based TiVo device has greater than 80 percent share, with Microsoft selling very few of its "Ultimate TV" appliance.

2.2.4   New Companies and New Businesses Use Open Source

When a new technology becomes available, there are many obstacles to its rapid deployment. For most existing businesses, the "better" is the enemy of the "good enough." First, if we have done the intellectual and physical work to build a satisfactory networking solution for our organization based on Windows 2000, then a better or cheaper solution, whether based on Windows 2003 or Linux, is an annoyance since we may have to do the work again. Second, any savings are probably negated by our sunk costs, at least until some major upgrade comes along.

Thus, the first places we could reasonably expect to see new technology deployed early are companies and businesses that are new in the last few years, or have grown so explosively that they are practically new. And we do see that these types of organizations have adopted open source software widely and quickly.

Dot-Coms

One obvious case is the dot-com industry. For all the disappointment around the "boom and bust" of this phenomenon, a number of powerful companies have come from the Internet industry. These companies have been disproportionately users of open source, starting obviously with Apache, as already discussed, but including open source operating systems, tools, and databases.

Amazon.com is an extensive Linux user, having converted from UNIX. The main online Amazon system is developed in C++. Amazon also uses Perl heavily for data integration.

Yahoo! is a heavy FreeBSD user. It also uses PHP and Perl languages, moving more to PHP, and the MySQL database. The high-volume Yahoo! Mail is all open source.

Google uses thousands of small commodity servers running Linux. Their home-grown systems management is written using the C++ and Perl development tools. They also use Python extensively.

The thousands of servers that Akamai has placed around the world to cache and accelerate content all run on Linux.

Hotmail became the largest free email service in the world while running on FreeBSD, although much, possibly all, of it now understandably runs on Windows 2000.

Slashdot, the news service, runs on Linux and is written in Perl. Slashdot is so heavily used that it regularly "slashdots" or swamps other high-volume sites when it points its readers to them. The Slashdot code is also available as an open source product (slash).

Bioinformatics

Bioinformatics is a rapidly growing industry characterized by scientists using powerful computers to perform gene sequencing, cladistics, computer-driven ecology, modeling of dynamic systems, and other computer-intensive processing. The power needed would have been the province of supercomputers and powerful UNIX workstations a few years ago; today it is all done with commodity systems, linked into grids if necessary. Professionals in this area will use a variety of programs written recently. Essentially all of these programs require Linux or UNIX. For example, the book *Developing Bioinformatics Computer Skills* (Gibas and Jambeck, O'Reilly) covers the industry widely and is confined to Linux/UNIX, including Perl for data manipulation and MySQL for database management.

Grid and High-Performance Computing

High-performance technical computing ("rocket science") has traditionally been a UNIX domain, although techniques leak over to the business world from academia, to Wall Street in the 1980s, and later to energy companies and large-scale retail analytics. This includes many systems with dozens of Linux servers running the "Beowolf" clusters, as well as some very large custom supercomputer systems.

Grid computing, which has evolved from this, is the growing use of loosely organized "grids" of computers, which can be accessed to solve difficult computational problems. Unlike a cluster, a grid can be joined and exited voluntarily, so capacity is dynamic. This is mostly done on Linux and UNIX systems today.

The brokerage company Reech Capital uses an inexpensive grid of 144 Xeon processor systems running Linux and Sungard software to calculate complex derivatives 100 times faster than a single machine. BP Americas uses Red Hat Linux systems on HP to perform seismic analysis for oil drilling.

Massive Multiplayer Games

The massive multiplayer game industry is a new business that needs high scalable performance and is very cost driven. These systems are built today using Linux clusters. Back-end databases are often Oracle on UNIX, but these are moving to clusters also. Electronic Arts, for example, has deployed Oracle RAC on Linux.

2.2.5   Open Source Is Broadly Adopted

Most top computer companies are strong advocates of open source software for significant elements of their products. This includes all of the top integrated systems companies, such as IBM, Hewlett-Packard, Apple, and Sun. IBM and HP make billions from Linux sales. Sun has several product lines based on Linux. The Apple Macintosh OS X operating system is based on the open source FreeBSD operating system.

All of the leading software companies, with the single exception of Microsoft, offer products based on open source. This includes Oracle, SAP, Computer Associates, PeopleSoft, Veritas, SAS, and Siebel.

There are many big corporate open source success stories, including Amazon, Google, eBay, and Industrial Light & Magic. These include some of the newest and largest applications, such as new scientific supercomputers based on Linux clusters, commercial Web megaservers, most bioinformatics, and all grid computing systems.

Many government organizations from Munich to Massachusetts, Brazil to China, NASA to the National Security Agency are making significant moves toward wholesale adoption of open source.

As of October 2003, according to the *Financial Times*, there had been 20 million downloads of OpenOffice.

In January 2004, the top database performance benchmark (TPC-C) was performed with the Oracle database on a 64-way Red Hat Enterprise Linux cluster. It achieved over a million tpmC at 5.50 per tpmC.

There are over 2,000 SAP installations on Linux. Oracle has over 500 customers on Linux.

PHP is the most used development language on the Web, having overtaken Microsoft Active Server Pages.

IBM has announced that it is moving all internal desktops to Red Hat Linux. It is using a mixed strategy, combining Notes, Office viewers, and Citrix. This is in progress in 2004, aiming for completion in 2005. IBM plans to transition all of its customers from the AIX operating system to Linux.

Sabre is replacing front-facing components of Travelocity, its Web-based booking system, with applications developed using Linux and MySQL. Sabre, the reservation system of American Airlines, was a pioneer of OLTP technology and runs the world's largest mainframe OLTP travel booking system.

Sherwin-Williams, the paint manufacturer, moved 10,000 systems from Windows to Turbolinux. AutoZone moved over 3,000 systems from SCO UNIX to Red Hat Linux. The U.S. Postal Service has 6,000 Linux systems installed in 250 mail distribution centers. McKesson serves billions of prescriptions annually at thousands of locations through a Linux-based application.

The Pentagon announced in February 2004 that the Army Research Lab (MSRC) is installing a Linux supercomputer system based on 1,066 dual Xeon processors (2,132 processors total).

Other large corporate adopters of open systems include:

- Ford
- L.L. Bean
- Delta Airlines
- DaimlerChrysler
- Dresdner Kleinwort Benson
- Hughes Network Services
- Merrill Lynch
- Deutsche Bank
- Telstra
- Cisco
- UBS Warburg
- Federal Aviation Authority

2.3   Examples of Open Source Systems

Four examples of high-volume open source sites that can be seen on the Web are Amazon, FedStats, Travelocity, and Slashdot.

Amazon

Originally, Amazon was mostly based on proprietary UNIX but many systems have migrated to Linux and important new systems are built with all open source software. This includes the customer management and recommendations sections. See Figure 2.8 for the Amazon recommendations page.

FedStats

The U.S. Census site, http://www.fedstats.gov/, is an excellent demonstration of what can be achieved using all open source software (Linux, Apache, MySQL, PHP, Perl) operating with large amounts of data. See Figure 2.9 for FedStats and Figure 2.10 for the related site MapStats.

Travelocity

Travelocity is a high-volume air and travel reservation site run by Sabre. The original reservation system run on NonStop equipment. The new ecommerce pricing system, which handles much higher processing requirements and customer volumes, uses all open source software including Linux and MySQL. See Figure 2.11.

Figure 2.8
Amazon recommendations page.

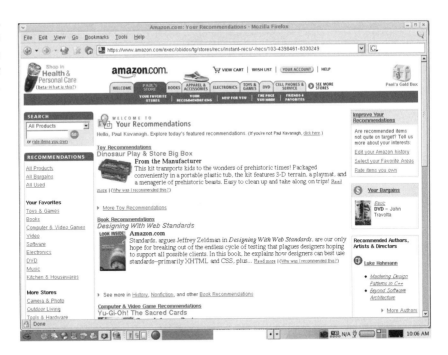

Figure 2.9
FedStats.

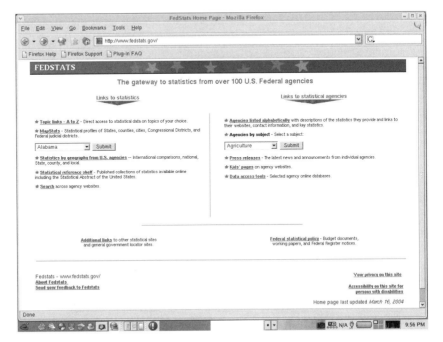

Figure 2.10
MapStats.

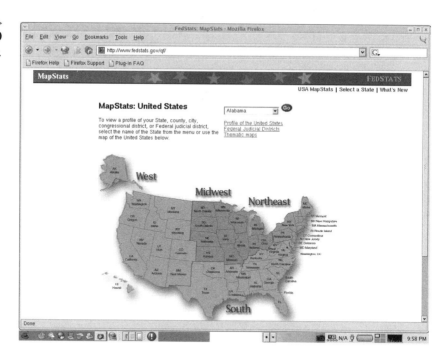

Figure 2.11
Trevelocity.

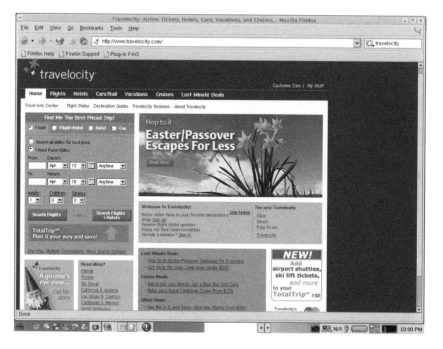

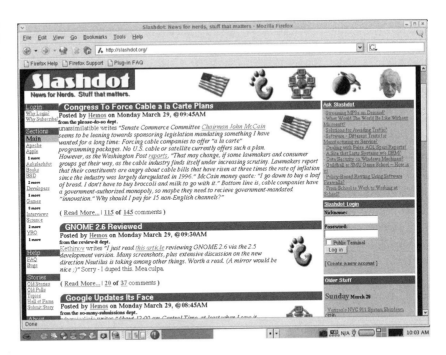

Figure 2.12
Slashdot.

Slashdot

Slashdot is one of the highest-volume database-driven news sites on the Web. It is totally open source, built in Linux, Apache, MySQL, and Perl. See Figure 2.12.

2.4   Summary

Open source software is here today. It is extensively used on the Internet backbone, by IBM, the U.S. government, Ford, Wal-Mart, Exxon, GM, Amazon.com, and Merrill Lynch, among others, in the United States, and by large enterprises and government organizations around the world. The products that are in widespread use (by millions of people every day) include:

- Linux and FreeBSD operating systems
- Apache Web server
- MySQL and PostgreSQL databases
- BIND and Sendmail, the primary systems used for Internet domain names and mail forwarding

- Samba and other tools for file and print sharing broadly across systems

- OpenOffice and other office suites

- GIMP and other professional tools

- OpenLDAP and other open tools for directory and security management

- GNU C++, Perl, PHP, Python, and other development languages

- Appliances for corporate and consumer use, such as TiVo, Linksys, Netgear, Sharp Zaurus, and SunCobalt and SunFire systems.

In some areas, such as embedded devices, Web servers, and engineering workstations, the open source choices are already the leading installed systems. In others, including infrastructure servers, application servers, and large academic clusters, open source is gaining the majority of the new install decisions. Not everyone can necessarily benefit by adopting these products today. Some may have sunk costs in existing solutions, and there can be large transitional costs in other cases. But open source solutions are sufficiently compelling that every organization should be looking at them as possibilities now.

3

Open Source: The Good, the Bad, and the Ugly

In this chapter, we will review arguments for and against open source software, and some other issues that are relevant.

3.1   What Is Good about Open Source

Advantages of using open source software include our ability to:

- View source code
- Change and redistribute source code
- Buy from different vendors and adopt new platforms
- Avoid proprietary information formats
- Allow integration between products
- Reduce software licensing cost and effort
- Develop and deploy effectively internationally
- Draw from a large pool of skilled professionals

3.1.1   Why Your Right to View Code Matters

There are reasons why you should have the ability to review source code, even though you don't expect to do it, don't want to do it, and may not even be able to (if you don't know C++ or Perl). If there is a problem with a system you are maintaining, you may not read the code but you will do the following:

- Check the documentation that describes how the system should work, including FAQs, to see if you are using the system correctly.

- Check support base or bug reports for the system for similar problems and solutions.

- Use search engines such as Google to search for similar problems and solutions.

These methods are all improved by source code availability.

The documentation is more likely to be specific and accurate since the author is not attempting to hide the implementation (or the fact he or she hasn't seen it). Write-ups of bug reports are more likely to describe the bug in terms of the code (and may include the proposed fix). Problems that appear similar on the surface will be correctly classified as identical or different once compared with the actual code error.

If these instantaneous methods fail, you will probably:

- Use mail lists or user groups to find people who've already solved the problem (but haven't reported it) or who have more advanced problem-solving skills.

- Use the support mechanism of your organization or your vendor to find people to do that.

At this point, even though you still don't plan to read the source code, the people you will be relying on will need to see it, and if you don't have the right to see it they very likely will not either.

In closed code organizations, it is quite common for employees in support and consulting positions not to have access to source code, because of concerns about theft. That is, employees of the same company may not have access to their own closed code. They often won't tell you this.

Support and consulting work is commonly contracted these days to third-party companies on a variety of terms. Since they are not employees, they are quite unlikely to have access to the closed code. Again, they may not tell you this.

The closed code that needs to be reviewed may not belong to the company you think. Oracle and IBM state that they prefer Linux to Windows (or Solaris), because their development and support staff then has access to the entire software stack. This is better, according to them, than having to go through Microsoft (or Sun) support for the bugs that may originate there. But this is the same objection, simply at the next level. And no doubt SAP says the same thing about the Sun and IBM database support. So we all want everyone else to be open to us, at the very least.

Let's emphasize that this is in no sense a theoretical issue. It is about getting work done day to day, under pressure, and with some guarantee of results. In most cases that work will be done by someone you hired. Here is an analogy: You probably don't sign contracts without an attorney's review or send tax forms without an accountant's review. It is your right to read these documents that allows your accountant or attorney to read them. In some other legal system, you might not have that right.

If you can read the source code yourself, it becomes more personal. The Free Software Movement originated in a printer driver that Richard Stallman was unable to fix because the printer manufacturer refused to let him have the source code. I have been personally frustrated on many occasions by problems caused by bugs in code I was not allowed to see by the software vendor, or by insufficient understanding of how the code is expected to work, such as what the meaning is of various parameters passed in. If you have been reduced a couple of times to hanging on a telephone waiting for someone who is often not a programmer to basically read bits of the code to you in a sort of guessing game, you would want to work with open source software too.

3.1.2   Why Your Right to Change and Redistribute Code Matters

There are reasons why you want to be able not only to view the source code, but to change it and possibly redistribute it.

First, code has to be kept up-to-date to be worth seeing, and that mechanism must be public. While only a small percentage of a large code base will have changed after a few months, it will be precisely those few percent that will have had the reported and fixed bugs. Your bug is probably in there as a fix or caused by a fix, and if not it is statistically likely to be close by because bugs are known to cluster. It is a waste of time looking through old code for current problems. There is other value in old code, such as to see general architecture or coding style or to learn the application. But for purposes of finding and correcting problems, only current code is satisfactory. As a practical matter, this means that some sort of code repository, such as CVS, which supports concurrent source code updates, is needed to make source code sufficiently current.

Second, as a practical matter, we have found that the ability for serious users to contribute is a real source of strength for the large open source projects such as Linux and Apache. It has allowed them to improve more rapidly than the largest and best closed code competitors, and much more than the average closed code product, which is usually very resource constrained. Although it may not be necessary for every open source product to allow broad contribution from users, and many closed code products have been successful over the years without it, it is wasteful to lose this when it is available.

Third, and most importantly, the ability to "fork" or spin off a completely new competing line of code is the guarantee that the code is open and available. The possibility of the "fork" means that if in the future some open source project falls into incompetent or malicious hands, or that the original authors don't want to maintain it or upgrade it, there is a choice. It will always be possible for another group to set up a rival program that can support the same existing customers and interfaces but start to develop in a new direction.

The "fork" is the last line of defense option of the open source world—an expensive choice, rarely used, with strong social pressure against it. But it is the mechanism that ensures that ownership of the product resides with the users, not the author. It means that if, for example, Red Hat Linux were to go out of business, another company or even your organization could pick it up and maintain it.

3.1.3 You Can Buy from Different Vendors and Adopt New Platforms

You do have to plan and build for a capability to buy from multiple vendors; if you do, your investment in software and business practices is safer than if you rely on one closed code platform. This has been proven repeatedly in the past.

In particular, systems based on "PC" commodity hardware have proven much less expensive than closed code single-vendor systems. Linux, of course, benefits from this because it runs on those commodity platforms. Hardware parts, training, support, and software such as drivers all generally cost more when you are restricted to a single vendor.

Freedom to choose can reduce costs through commoditization, but that is not all. It allows competition on function or style as well as price. There is also a considerable danger of obsolescence of computer platforms over time.

History has shown that it is a good idea to be prepared to move systems to new platforms and architectures, hardware, and software.

Open source is portable theoretically and practically. Theoretically, it is portable because the source code is available and the tools to build from the code (notably the GNU C/C++ compiler but much more) are available on many platforms and are also portable, so it can be done. Practically, we find that open source products are generally available on multiple platforms where this makes sense, so it actually is done.

Today, there are two major operating systems that are widely installed and still growing in installations on server and desktop computers: Windows and Linux. There are also three other types of systems that are important, although less widely installed:

- UNIX, mostly Mac OS X on desktops, and Solaris, HP-UX, and AIX on servers. Other UNIX systems sell in smaller volumes.

- IBM operating systems sold on IBM and compatible mainframes and AS/400s.

- Embedded and other tiny systems, including Palm Pilots, tablet PCs, appliances, and electronic items.

Windows is only available for Intel (previously Intel and Alpha); there is a version of Windows available for embedded systems on a variety of processors but it is a different code base, just branded Windows. Microsoft servers and tools such as SQL Server, Visual BASIC, and Internet Information Server are generally available only on Windows, with a few rare exceptions.

UNIX systems are only available for their respective vendor hardware. OS X is available only for Apple systems. Solaris is really only available for Sparc systems, since the Intel-based Solaris is a different code base with many missing high-end features. Other IBM operating systems are for specific IBM or plug-compatible hardware.

Only Linux is available on a wide range of hardware platforms from different vendors, using various processors, in many configurations. This includes all of those previously mentioned, as well as Intel, PowerPC, Sparc, IBM servers, and embedded systems. Open code servers and languages such as Apache, MySQL, Python, and Perl are available on Linux, but are also available on Windows, Mac OS X, Solaris, and other systems.

3.1.4 Open Source Avoids Proprietary Information Formats

It is unusual for open source to implement proprietary data formats, but it is not impossible. Open code could use proprietary keys to make data inaccessible even though the algorithms are public, as is done routinely for security reasons. Open code could also use legal means to protect data storage even though the algorithms are known, in the same way that Unisys did with the GIF format for years.

But the most common method used by closed code companies to implement proprietary formats is simply not to publish them, combined with changing the formats periodically and reserving the right to do so. Because open source code can be read (and copied), this method is not available to open source products. Generally, open source as a matter of principle avoids proprietary control also.

Unfortunately, it has been the general practice for vendors to develop proprietary formats that are not fully documented, and to reserve the right to change those formats. This is not usually defended as a right; it is most often argued that it is technically too difficult to publish the formats and maintain them over time in a consistent manner.

Information created by individuals and corporations belongs to them, or in some cases to broader bodies, so legal constraints on data access are unlikely to apply to individuals publishing their own information. Government information may belong to all people, for instance. This is not usually bounded by time and place.

Examples of proprietary data formats include Microsoft Office (Word/Excel/PowerPoint), and also enterprise server software such as SAP, PeopleSoft, and so on. Documents you create may last for years. It is not unusual to have to convert the formats several times. For example, at some time, you may want to show them on the Web or on a Palm Pilot. You should never pay a license fee to access your own data as many vendors require, and you should be sure that you can always access it.

3.1.5 Open Source Allows Integration between Products

With open source, because data and code specs and source code are available, you can always make things work together by examining these documents. With proprietary systems, you are dependent on the code owner to make changes (or not).

Proprietary systems are more likely than open source to offer canned and integrated "solutions." Unfortunately, these are rarely more than marketing fluff. They are unlikely to involve multiple vendors, except by using special and expensive integration engines. They are unlikely to work with older products from the same vendor, or if they do they may require special adapters at extra cost. And quite often, even current products from a single vendor will not work together as you would expect. In real life, you do have to put together your own system from many pieces to solve your issues. If the code is closed, you will probably be stymied.

If you purchase all of your systems from a single vendor, you may eliminate some integration problems, but most likely not all, unless you are somehow able to make a single purchase of everything you need at one time. Integration at any time may be limited and ad hoc. Over time, the formats and preferred integration methods change and integration is very limited.

Large companies such as IBM and Microsoft have their own integration issues, since they purchase technologies from outside software developers and bundle them together. Even when products are built in house, their in house groups may not use the same technology.

I will use Microsoft as an example here, but I could have used IBM, not that these two are worse than anyone else, but they have more products. Various Microsoft products use the following data stores:

- Jet database engine, which has at least two internal variants, based on, but not the same as, the database engine within Access.

- SQL Server, sometimes using the database in transparent ways, on other occasions obscuring the format to prevent user access (as in Commerce Server) or accessing only through unpublished stored procedures (Great Plains products).

- IIS uses a poorly documented "metabase," which has its own proprietary format.

- Windows registry (now deprecated but still used by many products and supported for compatibility).

- XML files with a variety of application-specific formats, not all published, and at least three different schema standards over time.

This is uncountable, but can easily be ten different formats in one organization.

In the real world, we buy products over time from different companies and keep them operating for years. Integration is a hard problem that we must deal with. Open standards and source code are essential parts from which the solutions to integration can be constructed. The alternatives using closed source are vendor-managed product integration and general-purpose integration engines. These are expensive, often disappointing in reach, can restrict our ability to choose products, and often do not work for the specific situations we need in a particular organization.

3.1.6   Open Source Licensing Is Simpler and Less Expensive

Open Source Is Less Expensive

Open source saves money over closed code software in almost all cases. The logic is simple. The software costs much less, while all other costs can be expected to be approximately the same or less unless some special circumstances apply. I'll use Linux in the following examples, but the same would apply to other products, such as MySQL.

Hardware costs are about the same between Windows and Linux. Sometimes, particular products outperform others. One reason many people are adopting Linux for file and print serving now is that in most cases, current Linux versions will serve more users than Windows on the same hardware, whereas two years ago they supported less.

Support and training costs vary greatly among organizations, but will be similar between open and closed code. Most often, you can expect to pay more for support or training around closed code, which is visible only to one vendor, since it has an effective monopoly. This is very common with smaller closed code software companies, which typically have very high margins on training and consulting.

It is possible to find a few cases where open source is not less expensive; although this is not easy, it is apparently a challenge that closed code vendors are always willing to step up to. The trick here is to use an expensive Linux or open source distribution and compare it to an inexpensive way of procuring the closed code alternative in a very precise way.

Perhaps an easier thing to do is to prepare "total cost of ownership" numbers, where the real advantage of open source in licensing costs is swamped by some other large numbers. This can be done in a variety of ways:

- Use expensive hardware (e.g., putting Linux on a mainframe).

- Use expensive development, management tools, or services in the Linux comparison.

- Use large numbers for development, training, support, or downtime; then estimate Linux as a little (or a lot) worse than the closed code solution in this area.

All of these things have been done in published reports.

The "best and final" method for demonstrating that open source is not less expensive is the incumbency trick. Some costs favor the incumbent over the newcomer. These costs will systematically favor Windows over Linux and Oracle over MySQL, and they can be large. Two of these are training and staffing.

Training is a big one-time cost for the newcomer product but a sunk cost for the incumbent. It is also easy to make training an arbitrarily large cost, particularly since it can apply to all users and can be combined with other soft numbers such as error rates or user satisfaction during transition.

Over the longer term, training is always with us and the more stable progress of open source software and availability of quality materials will tend to lower that cost over closed code. In the short run, imputing higher costs of training to open source is commonly "the last refuge of a scoundrel" attempting to prop up an expensive closed code software deal.

Staff costs for developers and administrators are another big cost for the newcomer. The incumbent product must already have trained people on staff supporting it. In general, Linux developers and administrators are widely available with good experience at reasonable rates. The skills to manage and develop for Apache, Linux, Perl, and MySQL are not greater than similar Microsoft or other systems, and they are more stable over time. These skills are what young people are learning, so if in a few places Microsoft skills are more common or less expensive, the trend is toward open source within the next few years. However, it is very possible that in a time of transition, some of these open source skills will be bid up in the short run, leading to apparently higher costs.

Open Source Licensing Is Simpler

Whatever the dollar cost of closed source software may be, another cost is licensing. Companies have to put staff and tracking programs in place to manage purchased licenses. The costs of noncompliance can be embarrassing and arbitrarily high, and will certainly involve dismissal for some systems administrators.

Furthermore, many people overbuy licenses because it is difficult to manage concurrent use. One reason so many companies choose the Microsoft licensing programs is that they are designed to be easy to administer by licensing all desktops, including many where the software is probably never used. This is very possibly by design; Microsoft has certainly never favored concurrent licensing, since at any time only a small percentage of most licensed software users are using the software..

You Control Software Upgrades

Using open source, there is no need to accept "upgrades" that break everything, such as those we have endured with Office, Exchange (with Active Directory), SQL Server, and Commerce Server. The need to upgrade on a vendor schedule leads to expensive unplanned migrations, getting locked into old versions (and losing the new features and bug fixes), or high and unpredictable licensing fees.

Another benefit from this lack of churn with open source is experienced developers; there are plenty of Perl, shell, and C programmers with five or ten years practical experience, but there are few five-year C#, VB.Net, or Java developers. And that five-year-old Perl code still works today alongside new code, unlike most five-year-old applications using Java application servers or COM components.

3.1.7   Open Source is a Good Solution for International Companies

Everyone in the world is not going to license closed code software at today's prices. Today, that has led to heavy use of unlicensed software in many countries.

If an organization is operating overseas, the cost of software may already be an issue. So what looks like overwhelming market share in the United States looks different in Germany or Japan, not to mention Brazil, India, or China. Many newer global competitors will not be paying the high fees to closed code companies that so many large U.S. companies pay.

The decision to make software available in a particular language and culture is a difficult one for a closed code company. It appears that we are beginning to see internationalization of open source products in marginal countries, where the resources are available to work in the local language.

Microsoft, for example, supports about fifty languages but there are many hundreds in use including a dozen each in India and China. Open source software can be translated into these languages by local resources even if it is not economically worthwhile from a central perspective.

Where an impact could be felt is in some specific locations, since closed source companies from areas such as California, Washington, and Massachusetts have tended to centralize consulting and support jobs there. If open source opens up opportunities, other U.S. areas and countries such as India, Brazil, China, and Germany hope to see open source as improving their local employment opportunities, although they may underestimate the power of existing clusters to maintain an edge in the complex sets of skills and relationships that underpin succesful software production.

3.1.8   There Is a Large Pool of Skilled Open Source Professionals

At the present time, with the majority of servers and an overwhelming majority of desktops running Windows, there is an approximate parity in cost and availability of skills between Linux and Windows. Some surveys or studies find one or the other is easier to staff, and there are substantial regional variations.

For other open source software, the situation varies. It is easier to find Apache than IIS experienced personnel. However, it is harder to find MySQL or Perl professionals than SQL Server or Visual BASIC professionals.

It is common today for an enterprise that is considering switching to using more open source to find that there will be additional costs associated with training or acquiring the new skills. In a particular U.S. commercial center, there may be a shortage of MySQL or Python developers, particularly if a large organization is actively seeking them. But these issues should be transitional. We went through similar disruptions when the market switched from Novell to Microsoft networking, or from network to relational databases. After a couple of years, the balance is restored.

In the case of Linux, the skills and training issue is helped immensely because Linux is really the same as UNIX from a skills perspective. Older UNIX professionals may have a little to learn about the new Linux GUIs and PC technologies such as wireless networking, but their core skills in C or shell programming survive. Large numbers of recent college graduates and professionals in the developing world are now exposed directly to Linux and open source as their primary computer skills, and these people are entering the workforce in great numbers.

The nature of open source makes it easier for a large motivated group to learn. Anyone who chooses has access to the code and can run it on inexpensive and widely available equipment. This is not true, for instance, of Oracle, WebLogic, or Solaris. In addition to source and executable code being freely available, it is also the nature of open source that documentation, books, and training are available very competitively and in many cases at no cost.

While there is approximate parity now, open source is likely to gain advantages over closed code internationally and over time.

3.2   Open Source Is Not Enough by Itself

It may be a good thing that a system is open source, but it is not sufficient. It is commonly argued that open source generally has certain good features by virtue of its construction—for example, that it is secure, virus free, reliable, or at least more so than closed code software. This certainly seems to be true of most of the well-known open source products discussed in this book, such as Apache and Linux. However, it is not necessarily true that all open source products are well written, let alone that any particular product is best suited to the purpose you have in mind. In fact, to make a point, you or I could take a lousy piece of undocumented and poorly tested code today, donate it to the community, and it would be on the Internet server Freshmeat tomorrow as "open source software" ready for download.

We will want to review any open source product for openness of each component and standard employed. Once we have an open source product we want to use, we will want to review at least the following elements:

- Platform portability (hardware, OS)
- Database portability (stored procedures, APIs)
- Language
- Data architecture
- Software quality (modular, documented)

3.2.1   Deployment Platform

We would prefer to see applications that can be deployed on standard, scalable computer hardware available from several different vendors and employing internal standard components obtainable in an open market process.

We would prefer applications that can support a range of operating systems, since this will provide the most choices. Ideally, this would include at least Linux, Windows, and other UNIX. Alternatively, we would prefer applications that run on an operating system available on a range of hardware and from multiple sources—in practice, this is Linux.

An acceptable alternative might be a widely deployed operating system from a single very strong vendor (e.g., Microsoft Windows, IBM zOS). In conventional practice, purchasers look for multiple sources for a key product, not a single strong supplier. But we need to recognize reality; there are products that run only on Windows or IBM zOS today.

As a general rule, if an application is not now available for multiple platforms it is probably not going to be in the future. However, in some cases, we might want to review an application for future portability. This would depend on the language chosen and avoiding specific ties to platform features.

3.2.2   Database Platform

If the application uses a database, we would like it at a minimum to use a standards-based (SQL) database and a consistent, well-designed current interface to that database's APIs and stored procedures.

It would be preferable to have a choice of databases, particularly because some databases require particular platforms for the underlying hardware and OS. This is not always going to be possible, since the extra work of supporting multiple databases is not always justified for an application.

Unfortunately, the SQL standard is not sufficient to ensure that an application does not have dependencies on a particular database. We will generally need to recognize the limits of SQL portability and review database design and access strategy to maximize it.

3.2.3   Software Language, Architecture, and Implementation

We want the application to be written in an open source language, preferably one that is portable between platforms. This set of languages generally includes C/C++, Perl, Python, PHP, and UNIX shell. Java is not an open source language. The Java specification is not open, although there are competing implementations of the language that are open source software. However, it is cross-platform, and much open source software is written in Java.

It is particularly important to review the software architecture to identify dependencies on code libraries, platform APIs, and so on. Most languages are portable until those issues are considered. For that reason, applications that are actually available today on multiple platforms are to be preferred over those that could theoretically be available. For example, an application written in Java for WebSphere is likely to be difficult to move to other platforms even though Java is portable.

It is also necessary that application software is modular, documented, and free of restrictions on use so that it can be revised if necessary. The well-known open source licenses will be free of such restrictions. Products need to be specifically reviewed for modularity, since we are looking to see if the system can be adapted to our anticipated needs, and for quality of documentation in the context of our expected users and scenarios of use.

3.2.4   Data Architecture

The important issues with application data architecture are that it allows external access to all data through well-understood standards—for example, SQL or XML—and that this access is documented with examples and is free of restrictions on use.

If the data is stored in SQL or XML but needs special programming or reverse engineering to get, or is not documented, that's a problem. There might be some efficiency and security considerations, and this could be a question of timing, but if the closed code vendor can get to this and you can't, then the vendor is hiding a code library that you need and calling it a trade secret, and that's not right.

In some cases, applications may impose per customer fees or license-based restrictions on access to data. So in these cases, you know where your data is, you have figured out how to get it and display it, and you still owe a fee or have to ask permission to use it. I would not want to explain this to my management.

Other questions to ask to test the openness of a system include:

■ For each vendor, what do I do if it goes bankrupt, tries to overcharge me, or ceases to support the product?

- What will it take to move the system to a platform an order of magnitude larger or smaller?

- How easily can I obtain a package or build a new application to add or replace functionality?

I first wrote this list in another book in 1994. At that time, systems could only approach these ideals to a limited extent, because significant systems were almost always built on closed code and open source was not then a serious option for business systems, or I hadn't realized it was.

An interesting question arises. Is open source necessary to achieve this? How can we determine these good qualities for a closed code product? For open source, we will review the product code and documentation to whatever level of detail we wish. For closed source products, it is not clear how we will do this.

Generally, for a closed source product, we will see documentation on use but only colored diagrams for the architecture. If we see the architecture in detail, it may not be correct. There have been incidents in the past of closed code vendors showing mock-ups and claiming they were completed code, announcing that a product is XML-based when it is not, or that a product is based on a new technology such as Java when it just uses thin wrappers to access older code. It is actually very common for security companies to claim closed code algorithms and so on, but actually have nothing to back these up. Consider the controversy over Windows "hidden APIs," which Microsoft allegedly used to obtain an edge for Office. Although I don't believe this, it was never really resolved. Open source has no hidden APIs by definition.

Further, how do you know that a particular database or operating system will be supported in the future, since that is a business decision by the vendor to be made at that time? A case in point is the history of Windows NT platform support. It was announced for Intel, Alpha, and MIPS, and then added PowerPC, but it wound up being Intel only after decisions by Microsoft (MIPS), Motorola (PowerPC), and Compaq (Alpha). With open source, you can make your own choices; of course, the economic drivers may push you to the same decision.

3.3 How Choosing Open Source Is More Difficult for You

There are some ways the computer business is structured that will make it more difficult for you to choose open source software and advocate it in your organization.

The business has traditionally consisted of large companies with a direct sales force and substantial marketing budgets. These are able to provide direct sales people in support of a corporate evaluation, and to feed a stream of independent reviews and trade journalism that generates demand for the products. The shape of the business also influences the structure of applications into "suites" or other forms of bundle.

Open source software does not have the direct sales force, the marketing budgets, or the incentive to bundle product. As a consequence, it can seem "weird," unless you are expecting this.

3.3.1 Open Source Has a Less Complete Level of Sales Support

No Direct Sales Model

There are not many products, particularly in the early stages of adoption, that sell themselves. Without a direct sales force, many products are unlikely to be adopted. Indeed, otherwise good products may not even be considered. Microsoft Test, for example, was a product as good as the competition, but it never sold since it was too inexpensive and had no direct sales force; eventually it was given away to Rational.

It is difficult to sell products that cost less than a threshold value through a direct sales force. This value is driven by simple arithmetic as applied to a sales pipeline. A single sales rep may be able to track a dozen realistic opportunities and close one or two a month. In this business, a rep may receive 5 percent to 8 percent of the sale. To make a good living on these numbers, each sale has to average around $100,000. This value has not changed substantially in a generation, although it fluctuates depending on whether times are bad or good.

The problem of funding a direct sales force makes it hard for open source products if they are sufficiently complex to require a direct sale. It is a particular problem if they must compete against a direct sales force, as do JBoss and MySQL. Databases and application servers are almost always sold directly. These two companies also follow dual licensing (they charge corporations), but they need to develop a set of training, consulting, systems integration, and support to get their overall package to a sustainable price.

This situation is a major reason why complete open source software solutions are rarely sold by themselves. What is most often sold is a hybrid involving a closed code or some other proprietary solution on top of or alongside open source, and this can pay for the expense of the sale. Examples of hybrids with closed code on top include WebSphere on Apache, Oracle on Linux, or SAP on Linux and MySQL. Examples with closed code or proprietary hardware alongside include IBM sponsorship of mainframe Linux, or Hewlett-Packard offering all new computers running Linux for file and print consolidation.

Selling from Inside

It can also be hard to be the direct sales force in this situation. The internal opponent has some advantages. It can always be present for meetings or presentations. It can usually provide examples relevant to the business, and it may have existing relationships and reputation that work in its favor.

With almost any large complex product, but particularly with integration products, such as Microsoft BizTalk, WebMethods, or Web service integration, it is usually necessary to write some custom code to solve one or more specific situations. The internal person has real advantages here, and has often developed a specific solution already if he or she can get the tools. Database and development tools such as SQL Server and Visual BASIC have often been successful against direct sales in these internal situations, and development tools often do well here also.

The sales support that a large vendor can offer (for or against) can include executive-level pressures. In some organizations, it is difficult to counter these from technical positions. A good vendor:

- Puts on sales demonstrations, provides references, and prepares information on costs and competitors

- Meets or bypasses objections from IT traditionalists

- Helps manage senior management buy-in

- Provides technical demonstrations and may help set up a tech lab

- Offers installation support and advice to evaluators

- May offer consulting or other help to make the first case successful

An important objective of this book is to provide this kind of ammunition for the internal change agent to use when competing against a direct sales force, both directly in the content of various chapters and indirectly by suggesting resources where this kind of information can be obtained and is always kept current.

3.3.2   Specific Product Reviews Will Not Favor Open Source

Product reviews are generally conducted fairly and in a reproducible manner by an independent company, and in that sense are fair. There is no shortage of general information from reviewers and vendors indicating that open source in general and Linux in particular are important upcoming trends. This book has already quoted several of these statements, and they continue to be published regularly. The views of companies such as Gartner and IDC have been very helpful in spreading the word in these areas to organizations that might otherwise have been uncertain or unnecessarily conservative.

However, specific reviews comparing an open source product to a closed code competitor are another matter. This type of review is generally commissioned by one party, and that party gets to select aspects of the review that are not explicitly stated but bear heavily on the results. This is the standard practice in the industry, and generally leads to a "rough justice" over time as different vendors sponsor reviews and comparisons at times and over issues of their choosing.

In the case of open source, the same process leads to a systematic bias against the open source product, because that product invariably has less money (and spends less on marketing). To look at this in more detail, there are four ways that specific product reviews can be misleading. The controlling party selects:

- The package of products under consideration

- The timing of the review against release dates

- The competitors to compare against and the versions of the product to compare

- The behavior being evaluated (e.g., performance, stability, ease of use)

Package of Products

The differences in the way open source and closed systems are packaged and sold can lead to misleading comparisons. Open source distributions generally include office suites, various personal tools, databases and other servers, and development tools, often several of each kind. These are generally automatically installed for you if you select a profile such as "professional" or "developer," and at no additional charge. Because the closed code vendors fund the reviews, they may choose to essentially define the functions to review as what they have included themselves and ignore the others.

Timing Reviews against Release Dates

There are differences in the timing of releases and the reviews. This one ought to balance out but it systematically favors the closed code vendors, because they fund the reviews and thus pick the timing. So the review will compare a late beta product with its new features against an older product from open source.

In one example, a study that focused on ease of installation did not compare the currently available versions of Windows Small Business Server (SBS) and Red Hat. At the time, Red Hat Enterprise Linux 2.1 was in production and SBS (based on Windows 2003 Server) was in beta. The study did not wait for a beta of RHEL 3, which is much easier to install.

Competitors and Product Versions

Another issue is product versioning. The same review which compared Red Hat Enterprise Linux 2.1 (RHEL) with Microsoft Small Business Server did not compare similar products. Small Business Server is a low-end version of Windows Server with restrictions on number of users and throughput, bundled with a limited-use version of the SQL Server database and some other products, such as a fax server and a wizard-based front end, which were included specifically to improve ease of installation for small businesses. RHEL is the version of Red Hat Linux designed and priced for use by large ("Enterprise") businesses, having, for instance, clustering and a choice of full-function database packages. RHEL should be compared with the more expensive Microsoft Windows Advanced Server. More relevantly, Small Business Server should have been compared with Red Hat Linux 9, which was a production release at the time. Red Hat Linux 9 was positioned for smaller and home businesses and was much easier to install.

Evaluation Criteria

Criteria being evaluated are selected by the reviewer to favor the comparison. This includes what is measured and which products are selected for competition. For example, Microsoft prefers to evaluate application development as .Net versus Java, because Java tools are more expensive and harder to develop with with than, say, PHP. When Oracle and IBM review application servers, they go against each other. They don't want to count the Microsoft product, because it is "free" (bundled into the OS), so they usually arrange for a review of "Java servers" or they don't count the Microsoft product as an application server.

When Microsoft reviews Web servers, it finds that it is the "commercial market leader." In this case, Microsoft, which has less than a 20 percent share, is choosing not to count Apache, which has a 65 percent share but is "free." Actually, Internet Information Server (IIS) is "free," according to Microsoft, since it is bundled into the operating system.

3.3.3   Open Source Products Are Not Bundled, Branded, or Integrated

Bundling is when several products come packaged together. There is generally some, often limited, integration. Branding is when several products are named similarly so that all can benefit from the reputation of some.

Bundling

Closed source products have several incentives to pursue bundled software (that is, to put together several solutions with incentives to buy them together), branding strategies (associate products with each other), or to create direct tie-ins between products. These incentives are as follows:

- Often, this is needed to bring the direct sales force sufficient revenue to keep operating.

- It is an advantage for a sales force to have more products to sell to the same customer they are calling on anyway.

- If individual product revenues rise and fall over time, a portfolio of products can smooth the results.

- People may need products to work together. If the products are closed source, the most likely way for them to work together efficiently is if one vendor, with access to the source, makes it happen.

This applies to almost every enhancement made over the years to Windows Server, such as the recent introduction of Active Directory or Sharepoint Team Services. Product suites such as Microsoft Office and Visual Studio have been very successful in bundling several products together. There is actually little reason for individual customers to choose these suites. Most developers work in a single language, and nobody uses all the tools in Visual Studio. Most serious professional users work mostly in only one of the Office products. Most people don't use all the products, but by making the bundle attractive all are sold to everyone. This is particularly attractive to a purchasing agent, who does not have to worry about what individual users are doing.

Other suites and studios from testing, network management, and database companies often make even less sense to customers. But the suites serve two purposes. The suite commands a good price by including enough function to cost many hundreds of dollars, and it reaches more people at a target organization by grouping together spreadsheet developers with presenters, for instance, or developers with testers.

Microsoft Exchange Server and SQL Server are both cases of single-function products, mail and database servers, that have both chosen to bundle several functions together to increase overall sales. In the case of Exchange, this has extended beyond mail to include instant messaging, collaboration, forms, and so on. With SQL Server, the product expanded beyond database to include analysis and data transformation services.

Branding

Microsoft has historically sold three different operating systems under the Windows brand: Windows 98/ME (now obsolete), Windows NT/2000/ XP, and Windows CE. This is a branding strategy. There are some common characteristics, such as a similar look, and an attempt to make tools such as SQL and VB run across the platforms, but these are in fact three totally different code bases.

This can also be seen in branding strategies such as IBM WebSphere and Tivoli, or the Sun Java Desktop. The result can be, in some cases, an appearance of integration, similarity, or "synergy" from the brand, but this is not very useful in reality. There are completely incompatible competing transaction manager products packaged together in WebSphere, and there is very little Java in the Java Desktop, whose important elements are Gnome, Mozilla, Evolution, and OpenOffice.

In contrast, the Linux that runs across platforms from large clustered servers to desktops to small appliances is the same code base, with the same kernel and tools.

Different open source software products often work well together because they tend to use the same standards, but that is not always communicated by product naming or by any sort of marketing effort. So we must look past brands to the components, standards, and integration methods that we need.

Integration

The level of integration offered by closed code platforms is often disappointing, particularly if you assume it. In particular, if what you want is not available you may have no way to proceed at all. Closed code platforms often offer the integration they do because they are closed; you need integration and you can't do it without access to the code, but they won't let you access it, so they have to do it for you. And, of course, integration between closed code products from two vendors is very difficult. It is best to approach any two products with a needs analysis and a review of what is available.

Open source can appear harder for customers to integrate, because it is more likely to achieve "working together" by making separate parts work using open standards. Such a solution is often a little more difficult to understand and set up, but it is robust enough to support a variety of decisions over time. Integration between databases and development tools is generally high. Open source products generally offer UNIX philosophy-style integration methods; recent products will have XML-based information exchange. Because source code is available, you should be able to make things work at some effort level.

If you feel comfortable and able to go entirely with a single closed code platform vendor, you may be able to get the integration you need. If you acquire all systems from one large vendor such as SAP, Microsoft, Oracle, or IBM, particularly if you acquire them all at the same time, then chances are you will be able to achieve some level of integration. It does need to be specifically checked for. Single sign-on is a clear case where vendors have an incentive to make their products work together within a family, and the result has often not been good for the customer but just another way to be locked in to a single vendor. The single-vendor approach is likely to fail the first time you need to select another product on functional grounds, and the failure puts you right back to the beginning, doing your own integration.

3.4   What Others Say about Open Source

These are some questions we hear repeatedly, often asked by vendors who compete with open source software. Those questions include whether open source is financially viable, if it will fall apart or fade away, and if it is really less expensive.

Can Vendors Make Money from Open Source?

This question is most often asked by vendors that are competing with open source products. Customers are usually untroubled by lower prices in products they buy, if arrived at legally.

It turns out that many vendors are making significant revenues from Linux today. Hardware and systems integration companies are content. IBM and HP are reporting record revenues from profitable hardware and services related to Linux. In 2002, HP reported $2B in "Linux-related revenue." IBM reported $1.5B from Linux in 2002 and expects to report over $3.5B in 2004.

Among software-only companies, Red Hat is profitable selling only Linux-related products and services, and MySQL is profitable selling only SQL-related products and services. While there are many ways to run a software-related business, the most common is to offer a mix of consulting, training, integration, and support services in addition to license or distribution fees. This is the model of open source companies MySQL and Red Hat. It is also the model of primarily closed code IBM and Oracle, which make more money from services than from software licensing. It is also why IBM and Oracle, and almost every other closed code company, are not afraid of the open source model.

Among service companies, little will change. Although Microsoft makes its money mostly from licensing fees, the typical Microsoft Solution Provider today makes no money from licensing fees and actually does not sell the product in the United States. All revenue for these companies, of which there are thousands around the world, comes from charging fees for services. This is a common computer industry model, also true of many IBM business partners and others. It makes no difference to this type of company if it is working with Office and Windows or OpenOffice and FreeBSD.

What If Linux "Fractures" Like UNIX?

The specific reasons for the fracturing of UNIX are complicated and do not appear to be present with Linux.

One problem with UNIX was the trademark issue. Linux can be freely used without trademark acknowledgment to another company so there is not the name fragmentation around Linux that occurred with UNIX, which was marketed variously as Solaris, HP-UX, Xenix, Irix, AIX, Tru64, and SCO Xenix, among others.

Companies competed to enhance UNIX with proprietary improvements that were only available on their systems. Linux licensing requires enhancements to be made available to put back into the (core) code base, so the technical divergences that happened in UNIX cannot occur. It also appears that UNIX vendors discovered that their efforts to create proprietary enhancements at the operating system level were very expensive and did not give them a good return, at least according to IBM and Hewlett-Packard.

Is Open Source Really Cheaper When You Consider All the Costs?

Vendors may point out that if you price a system including middleware, such as IBM WebSphere or BEA WebLogic; database software, such as Oracle; or hardware, such as a mainframe, a solution involving open source may not always be cheaper (or much cheaper) than a system without open source.

Maybe it is not always cheaper in those cases. Customers don't always want cheaper. Maybe they like the solutions involving WebSphere, WebLogic, Oracle, or Linux on a mainframe and think they are worth the money.

On the other hand, you can certainly build systems using open source products without expensive middleware and do a great many things with them, and this book will cover many of these. Further, in the expensive hybrid systems mentioned previously, the open source is always providing inexpensive and flexible elements to the solution and is never specifically the cause of the high cost.

3.5   Summary

There are some differences in buying open source, because it is marketed and sold in a different way. But there are very real advantages to these products. Considered separately, several are simply the best price/performance available in their category. Considered together, open source software offers a group of integrated solutions to many common problems faced by large enterprises.

In areas such as embedded devices, Web servers, engineering workstations, and large clusters, open source systems are already the market-leading choices. In other areas, such as simple application development, transactional databases, and corporate infrastructure servers, it appears that open source will be the market leader or pressing for it within the next two years. In other areas, such as enterprise applications, open source is at an earlier stage and only companies wanting to show technology leadership will be deploying it today.

At its best, the open source process has demonstrated an ability to catch and overtake closed code enhancements while exposing code to massive testing, leading to a great combination of customer value and reliability.

4

Five Immediate Open Source Opportunities

At this point, we have looked at the history and composition of open source, the extent to which open source is already deployed, the successes others have had, and the issues to consider in using it. Now it is time to ask questions in more detail:

- What business opportunities does open source software offer to a typical organization?
- Are there some opportunities that are "low-hanging fruit," that is, easier to take advantage of immediately?
- Which of these opportunities are lowest in risk and biggest in potential payoff?
- Which of these opportunities might be best to avoid and in what circumstances?

The following sections look at a group of the best open source deployment ideas that can be implemented in an organization today. These, in rough order of relevance, consist of:

- Create an open source lab.
- Migrate file, print, and network infrastructure to open source.
- Build one or more Web applications using Apache and related tools.
- Bring new open source desktop and Web systems to the underserved.
- Migrate applications and databases from other systems to Linux.

These opportunities should be relevant to most organizations. The less immediate or more problematic opportunities are in the next chapter.

4.1 Create an Open Source Lab

The first step to take is to set up an open source lab. This supports all the activities that follow, in this book and in the organization, so it is a critical beginning. From experience with other migrations, such as in the personal computer and network eras, we know that using a lab is a pivotal move. It is a first step to take for an organization that is considering open source.

The lab is really a communication tool to discover useful information, activity, and resources and bring it to the attention of decision makers and professionals who can act on it. Figure 4.1 shows the various open source elements on display that are used for communicating with key decision makers, including end users, IT professionals, and executives. It can be a good place to conduct training in relevant open source skills for developers, administrators, users, and executives.

The lab will contain and demonstrate the basic elements of open source software. This should be dedicated space, but does not need to be large and won't need much equipment, at least not unless you get into training on a serious scale. You can use this lab to test the possibilities and limitations of open source, and compare management, use, and running costs to the alter-

Figure 4.1
Open source lab.

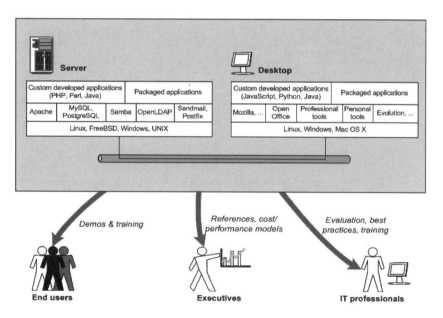

natives that your organization has used. It is a place to test configurations and migrations, including such things as printers and device drivers, and publish papers on how to do that.

This makes future decisions simpler, since they can be tested and demonstrated in the lab. It is also a vehicle for training professionals and end users. Specific issues and problems of your organization can be tackled, resolved, and the solutions demonstrated. This creates a track record of success to build on.

If cost is a concern, the lab can be kept very small and use only used equipment. If there is an existing lab, it may well become a corner of that. It is generally useful to have some space available nearby that you can control, so there should be a lab of some sort, but if space is tight, alternative ways to execute some of the work recommended for the lab include using external expertise, such as a consultant or help from a user group, to achieve some of the goals. Training and other tasks that involve large amounts of space and equipment can be subcontracted to organizations that have such space and equipment.

4.1.1 Review Existing Work

Review existing work to see where open source is already in use in the organization. Identify and involve evangelists and early adopters from within the organization. This begins with identifying areas where open source has already been adopted and finding out who was responsible.

Among the lessons we have learned from the adoption of personal computers and local area networks are the possibilities of bottom-up, or guerrilla, techniques of persuasion. Mainframes and big database servers are expensive, so they always have to be sold from the top down, with boardroom meetings and budget requisitions. With less expensive assets, sometimes things just happen. If you can identify early adopters, who just went ahead and introduced solutions without asking for permission, you may have found useful assets for future deployment.

Look for existing use of open source products in your own organization, such as:

- Outsourced services such as Web sites or Web services that may use open source

- Software packages that have been installed on open source or are under consideration and could be so installed

- Departments or divisions that have made or are considering unilateral moves
- Individual evangelists or developers who are considering or using open source

If there are guerrilla departments or individuals who have already deployed open source, the likeliest candidates are:

- Small Web sites using Apache and PHP
- Small databases using MySQL
- Scripting using Perl or UNIX shell scripts on Windows
- Use of Samba for Windows file sharing
- Individual Linux desktops
- Appliance servers for Web, caching, network, storage, and firewall/security

At the least, this research will provide a baseline against which to measure future activity. For example, it will be interesting to see the percentage of the budget being spent on open source software and whether that percentage is growing, as well as the percentage of people with experience developing, deploying, and using open source.

Many organizations turn up references that are particularly relevant to them because they are internal. Further, where successful open source implementations are found, you have probably also found internal technical resources or evangelists who can help in the future.

Getting this research started can be a reasonably quick activity. For someone who is enthusiastic about this, it will take no more than a few telephone calls until an interesting case is found and then maybe some interviews.

4.1.2 Train Developers to Program in Open Source Languages

We can train Microsoft Visual BASIC developers to develop in the open source programming languages PHP or Python. These languages are easy to learn and productive to use, and there is no charge for their installation or use by developers or end users. They can be learned and used on Windows, since they run as well on Windows as any other language.

ASP developers should look at PHP for Web development. PHP is more widely used than ASP, is cross-platform (works on Windows), and is powerful and easy to learn. VB developers should look at Python for interactive development. Python is similar to Visual BASIC in many respects. It is easy to install on Windows, and its Windows implementation is stable, well documented, and well integrated with Windows. Python is installed by default on Linux and Mac OS X. Developers using Python can be as productive in a week or two as they were in Visual BASIC and are capable of producing applications that can run equally well on Windows, Linux, Mac, and other platforms.

The first developers to be trained should be those who can do some new development soon. So they should be in areas calling for rapid application development, where introduction of open source or heterogeneous systems is possible in the next one to two years. A particularly good reason to consider this is if older applications are being phased out and training is being considered in .Net or Java/JSP.

As an alternative, Perl is a good language to choose if the applications involve administrative scripting—for instance, if they would have been done in Windows Scripting Host, data management, or using SQL Data Transformation Services on Windows. Perl is easy to install, runs well, and is frequently used on Windows, but it is less VB-like than Python, more resembling shell scripts or the DOS batch language. Shell scripting is also a possibility here.

4.2   Migrate Infrastructure to Samba and OpenLDAP

4.2.1   File and Print Servers

According to the Gartner report "Fear the Penguin" (January 2003), by 2004 most organizations will, as a standard practice, be deploying file and print servers based on Linux. Essentially, this means using Samba for file and print sharing. See Figure 4.2.

Linux servers can use Samba combined with print management such as CUPS to serve Windows clients without change to the clients. This system supports other desktops also, since Samba clients (and servers) ship with current Linux and Mac systems. In fact, this does not have to be a Linux

Figure 4.2
*File and print
infrastructure.*

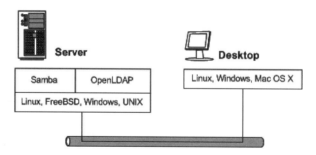

server. It could be any UNIX system, including Mac OS X or FreeBSD, or it could be network-attached storage appliances. But Linux is probably going to offer the best price/performance.

The big payoff for this move is that there are no client access licenses (CALs) to pay for and keep track of. Windows CALs for file, print, and directory services can be significant for large organizations.

This will work for many organizations with only trivial effort, but not for all. The big problem that has to be analyzed with this idea is the problem of user authentication—of how much you need to rely on a centralized directory for security. Briefly, we'll just note for now that Samba 2 supports NT4 authentication, and Samba 3 supports Active Directory. We will discuss the details in a following section.

Most organizations now have many smaller servers doing these functions. They may have successfully standardized on Windows NT4 or Windows 2000, while others have standardized on Novell 3.2 or 4.1, a version of UNIX, or even OS/2. Most organizations are not using all of these, of course, but some are and most are using more than one.

All of these situations are coming toward end of life in the next couple of years, with costs amortized and functionality up for review. These older systems will usually have many small servers and can be candidates for consolidation, in addition to being perceived by their users as plainly obsolete.

Table 4.1, which is based on some private information gained in 2003, shows the approximate composition of the installed base in thousands of servers in January 2003, as well as those that are file/print servers exclusively.

Hypothetical Analysis

The current Linux run rate is higher than UNIX and Novell combined, and is forecast to match Windows during 2004. As UNIX systems used for file and print age, the natural migration path for these systems is Linux. This is also true for Novell systems now that Novell is clearly a Linux company fol-

Table 4.1 *Installed Server Systems 2003*

Server OS	# Installed (millions)	# File/Print (millions)
Windows	9.5	6.3
Novell	3.3	3.3
UNIX	3	1.35
Linux	2.3	N/A

lowing the recent acquisitions of Ximian and SuSE. Organizations with significant current Novell use are likely to adopt Linux going forward.

If the existing Novell and UNIX file/print systems were all migrated to Linux over the next two years, and if forecasts that Linux server shipments will match Windows this year are correct, then by the end of 2005 the majority of file/print servers would be on Linux even if all Windows systems are unchanged.

But there is reason to think many Windows systems could be migrated to Linux. In 2002, approximately half of the Windows servers were Windows 2000 or later, the other half being Windows NT. Most Windows 2000 systems, which will have been deployed in volume in 2001 at the earliest, are probably too new for wholesale replacement. We will talk later about what can be done to prepare now to ensure that future migration is not impeded by decisions taken today.

Because Windows allows systems on NT4 to authenticate against Active Directory, it is difficult to determine what percentage of the NT systems is included in Active Directory. We know that many Windows 2000 sites don't use most AD features. If most of the Windows NT systems were installed at the time of NT authentication and then left alone, then less than half the installed systems are probably using Active Directory.

So approximately half of the Windows systems, over 3 million servers, are simple Windows NT4 systems serving file and print services with NT4 authentication, which provides easy migration targets to Linux and Samba.

Figure 4.3 is based on Table 4.1 but splits the Windows systems between NT and 2000. All but the Windows 2000 segment in this diagram can be easily migrated to Linux.

Figure 4.3
*File/print installed
systems.*

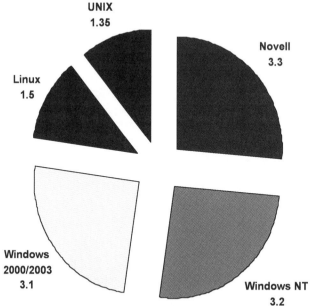

In replacing infrastructure servers, we can choose to:

- Continue to use a distributed design but use Linux servers.
- Consolidate onto fewer larger platforms.
- Replace servers with network-attached storage.
- Combine all three strategies.

Many Small Linux Boxes

The problems of managing many small computer servers for file and print serving are well understood, which is what generates interest in the alternatives. The advantage of this is that we can do a piecemeal upgrade in place, as opposed to trying to buy all new systems. Since Linux systems cost little and will probably outperform the software they are replacing, we get better performance at almost no cost.

Consolidation

Server consolidation is very likely to be a piece of the solution, because it puts configuration and updates under better control. The arithmetic of consolidation can be attractive, but unfortunately organizational boundaries and geography often prevent us from getting the full benefits because some small servers just need to be in remote locations or outlying divisions. Also, vendors price consolidation to reap much of the benefit for themselves; for example, a Microsoft enterprise-class operating system that can replace three servers costs about three times as much as the standard server, and larger hardware is often more costly than smaller. Finally, consolidation is popular with vendors because it generally means buying all new hardware, when much of the older equipment is a sunk cost and may be quite serviceable. Typical organizations should see fairly constant file and print use unless they are expanding employment.

Network-Attached Storage

Network-attached storage (NAS) offers management and cost advantages, although once again actual geography and the need to replace hardware that is a sunk cost can eat up the advantages.

4.2.2   Manage Use of Windows Proprietary Features

The goal here is for those organizations that are not able to make a large-scale move from Windows today to prepare the ground for a move away from Windows to open source when the time is right. This could be in response to a business change, license upgrade, or just when systems are ready for replacement.

We will postpone new licensing as far as possible. We will postpone further use of Active Directory, and look at open alternatives for directory and security. This has the benefit of potentially reducing licensing fees while making integration with non-Windows systems simpler.

We will avoid upgrades in general, as they are only justified by new features. We will stay on NT4 rather than Win2K, and on Exchange 5.5 rather than 2000. We will prepare the ground for open source types of support by looking at community support options over, for example, MS Premier Support.

Systems management tools should be built using open source development tools such as Python, not platform-specific APIs, and tools that are purchased should be open source or cross-platform if possible, or else inexpensive if platform specific. Systems management in particular is an area where good people inside good companies often make large and well-designed investments, only to find themselves trapped within proprietary code.

4.2.3   **Train Administrators in Linux and Samba**

We should train MCSEs in Linux, including Samba and CUPS (file and print sharing), and, if appropriate, OpenLDAP and mail administration.

There are about a half million MCSEs and 1.5M MCPs. These people are often advocates for the technology skills they have now, particularly since it may have taken significant time and money to acquire them. It will be helpful to teach them the open source equivalents.

Microsoft administrators spend a great deal of time setting up file and print services, working with Active Directory and Exchange. Linux and Samba are the open source equivalents.

Any personnel involved in any new or updated deployment of file/print servers should be considered for this.

4.3   **Build Some LAMP Applications**

The Gartner report "Fear the Penguin" (January 2003) forecasts that by 2004, most organizations will be deploying simple applications and four-way clusters on Linux. The single largest reason companies deploy Linux today is for Web development.

An excellent first step is to build one or two simple applications using Linux and Apache with MySQL or PostgreSQL as a database and PHP, Perl, or Python as a development language. This combination, known as LAMP, allows you to build a pure open source system quickly. You are then free to compare the ease of construction and maintenance and the running costs to alternatives that your organization has used. Hopefully this will demonstrate that an open source system is reliable to run, simple to build, and inexpensive to buy and operate. See Figure 4.4.

According to reports on module installation published by the Web site Security Space (www.securityspace.com, March 2004), the Web development language PHP is used at over 50 percent of Apache sites, Perl at 16 percent, and Python at about 1 percent. The PHP number is growing steadily, the Perl number shrinking from a high of about 35 percent, and the Python number is stable. So most people use PHP as the development language with Apache.

MySQL is a powerful database that is easy to install and learn to use, and the LAMP combination makes a nice clean story in terms of licensing and costs, particularly for distribution outside your organization. An alternative open source database is PostgreSQL.

Figure 4.4
LAMP.

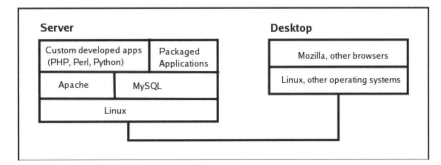

Some organizations have database standards that are difficult to change. If you work in one of those, I would not hesitate to use Oracle, DB2, or SQL Server as the database. Connecting PHP, Perl, or Python to any of these is an easy technical task.

Web Applications

For most people, these will be Web applications using PHP with Apache. They could equally well be external-facing sites, such as Web presence or ecommerce; business to business; or internal-facing sites, such as an employee portal.

Client/Server Applications

Client/server applications can be built also, if that's what you need. Everybody builds Web applications these days, but there is still a type of application that can be less suitable to the Web and more appropriate for client/server. Such an application will have rich information presentation and/or heavy data entry and editing and be aimed at an in-house group whose equipment we control, for example:

- Authors
- Call center
- Customer relationship management
- Decision support or spreadsheets
- Engineering workstations and CAD
- Analysis (financial, mathematical, economic, etc.)
- Medical

Generally, LAMP client/server applications use Python or Perl as the development language. Python is a good choice for rich interactive applications such as these.

Selecting the First System

At this time, you are not likely to be building the first Web application for a company of any size. Likely opportunities to try the new approach may include:

- Building a new Web site or application
- Adding significant new functionality to an existing site or application
- Migrating an application developed with obsolete tools
- Migrating Web development, such as ASP to ASP.Net or JSP
- Development or management of the site is being moved, such as out-sourced or brought back in house

We will be using the first systems to prove something about open source. We should, therefore, avoid toy systems so simple and small that they could have been built in any technology, as well as pilots in the sense of systems that will not be deployed, since neither proves anything and we don't want to throw any work away.

The system should be a good fit to the technology. When completed, it should demonstrate aspects of the technology that are compelling, but this is often impractical. For a LAMP system, this probably just implies that it should be a reasonably interesting and attractive Web site.

The system introduction should not be time critical, because a first-time system needs to allow extra time for training, migration, and mistakes that will not occur on a second or subsequent deployment. It should have a good return on investment for the same reason—so that even if the cost goes over, the ROI is still good enough to justify the system. Preferably, the system should be deployable in phases. A first system may learn valuable lessons early on that will influence later deployment.

Since there is always controversy around the new technology, it is best to ensure early success. It is usually best to avoid attacking the most complex, unmaintainable, innovative, obsolete, or mission-critical problem for the first system. Instead, it is better to pick something that has an excellent chance of succeeding if merely reasonable professional work is done. If you do tackle one of these, you will have to split it into pieces, as discussed previously, so you can start delivering successes early.

Having said all of this, there is no general need to avoid complex, technically advanced systems. Some of the greatest successes of open source systems have been on the leading edge. Sometimes the opportunity that is available calls for heroic effort and risk, and someone has to answer it. Linux, Apache, Amazon, and Google were those types of opportunities. There will be others.

4.4 Bring New Desktop Systems to the Underserved

Simply make open source software available to users who currently don't have and cannot afford a current licensed set of desktop software, including Office, Visio, Photoshop, SQL Server, and Visual Studio. There are no migration costs. The systems will exceed expectations. The software costs are in line with the likely vehicles (cheaper, older, or shared systems) instead of dwarfing them as the closed code software prices would. The hardware needs can typically be met by an older computer. See Figure 4.5.

Users who do not have desktop software today include many in these categories:

- New and small businesses
- Franchised businesses or dealerships, and other business partners
- Customers and others accessing our Web site
- Our home, family, and neighbors
- Community organizations, such as schools and healthcare
- Retail, distribution, and manufacturing workers

Unlike "educational" (e.g., MS Office Student & Teacher Edition) or "charitable" or "donated" closed code software, with open source there are no licensing restrictions or other provisions that will lead to higher expenses down the line. For example, if a student at a college or community center uses Office or Visual Studio to develop an application that is distributed to other schools, he or she may have to pay licensing fees, or the other schools may have to license Office. Or, when you go back next year to get more copies, with closed code the discount or donation may be used up; the open source will still be free. Other groups that have typically been underserved with licensed software include:

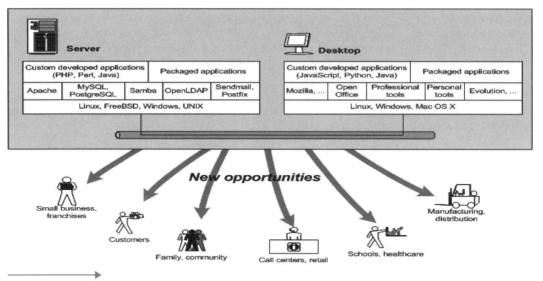

Figure 4.5   *New systems.*

- Call centers

- Manufacturing and distribution

- Retail and hospitality

- Government

- Education

- Healthcare

In the United States alone, these are very large groups, including millions of workers we may be able to empower with better tools at reasonable costs using open source.

We will also consider the special cases of opportunities in developing countries, as well as piracy. These somewhat overlapping groups (because few people in developing countries are paying for software) must be conservatively estimated as constituting tens to hundreds of millions of potential customers for open source software.

4.4.1   New and Small Businesses

New, small, and home office businesses have the opportunity to set up without migration costs, and without the difficulty of communicating change to a large workforce. Some will choose to go directly to an open source stack. This is particularly the case with professional workers who can choose their tools.

The major obstacle to open source adoption for small businesses is their business partners. Often, small businesses do much of their transactions with a few companies, which may be the head office, franchiser, or publisher, and may control the environment.

4.4.2   Franchises

With many retail operations, most of the stores are not wholly owned subsidiaries but instead are franchised. In fast food and hospitality, there are often regional large franchisees that operate dozens or hundreds of stores for one or several franchisers. A restaurant operating company might operate 200 Burger Kings in the Midwest, for instance. A hotel operator might run a collection of Quality hotels for one franchiser and Marriott hotels for another. Franchising is also very common among automobile dealers.

In the franchise situation, it can be difficult to specify particular systems consistently, since the organization buying the systems is not the one specifying. This can lead to several problems:

- Similar systems in different stores implemented with different platforms, so they don't work with central systems that must support them

- Different systems in a store implemented with different platforms, so they don't work together in the store

- Lack of ability to get volume discounts or other leverage, because hundreds or thousands of purchases are split into many small purchases across many organizations

Open source software may offer a way through in the franchise area, by allowing acquisition of software at a reasonable price—for instance, Open-Office—and software that can be customized as needed by differing participating organizations.

4.4.3 **Call Centers**

Approximately 2 percent of the U.S. workforce works in call center or data entry functions. Call centers generally have hundreds of workers on a few dedicated applications. They have these issues:

- Applications are sometimes on legacy boxes
- Need to keep cost low
- Management of workstations should be centralized and simplified, with no unnecessary extra applications or customization

Call center applications often need multiple screens to access legacy systems. This is common in telephone company applications, banking, and insurance, for example. If legacy applications are involved, then screen-scraping, or putting a pretty front end on a "green screen" application, is common. This can become quite sophisticated, so a smart workstation can drive around a bunch of older applications. Because of the need to show several systems concurrently on a screen, some call center systems have used very large displays to show multiple windows, often including the outbound Web site, when talking to customers. Some bought UNIX workstations in the past just to support the large displays.

Often, call center applications are custom developed per campaign—for instance, tied to a particular run of television commercials or telemarketing calls. So the quick development and deployment of the rapid scripting languages PHP and Python can work well here. PHP will be good if the application is Web based. Some call centers want very tight control over the GUI, in which case we would use Python.

Call center applications are generally database intensive. But the database need is most often not monolithic, since most likely a large center will access many related databases for different campaigns and products. If new custom applications are developed, then data propagation out of legacy systems to relational databases is likely. Typically the front system will maintain copies of customer records and catalogs and then push orders or status changes through to the back end.

In some cases there is a requirement for knowledge worker support using email, office software, or image display—but mostly not for creation, just for reading. Most call centers don't choose to license office suites because of the expense.

For call centers, which operate on slender margins, open source has the right licensing model and costs. It is also an advantage in this environment to be able to control the build, so as to keep games and other undesirable software off and even possibly to manage activity in detail.

Turnover is very high, in general, for this industry, because when taking on a new contract, very often an entire new workforce is hired and trained. So training is a constant and not a switching cost. It is as easy for an incoming group that is new to the situation to learn the application, scripts, and products using OpenOffice and Linux as anything else. In any case, the call center employee generally lives inside the application.

4.4.4 Retail, Food Service, and Hospitality

Retail includes companies such as Office Depot, PetsMart, and Wal-Mart, which operate many hundreds or thousands of stores, as well as individual stores and smaller chains, which may have one or a few sites. Automobile dealers are a large retail category in themselves, and one that has often not had very effective computer systems.

Food service includes less expensive eat-in restaurant chains, such as Red Lobster, and fast-food companies, such as Burger King, as well as high-end restaurants. The hospitality sector includes hotels, casinos, cruise lines, and other places where people stay. I will call the location of the point-of-sale system (POS) in all of these cases a "store" in the following text, although it might be a restaurant, hotel, or other location.

These systems typically have many very inexpensive systems placed across a larger number of sites with a few systems per site. For example, a mid-sized retail organization may have tens to hundreds of locations, and hundreds to thousands of systems. The cost of the system must be low, because there are so very many of them and because per store margins are usually low in these businesses.

A typical retailer would like to be stable over many years, as it is very difficult and undesirable to visit a location to upgrade a system in place. There should be, as far as possible, no on-site maintenance. Instead, systems should be managed remotely as much as possible, the rest by publishing simple daily and periodic procedures or talking staff through a simple process in an emergency. Every location needs to be built the same, or according to a few basic blueprints, since there is neither the money nor the time to conduct separate training or installation at different locations.

There is often a need to maintain the organization's own custom build. The most important reason for this is for stability, because systems need to work reliably at remote locations without maintenance. Footprint also matters; since the systems need to be inexpensive and are often old, they may have small amounts of memory and disk storage.

Applications in retail are primarily dedicated and customized for the particular retailer, purchased from specialized vendors that develop point-of-sale and store systems. Those systems are generally "locked down," for the ease of maintenance reasons already cited and also for fraud prevention.

Applications need to be easy to learn to use, since retail locations have very large numbers of staff and turn them over very quickly. On the other hand, these organizations do expect to conduct training from scratch for every hire, so the systems do not need to be particularly standard.

There is value in office software for retail managers, although most of these organizations have not wanted to license Microsoft Office broadly at the store level. Retail stores will have several managers per location, often sharing systems. There could be value in Web-based and multimedia applications for training, since these organizations employ thousands of new staff every year. There could also possibly be a use for mail and other social software to build a stronger community internally or to enable interaction with customer communities—for example, customers generated by applications such as Meetup.com.

A specific problem in retail that comes up repeatedly is the packaging of operating system and server products by closed code vendors. This packaging is designed to get the best price for servers, particularly from large organizations, while allowing certain small businesses to get some use from inexpensive Web and database servers running on workstations based on the same code base. That is done by specifying limited numbers of connections, database size, and so on. The result can be a retail organization that falls "between the cracks," behaving like a small business (which the store may or may not legally be), but wanting to standardize on "corporate" products like the large company that the parent legally is.

Most retail systems are transactional and anonymous, but in hospitality there is a move toward personalization that is still not completed. Hotels, for example, generally may know your credit card number and bed or smoking preference, but will not know the type of food and drink you like. Cruise lines will usually lose all personal information between voyages, although repeat customers are important to them; casinos, on the other hand, will not.

Retail systems are a good market for a low-cost, manageable front-end system that integrates well. They usually have an understood set of applications. They are very good Linux and open source opportunities.

4.4.5   Government, Healthcare, and Education

Government, healthcare, and educational systems all share similar problems across geographies and have no good reason not to cooperate. Closed code software companies perform a service by developing a solution at considerable investment cost in one locale, and then selling it in others. By cooperating, these organizations can smooth and sponsor that process.

Government

It is not common to think of governments as technology leaders, particularly in modern American discourse, but government is often the only vehicle for funding early technologies. Much of the early development of computers, PCs, and the Internet was government funded, often related to aerospace (e.g., NASA) or defense (e.g., DARPA). In aerospace and defense, government can often have a leadership role and be very generous at funding research. This can also happen in healthcare and education in some political environments.

Government is a very good fit in some ways to open source at later stages. Government customers outside of favored programs in defense and aerospace are often acutely concerned about cost. Governments have special motivation to employ open source, including the massive scale of the systems, and often legislation that may require access from "legacy systems." They are likely to have a very large number of users, typically orders of magnitude higher than businesses. Government acquisition cycles often emphasize cost predictability, perhaps from a variety of suppliers over years, over immediate cost savings, so multiple suppliers and consistent pricing may be especially important. Governments often have some unusual requirements, also. They combine some extreme needs for freedom of information with extreme issues of security and privacy. Voting is a special case of these extreme requirements; almost everyone in a territory is processed on the same day, with requirements of privacy and likelihood of fraud that are higher than a commercial credit card or gambling system, and with severe cost constraints.

Of course, not all government issues are on such large scales. There are opportunities for open source at all levels: national government, state/province, city, even subdevelopment (local calendaring and newsletters). Several of the previous points still apply; since government often offers mandatory services to all citizens, price/performance and scalability are always an issue. Others become more important; a lot could be spent on a national voting system if necessary, but reasonable development costs and times are particularly important at smaller scales of government.

Governments deal with issues of fairness. These often suggest use of open standards, nonuse of closed code viewing software, and some requirements that information can be accessed without special software or hardware. There are some special opportunities for government in building communities using social software and groupware.

Government systems have varying reasons to conduct these migrations. First, they may simply be cases of issues discussed elsewhere in this book. Some government agencies may not have been license compliant, for example. Perhaps all of these are foreign governments, but possibly not. Other governments may have fallen somewhat behind in versions—for instance, running Windows NT4 or old versions of Office—so that they are now in a situation to make a sweeping migration to open source to catch up.

Governments often have a funding cycle that is out of phase with software changes, so that it can be difficult to justify annual maintenance fees or unexpected licensing increases. So, government agencies sometimes make large moves after several years of waiting. Also, government agencies often make very large purchases, so they may be very motivated by the cost savings that can occur.

Some government functions seem well suited to open source software. For example, governments may be mandated to allow everyone access to files, a mailbox, voting, and so on, usually without requiring technology restrictions or expenses on the part of the users. And these may extend easily to millions of users. Also, because of the way government funds much research activity, it may be appropriate to demand that it be placed in the public domain or open sourced.

Government agencies are important and influential information publishers. The U.S. government is the world's largest publisher, for example. This subject is a massive tracking job in itself.

In the following text, some governments and agencies are mentioned that are known to be conducting open source deployments, evaluations, and migrations. Any one of us, whether an open source advocate or opponent, needs to be especially wary of these reports. Any fact could be out-of-date or inaccurate, but reports about government evaluations are doubly cursed. Some of these may turn out to be only evaluations that fail and are not adopted; some deployments will fail; some will take a long time to succeed or will succeed only partially; and those that succeed will eventually be superseded by something else. Any reports will probably be tainted by the bias of the observer; biased reporting is even more common when dealing with governments, particularly foreign governments, than with companies. These reports should be compared with the reports we often read about governments defeating crime or disease, or being overwhelmed by it.

China has announced plans to deploy millions of copies of Sun's Java Desktop System, which is based on Linux, OpenOffice, and Gnome. Although this plan is in early stages, more than a million systems already shipped in China with Linux installed in 2002. Brazil, Mexico, Denmark, Peru, France, and Italy have national plans involving many government agencies.

Germany has published migration standards to open source, and many agencies are migrating to open source, with some complete and some in early stages. The city of Munich migration from Office is well publicized.

In Austria, the IT & Communication Board, Census Board, and Ministry of Finance have migrated and others are under way.

The United Kingdom has been investigating open source since October 2003, and has several agencies under way, including the Department for Work & Pensions and the water industry regulator.

South Korea has plans to replace Windows OS and software (20 percent server, 30 percent desktop) with open source replacements, saving $300M/year by 2007.

Among U.S. agencies, the NSA uses its own version of the Linux kernel. The U.S. Census Bureau has developed new systems using Linux, Apache, MySQL, Perl, and PHP.

In the United States, there is now an organization where government entities can exchange information on open source software.

Healthcare and Education

In many countries, healthcare and education are wholly or partially part of the government. In any case, many of the issues, such as very large scale and irregular and inadequate funding, are the same. Cost is the largest issue in healthcare; it has been growing at such a high rate over the last 20 or 30 years that early attempts at managing the problem have stalled. Healthcare also has a very particular problem of allowing many parties cooperating around an individual set of records, while managing privacy. The various parties do not have a high level of trust in each other.

There is an open source healthcare vertical solution called OpenVista, from a company called Medsphere. Medsphere offers integration and services around the highly scalable MUMPS-based VA-developed software for hospital management.

Education systems typically have very large numbers. Giving a mailbox to every child in a school district, for example, can lead to very large volumes of mail traffic far above corporate levels. There is a bug training and ease-of-use problem, since training is often not commensurate with the systems deployed. There is a fairness issue. Private schools and universities may mandate computer and software, but this is often difficult for public schools. If we are going to give computers to high school children, we want to know that they can all use the same office suite. If we require them for design students, we want to know that they all have equal access to PhotoShop or Visual C++. This has been typically handled by educational discounts, but these have been partial and sporadic and cause problems if, for instance, design students moonlight, or if the educational versions have limitations. Open source software is a good response to some of these issues.

4.4.6 Unlicensed Software

Open Source Is a Legitimate Alternative to Piracy

An important case for open source is organizations that have not currently purchased a satisfactory system based on Windows.

There is a large group of organizations that never licensed the software they are using. According to the industry group Business Software Alliance (BSA), 40 percent of the world's software is not legitimately licensed. This rises to higher than 90 percent in some countries. Even in the United States, the BSA reports unlicensed software use of 25 percent nationwide and over 40 percent in some southern states.

All these systems are an immediate candidate for open source. Open source provides immediate legitimacy, allowing use of proven channels of support (including payment). It also offers fair competition, unlike piracy, since businesses in the United States or elsewhere have the same opportunity to lower costs using legitimate licenses.

The implication is that forty percent of the software in the world and 25 percent in the United States should be replaced now by open source in order to reach legal compliance at a reasonable cost.

Piracy Touches Most People

While software piracy is unusual in larger U.S. organizations, and many professionals may not have experienced it there, it is common in smaller businesses, in situations such as franchise operations, among students, and in the home in general. I think we have all seen this going on at a small business or a neighbor's house. There are large flea markets outside every U.S. city every summer weekend selling this stuff.

In some cases an organization may not actually have been using unlicensed software. It may simply be unable to prove that it was not. One well-known instance is Ernie Ball, the California manufacturer of guitar strings and guitars. A raid by armed U.S. marshals in 2000 found six unlicensed copies of Microsoft Office. The company had a $65,000 fine imposed on it, incurred $35,000 in legal fees, and received unwelcome publicity. Subsequently, Ernie Ball switched from Microsoft Windows and Office to Red Hat Linux and OpenOffice. The company says that it never used the illegal software; six old computers, out of 72 in the company, had simply been handed down to engineering with the software still on them. Understandably, Ernie Ball admits that the decision to switch was an emotional one originally, but the company is now saving $80K to $100K a year. So you don't necessarily have to think of yourself as a "software pirate" to be found guilty as one.

A personal case to consider might be donating an old computer to a local community center, or helping a neighbor's child with his or her homework. Either of these activities could easily involve you in "software piracy"—for instance, if you did not provably wipe the hard drive clean, or if the neighbor has installed Microsoft Office without a valid license and you help to set it up. If you use open source software, you are defended against this. When you donate the system, you can load it with Linux, OpenOffice, and other open source software and make sure it is a fully functional system. When you help with the homework, you can bring a CD with OpenOffice and install it, then open any Word or Excel files with that.

4.4.7   International Opportunities

Consider the new systems that will be deployed internationally over the next few years. The computer industry continues to develop systems faster than the old ones go obsolete, and the price continues to drop.

In developing countries, large growth in systems used and shared and telecommunications advances will allow many more people access to computers and the Internet. Iraq, for instance, has gone from 5,000 to 50,000 in a year with a potential to reach 5 million in a few years. The numbers for Brazil are much larger. Many systems in these parts of the world will be candidates for open source on economic grounds, and they know it, which is why China and Brazil are taking a lead.

In line with the precept "teach a man to fish," open source may empower some of these groups to come up with their own solutions. In developing countries, people have learned to make wheelchairs and other useful items for a fraction of the cost of those made in a developed country. These products are also better suited to the conditions. Why should the same not be true of Web sites and spreadsheets?

Open source allows countries to create their own versions of software in their own language and culture, even where there may not be an economic market by traditional standards. Large software may be localized into 50 to 100 languages, but there are many more languages than that. If Kurds or Basque people want their software in their own language, open source is the way they will get it.

Thinking More Broadly

We can take the idea of the underserved much further. We know that when a new technology is introduced, we tend to use it initially to replace previous technologies in similar uses. Only later are breakthrough uses conceived. It is not usual for this process to take a generation or two. The Web is only ten years old, and widespread use of open source is younger than that. This sounds crazy, but we probably have not yet thought of most of the important things that can be done with open source.

4.5 Migrate Applications and Databases to Open Source

There are many applications and databases on older and smaller servers that have been rendered obsolete by the Web.

We discussed the statistics of installed servers previously. The same analysis of the server installed base reveals that 25 percent of Windows servers and 40 percent of UNIX servers are application and database servers. This is approximately 2.4M Windows servers and 1.2M UNIX servers. There are also a smaller number of mainframe servers with a lot of big applications and databases on them that will need to get moved to new technology at some point. Most of these applications were written before the Web with databases and tools that are now obsolete. They will need to be migrated.

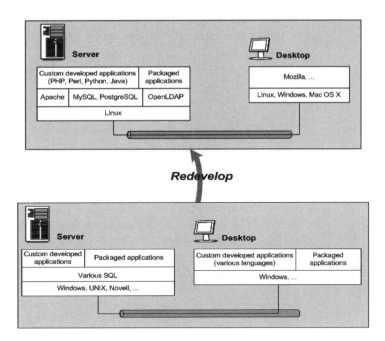

Figure 4.6
*LAMP
redeveloped.*

The obvious target for most of them is LAMP. Because of their age and size, they should be an easy fit for the technologies. In some cases, database schemata or code logic may be saved, but generally the simplest way to go is a new application. See Figure 4.6.

If a system is just old and a sunk cost, it is not likely to be migrated until something happens to make it suddenly expensive or needing to change. Specific reasons to migrate include:

- The old system is obsolete and the manufacturer is cutting off support.

- The old system needs an expensive upgrade by some date or will cease to work.

- The company is merging, splitting, or downsizing and would pay disproportionate costs to stay on system.

- The system is essential but particularly difficult to maintain or ineffective in supporting customer needs.

This opportunity is large, but it is riskier than the opportunities of infrastructure or new development. Everything said earlier about the risks of migration applies here. However ugly the system may look, it has apparently been working up to now. Unlike file and print servers, which can be approached piecemeal, database and application servers are often critical to the business and very difficult to tackle. The path to incrementally improve that system without risk may be difficult or impossible to follow. Sometimes the reason a big system has been left behind on an older database and platform is that smarter or luckier people than us recognized the risk and avoided it until we got here.

4.5.1 Evaluate Open Source Databases

While most companies will continue to use a nonopen source database, usually one or more of DB2, Oracle, and SQL Server, there are situations for almost every organization where an open source database will be adequate to the task, less expensive, have a smaller installed footprint, and be easier to manage. Some organizations may have the opportunity to move entirely to open source databases.

Accordingly, organizations should evaluate MySQL and PostgreSQL and determine the performance and risk criteria they will be comfortable with when deploying them.

Although there are obvious advantages to standardizing on one database, Web server, and application server in order to simplify intercommunication, training, remote offices, and so on, many companies will have more than one because of legacy, outsourcing, or packaging (some Apache/JBoss, some IIS/.Net). Others may use different systems at different scales, such as Oracle/Sun for larger systems and MySQL/Linux for smaller systems.

4.5.2 Replace Small and Old Database Applications with Open Source

Because open source databases are not expensive, they can replace the category of systems that could not be built with Oracle or SQL Server for price reasons in the past, but were built with Access, Paradox, Progress, Borland Interbase, xBase databases (such as FoxPro), and other personal databases. Many of these were shared-file systems, which were never very satisfactory as database servers, tending to corruption with multiple users and with generally poor performance and weak SQL standards support. Several of the products are no longer sold or supported.

Another class of database is the older minicomputer database, whether relational or more limited. If this is several years old, it is certainly within reach of an open source product such as MySQL to outperform it. This group includes older versions of Informix, Ingres, Btrieve, and SQL Server 6.x (possibly 7.x).

Generally, the front-end code on an older database system such as this has to be redone. The front-end tools sold a few years ago have almost all disappeared, and you would not want to use them anyway. Most were proprietary and eccentric and had all the limitations of client/server tools of their era. The best possible find might be VB3 or VC++ with MFC, early ASP/HTML, or Access, all of which need a big rewrite to bring them up-to-date.

So, the general plan will be to migrate the database schema to the new database—for instance, MySQL—and redevelop it as a new LAMP application.

4.5.3   Migrate UNIX to Linux

Another migration to consider is the UNIX workstation. Millions of these were installed from the 1980s on for engineering workstations, including mechanical CAD, software development, and so on. Manufacturers included Apollo, Sun, HP, IBM, Silicon Graphics, and others. Early on, these systems may have cost $50,000 to $100,000 apiece. A five-year-old system that cost $20K to $30K can be replaced now for $2,000. Ultimately, as they repeatedly fell in price in competition with commodity hardware, and their advanced 3D graphics systems were licensed for game systems such as the Gamecube and Playstation, these systems became replaceable with commodity personal computers.

Linux brings the power of the PC commodity model to UNIX workstations. The personal computer platform now has 3D graphics accelerators. All of these systems can be replaced with Linux when the time is right. They can also be replaced with Windows systems, and Microsoft goes after these opportunities hard, but the migration is obviously more difficult than to Linux. Microsoft sells into this market with UNIX services for batch utilities and software that runs all the UNIX APIs. But, of course, it's easier to migrate to Linux than to Windows, and the system will work better, too. UNIX emulation products on Windows are quite serviceable, but they hardly match Linux and lead to hard-to-administer systems that are neither properly UNIX nor Windows. The API emulation product has performance issues, too.

Much of Wall Street is doing this move, including Merrill Lynch. Another example of UNIX migration is Industrial Light & Magic, which has hundreds of Linux workstations. Dreamworks produced the movie *Sinbad* on all Linux workstations and rendering machines (over 1,000 systems).

Let's not forget that most UNIX workstation environments had a lot of servers installed in support, performing file/print, mail, and database services. If you get the front end, these are going to go over to Linux very nicely.

SCO Xenix (later UNIX) was the low-end (mass-market, inexpensive) system and is already largely replaced. This was the old Santa Cruz Operation (SCO) company in California that reinvented itself as Tarantella. Autozone is a case of a large company that successfully converted from SCO UNIX to Linux in 1999.

If we have a package that is running on an old UNIX system, then, if that system is still actively maintained, it is probably available on Linux now, and we have an opportunity to migrate from UNIX to Linux with no other changes. One option is to move to Linux on the proprietary UNIX server, and then migrate to commodity hardware later as appropriate. This may be worth considering, since that server will be an expensive sunk cost and may have valuable peripherals attached.

Database Migration

One important special case of packages that can be moved from UNIX to Linux is database servers, of course. Most people will not migrate their databases between database products, since it is far too much work. Differences in large issues, such as stored procedures, and even small issues of syntax trip you up without extensive retesting. However, it is certainly possible to migrate Oracle and DB2 systems already on UNIX to Linux. This is not likely to cause major problems of conversion. Given the economics, in the mid-market area it seems unlikely that many existing systems will be migrated to Linux, but systems that need to purchase new hardware and systems that must scale down (perhaps for distribution) would be fits.

4.5.4 Evaluate and Purchase Packages on Linux

Looking at the major software vendors, we see that most of them support Linux fully on their core products, while the portfolio-type companies support it on some products. The four leading software companies other than Microsoft are IBM, SAP, Oracle, and Computer Associates, and they are all enthusiastic supporters of Linux and other open source products:

- IBM: most core products run on Linux
- SAP: core products, including the mySAP Business Suite, support SuSE and Red Hat Linux

- Oracle: core products run on Linux

- Computer Associates: offers a full range of enterprise management, data management, change management portal, security, and storage solutions for Linux, including Unicenter and the Ingres database

- Cadence: electronic design systems run on Linux, including clusters

- PeopleSoft: enterprise business logic and background servers run on Linux

- BMC: core products, including MAINVIEW, Patrol, and Deployment Manager, support Linux

- SAS: products run on Linux, among many platforms

- Verisign: products fully support Linux

- Symantec, Compuware, Sungard: support Linux in some product lines

If our organization is looking at these packages, we can consider selecting Linux to run them. The availability of these packages helps to legitimize Linux and may help organizations trying to simplify to a few standard operating systems. Of course, it is unlikely that deploying these kinds of packages on Linux rather than any other operating system will save very much money.

4.5.5 Enterprise Application Software

From 1970 onward, there were substantial sales of enterprise packaged software, originally on mainframes. In the 1990s, there was a surge of growth in sales of a new generation of packaged software. This was built using client/server technologies and focused around suites of software for enterprise requirements planning (ERP) and customer relationship management (CRM). Sales of these products have stalled or, in some cases, collapsed since the year 2000. Sales of major CRM companies have fallen by half, and large but less catastrophic drops in sales of ERP and other large software products have occurred.

Initially, there were many companies in this area—but the field has consolidated, with the leaders now being SAP, PeopleSoft, and Oracle in ERP and Siebel in CRM. Apparently Microsoft intends to be a player in this area after acquiring the ERP suite vendors Great Plains, Solomon, and Navision and introducing a CRM product.

Acquisition of an ERP or CRM product typically drives technology choices right through the business, since the package is so large and influential that application server, database, and infrastructure platforms chosen for it usually will become the standards for other developments at the same time.

SAP, PeopleSoft, and Oracle all offer their entire product lines on Linux. So it is possible to install ERP (and CRM) systems on a Linux platform. SAP also offers support for the open source database Max DB from MySQL, formerly the SAP database.

There do not appear to be any large open source ERP or CRM products—that is, products that would be comparable to SAP, PeopleSoft, Oracle, or Siebel. There are some smaller systems, such as Compiere and Open For Business (OFB). Compiere is based on Java and Oracle, with an open source database in the planning stages. Neither of these products has an enterprise-level customer, or a very complete set of modules.

Do You Need Integrated ERP or CRM?

You may not need all of the features of an ERP package. Most customers buy only a few components (if only because of the cost). Perhaps the bundling was an artifact of commercial software.

All commercial companies have tended to grow by acquiring products that are related. Further, in a closed code software model, integration tends to happen because the software firm has the only access to data. In an open source model, customers or third parties can access data and create complementary modules. A similar situation can arise with the up-sell of an ERP or CRM vendor adding portal, data warehouse, or other products. This might leverage economies of scale, but more likely exploits the direct sales relationship and the closed code data formats of these types of products.

So, customers who just need something like Quickbooks for accounting, or on a larger scale Great Plains, might have some open source choices. Similarly, customers who need just call center, customer service management, or sales force automation might find single products, particularly for smaller businesses. Two products to consider are Tutos and SQL-Ledger.

4.6   Summary

Open source offers several business opportunities. The following is a summary of this chapter, with the ideas that will work for most people simply stated.

For most people, the first thing we can do is to set up an open source lab, and use the lab as a base to review and publicize open source activity, evaluate or create and test solutions, and train technical and user personnel. The lab should deploy the Linux distributions and other software on which you would like to standardize. This prepares the path for the other steps. We can train developers in one or two open source languages, probably Python and PHP, and train administrators in Linux, Samba, OpenLDAP, and Perl or Python scripting.

We can migrate infrastructure servers to open source using a combination of Samba on Linux servers and network-attached storage appliances. This saves money on client licensing and simplifies management. We can start with simple file/print sharing without strong security concerns. If we have directory-based security needs, we need to choose between using Samba 3 to support Active Directory or consider deploying OpenLDAP as a replacement for or alongside the closed source directory.

We can build one or more LAMP applications. This tool set speeds and simplifies development and can save money over alternatives. The most likely simple success will be to build some PHP Web applications using Apache and either MySQL or whichever database you currently use. These could be new applications or rewrites of old code trapped on obsolete platforms or databases.

We can investigate and begin bringing new open source systems to the underserved. We may be able to open up opportunities for solutions that were not possible before. Likely groups to consider include franchisees; business partners; customers; employees in factories, warehouses, and stores; and the local community. In such groups we may have influence but cannot control the operating environment or software purchasing. Offering office suites, image manipulation, or email and messaging without expensive licensing fees may allow us to offer systems or exchange information without great expense.

We can migrate applications and databases from other operating systems, such as UNIX and Novell, to Linux and one or two standardized databases. This can simplify system and application management and take out some old recurring costs. If it is a database that we are planning on continuing to use, such as Oracle, we can migrate to Oracle on Linux. If it is an obsolete or deprecated database system, such as Progress, Btrieve, or Access, we can move it to MySQL or PostgreSQL. For applications we wish to replace, we can look at new packages running on Linux or develop new Web applications using LAMP.

When making evaluation decisions, we should look at Linux for even the largest and most complex choices, such as SAP. There are not open source alternatives in all industries and for all applications, but there are in many. Because of the differing sales channels of open source, they may not be the most obvious, and a specific search should be conducted to identify open source solutions that may be available.

5

Five More Open Source Opportunities

5.1 Introduction

The opportunities discussed in the previous chapter were:

- Create an open source lab and use it to evaluate and evangelize open source systems.

- Migrate file, print, and network infrastructure to open source systems.

- Build one or more dynamic Web applications using Apache and open source languages.

- Bring new open source desktop and Web systems to the underserved.

- Migrate applications and databases from other systems to Linux.

These are activities that are technically possible today, well suited to the open source technologies, can be approached in stages, and have low or no switching costs. The categories are pretty well defined and the opportunities will work for different sizes of organizations.

The next group consists of opportunities that have more difficulties or restrictions than the ones in the previous chapter and may be more appropriate to some groups of customers than others. They are:

- Set up and administer an open directory to centrally manage the authentication of various systems.

- Migrate email servers to standards-based open source platforms.

- Evaluate and select open source groupware and collaboration tools.

- Develop and manage complex Web sites with open source content management portals.

- Evaluate and manage office and desktop software with a plan to migrate to open source as appropriate.

An open directory is an enabling technology for many of the other activities, including email, identity-driven portals, and most ecommerce and complex applications, but it does require integration skills. Email migration is simple in some cases, and Linux does it well, but if some Exchange or Notes features are used, there may be high switching costs. Groupware, particularly software for building communities, is an interesting candidate. The category is not clearly defined, customer requirements vary, and the different products differ in features and approach, so requirements need to be carefully studied. Complex Web site development, such as content management and portals, is an interesting case, since it is on the border between build and buy, which is a good place for open source.

For some, there may be a chance to begin open source initiatives in your industry or area of special interest. Every open source product began with someone satisfying an unmet need. While most open source products today are system software, future products will probably come increasingly from the business application area as well.

5.1.1   Customization and Integration

In many situations, we find ourselves purchasing a product or products that will involve us in some custom development or integration. If we are buying a product or group of products as the basis of an architecture that we will extend and integrate, then we are actually buying two things: the products and an architecture for development. Portals, application servers, and integration engines are clear examples of this; any large piece of application software, such as ERP or CRM, is also in practice. It is becoming increasingly clear that SAP and Oracle, for example, are as much development environments as sets of application products.

This type of decision, on the boundary between "build" and "buy," is a logically attractive spot for open source. When we are buying packages not for installation as a black box, but to customize and integrate into a solution, it is very useful to have access to the source, as we would if we had developed it. The code can serve as a model for our own development and also allow integration and extension under our control.

Open source software is very suitable to customization. First, since we have the source code, we can change it or extend it with no questions asked. Second, there is an opportunity for us to work with the developers to request improvements from them, including sponsoring changes.

5.1.2 Organization Size

As Figure 5.1 illustrates, companies vary tremendously in size, and their integration needs and capacity for custom development vary accordingly. The numbers are, of course, estimates. In particular, businesses such as dot-coms, or financial or technology companies, spend higher percentages on IT, so they behave like a conventional company that is much larger.

Larger companies are used to managing multiple environments, often with mainframes, and performing custom development and integration. Smaller organizations often do not have the staff and budget to do that effectively except in critical parts of the business, and they will emphasize more package acquisition and outsourcing.

Open source software, as a new and disruptive technology, fits in some of these organization sizes better than others. The largest companies can adopt new technologies and build custom systems, such as the clustered Linux analytical systems used at brokerage houses and for oil discovery, or

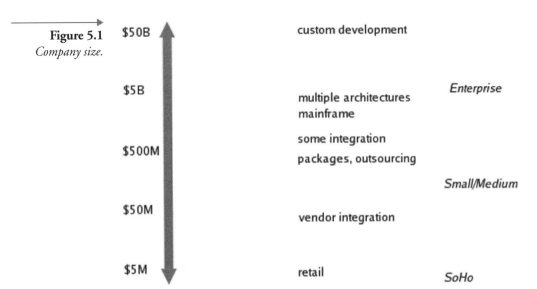

Figure 5.1
Company size.

Google and Amazon. Most large organizations can perform all of the actions in the previous chapter, and many of those in this one.

For very small organizations, open source systems may be installed where they had nothing in place before. For organizations in between, the situation may be more difficult. For mid-sized companies, the option of allowing one supplier to do the integration can be an attractive business proposition. For companies of $100M or so, this may mean purchasing all systems from one supplier, such as Microsoft, and allowing that integration to simplify their operations. For companies in the billions, where IT is not a core asset, this may mean hiring companies such as IBM Global Services or EDS and outsourcing operations.

5.2   Directory Services

The biggest cost benefit from infrastructure migration often comes from eliminating the directory element from Windows, since the client access license (CAL) for directory access is the most expensive software element of file storage. This also has a benefit in reduction of lock-in, as an open directory will support many different products from many vendors. The best argument for OpenLDAP is that the directory, touching so many systems and containing your proprietary information, is a very logical place to maintain open standards.

The choices for directory services are the open source OpenLDAP and closed code products, including:

- Novell eDirectory

- Sun ONE Directory Server

- IBM Directory Server

- Microsoft Active Directory

All of these are expensive compared with OpenLDAP. Microsoft Active Directory will not run on Linux, but it can support other servers and clients as an LDAP directory, so it deserves to be included. In some strategies, we will continue to use Active Directory and another directory server in a mixed infrastructure environment, and we will want them to work together.

We will need to survey the organization to find out what aspects of the directory people really use. This is certainly the case if Active Directory or any other modern directory software is being used, because they can optionally support many different activities. Fortunately, from a migration perspective, most organizations seem to do only what they need to.

5.2.1 Migration and Interoperability

Unfortunately, for many organizations interoperability will be the hardest part of the problem, as usual. There are tools to migrate directory content on a one-shot basis, and it is not especially difficult to get or build a tool to replicate directory information from a master directory to a copy, as you may do in some cases when introducing Samba to a Windows environment.

In some cases, it may be necessary to have two or more directories, which are both masters (e.g., Active Directory and Open LDAP), and a process for synchronizing them. This is unattractive, since whatever you call it, this really means adding a third directory to the mix, but there are several products that support this if it must be done. Many large organizations have to do this as a consequence of acquisitions or legacy systems.

5.3 Email

Email is the third most common use of Linux servers, after security (firewall and intrusion detection) and Web serving. A new Linux installation with email is easy to set up. This is not surprising, since email has been a part of UNIX since the earliest distributions. Every Linux system can be configured as an email server and/or client, with several options available for each. These Linux mail choices are the same in concept, but are also actually the same programs as the mail choices on other UNIX systems.

5.3.1 UNIX Mail Systems

Open source servers, such as Sendmail, Postfix, and Exim, and clients, such as Oak, Pine, and Eudora, have long been available on Solaris, AIX, and other UNIX systems. Commercial UNIX mail servers, such as HP Open-Mail, now sold through licensees such as Samsung Contact, also run on Linux.

That is not to say that there have not been recent improvements on Linux, such as Evolution, a new mail client unique to Linux, and Horde, a Web-based mail server.

5.3.2 **Migration**

Email can have all of the migration problems of a desktop application, including end-user reliance and familiarity, with the migration problems of a complex data center application that has integration and third-party tools issues. It is high risk, because in modern organizations email is a mission-critical application. Whether migration is possible depends on the organization, the pattern of use and expectations of users, and the willingness of administrators to adopt new tools.

Since email has client and server components, migration can involve replacing either or both. Replacing clients is discussed in section 5.6. Replacing servers involves careful procedures to retain messages and mailboxes; there are some tools available to help with this. Servers can be replaced while leaving the clients in place, or clients can be changed concurrently. Client settings will need to be changed, and some client behavior may change, depending on the migration.

The most common email servers on the Internet, according to an analysis by the email vendor Qmail, are:

- Sendmail, 42%
- Other UNIX mail servers, 22%
- Microsoft Exchange, 18%
- Other servers, 18%

It is reasonably simple if you need to migrate mail from UNIX to Linux systems. You almost certainly have the option of directly using the same mail server and client and just setting up the server platform on Linux and supporting the clients unchanged. Of course, as with any migration, you would need to back up the mail store, test the whole plan, and so on. In addition, you can look into alternative server and client software.

5.3.3 **PC-Based Mail Systems**

The tradition of mail in PC networks is different from UNIX. In the 1980s, when local area networks (LANs) were being installed, mail servers were supplied by the LAN suppliers Microsoft, Novell, and IBM. The products were originally built around LANs with weaker standards and Internet support and less scalability than UNIX systems, but they were generally easier to administer and use. These products, now Microsoft Exchange, IBM/Lotus Notes, and Novell Groupwise, have now incorporated Internet and mail standards such as IMAP and are capable of large scale. They have also extended the services they provide beyond mail to include other related activities, and there lies a problem for migration. These extended activities are useful, but they are different in each mail system and there are no standards for them. In a word, these extensions are proprietary, but many organizations rely on them.

If an organization uses one of these mail servers to provide a basic set of mail functions, it should not be a large challenge to migrate it. However, if it uses the proprietary groupware functions of Notes, Groupwise, or Exchange, there will be issues that could make the effort difficult or impossible. As with Microsoft Office, a full open source mail implementation that will meet most needs is not difficult to do. However, setting up the exact look and feel of an existing Microsoft Exchange and Outlook system is difficult in detail.

Exchange and Notes are problematic to replace because they bundle several functions together in their own unique ways. Lotus Notes, for instance, combines forms, small databases, replication, and user application development in a unique way. There are generally no direct equivalents in groupware functions. Lotus Notes databases and forms and Microsoft Exchange public folders and forms will need to be replaced, either by custom Web applications or by open source groupware.

Groupwise also differs in detail and is always linked to the Novell directory. Novell is now a major Linux vendor, and Novell users may want to look at a migration to Novell directory and Groupwise on Linux as an alternative.

5.3.4 Replacing Exchange

It is possible to replace Exchange with all open source products. Exchange itself is an integration of several different functions, and to replace it fully it is necessary to do similar integration. These functions are:

- Message send and receive

- Message store and index

- Global directory (Active Directory) integration for authentication and employee lookups

- Centralized store for personal information (contacts, calendar, tasks)
- Public folders (simple document management, discussions)

Exchange also supports optional browser-based mail access (Outlook Web Access). In addition, Exchange sites must generally make decisions on tools for spam filtering and message management, such as aging, quotas, and so on.

If it is possible to separate these functions and approach them with appropriate tools, then we are not locked into Exchange and can do this. If we must make everything appear as a single program with the same behavior, then we may do a fairly good job but will probably be perceived as falling short of expectations.

Table 5.1 shows the Exchange functions and some choices for open source programs that map to them.

As the table indicates, it is possible to provide functionality equivalent to all of the functions in Exchange, including the additional products that are normally used with Exchange. It should be apparent immediately that although this migration can be done, it will involve an integration effort that many organizations may not be ready for.

Table 5.1 *Mapping Microsoft to Open Source Mail*

Function/Service	Microsoft	Open Source
Message Send	Exchange	Postfix
Message Retrieve, Store	Exchange	Courier-IMAP, Cyrus IMAPD
User Lookup	Active Directory/Exchange	OpenLDAP
Web-based mail	Outlook Web Access	Horde
Groupware	Exchange forms, public folders	LAMP with OpenLDAP
Spam filtering	Third-party product	SpamAssassin
Message management functions	Third party, VB scripting to Exchange API	Python scripting, Procmail

5.3.5 Integrated Exchange Replacements

If you are on Exchange now and want to find a comprehensive product to move to, as opposed to the custom integration solution, there are at least two good choices. There is an open source product, Exchange4Linux, which is probably a replacement for Exchange in smaller organizations with a few hundred email users.

Organizations with many thousands of users that want to move from Exchange to a Linux platform may want to look at the closed code product Scalix. Scalix has licensed HP OpenMail, integrates the other functions discussed previously, and offers services such as migration from Exchange. An alternative is Samsung Contact, also based on HP OpenMail.

5.4 Groupware and Collaboration

The open source community has been effective at building tools that support the community. A promising possibility is to look at these community tools to perform a currently unserved function in your organization. In addition to looking at equivalents to commercial categories, such as content management, portals, and ecommerce software, this is an area where there are opportunities to look at open source software that may approach problems of collaboration and social interaction in a fresh way. This includes wikis, Weblogs, Real Simple Syndication (RSS), and other software for building and connecting communities.

5.4.1 Wiki

The wiki (see http://wiki.org/wiki.cgi?WelcomeVisitors), first created in 1995 by Ward Cunningham, allows users to read, create, and edit Web pages on a site using any browser. This includes not only content, but also organization such as new pages and links. This is one of the simplest forms of content publishing. Any user can usually participate. There are now thousands of wikis, built using dozens of different software packages (wiki engines). A master list of wiki engines is at http://c2.com/cgi/wiki?WikiEngines.

Good implementations among many available in different languages include Qwiki and the powerful Twiki, aimed at corporate intranets (Perl); TikiWiki and MediaWiki (PHP); Zwiki (Python); SnipSnap; and VeryQuickWiki (Java). Originally, security and workflow were simple or nonexistent, but many systems now support these needs quite well, so this category now somewhat overlaps with the content management products discussed in the next section.

Figures 5.2 and 5.3 show examples of wiki sites based on TikiWiki and SnipSnap.

In Microsoft terms, the wiki is functionally similar to Sharepoint Team Services, which was probably influenced by it, and also to shared folders in Exchange and WebDAV publishing features, which are in a few Microsoft products. A wiki has some similarity to simple Notes/Domino databases, but it is easier to administer.

Different implementations differ in storage formats, so migration will usually need to be arranged semimanually by writing scripts. Interoperability is usually impractical, since these tools differ and it is always easier to start over.

Everyone has the problem of interoperability between mail and wiki posting. This problem exists in Exchange and Notes as well. Some information gets in mail threads and some information gets on the Web pages, without any strong distinction. People wind up copying mail threads to public folders, making FAQ documents, writing scripts to collect mail

Figure 5.2
TikiWiki.

Figure 5.3
SnipSnap.

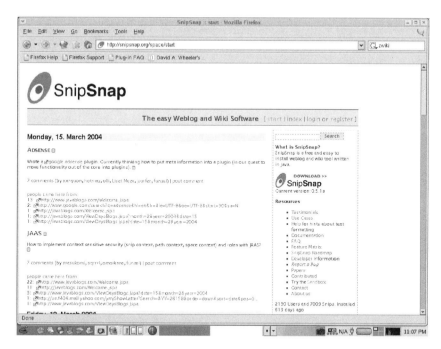

threads, and so on. Fortunately, as long as the software allows people to copy stuff freely, this seems to work out.

5.4.2 Other Community Software

The bulletin board package phpBB is a discussion forum, which has been around for several years and is very popular. It is written in PHP and uses MySQL, PostgreSQL, or SQL Server.

Scoop was written to support the discussion site Kuro5hin (http://www.kuro5hin.org). Scoop is written with Perl, Apache, and MySQL. This is used mostly for discussion sites, sometimes for simple content management. See Figure 5.4.

The heavily used discussion site Slashdot (http://slashdot.org) also makes the software that underlies the site available as the open source product Slash. Slash is written in Perl, and is apparently fairly complex, but it certainly has excellent performance. If you are looking for that functionality and look and have Perl maintenance skills available, it is a possibility. See Figure 5.5.

Figure 5.4
Scoop.

Figure 5.5
Slashdot.

5.4.3   **Weblogs**

Weblogs ("blogs") are a common method for building community; they went increasingly mainstream this year as the political community adopted them. There are several choices of software for creating Weblogs. Movable Type, probably the leader, is dual licensed, written in Perl with BDB or MySQL. Movable Type offers a Web service version, TypePad. Another Weblog product is b2, which is open source software written in PHP with MySQL.

Real Simple Syndication (RSS) is a standard for consolidating data from many feeds into a single viewer. Good Weblog software supports RSS.

Figures 5.6 and 5.7 are sample pages of blogs developed with Movable Type and b2, respectively.

5.4.4   **Instant Messaging**

Instant messaging (IM) is an application with high growth. In some places it is supplanting email, since it is faster and works well with cell phones. Consumer IM has been damaged by competition between proprietary formats. Possibly open source software can resolve this eventually. The GAIM instant messaging client works with many server formats, while the open

Figure 5.6
Movable Type.

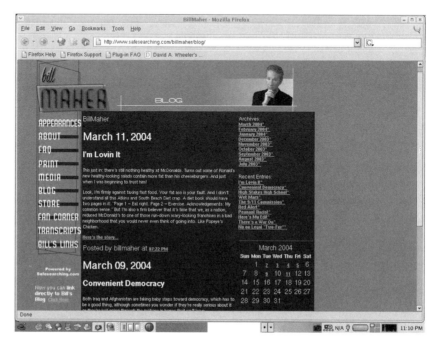

Figure 5.7
b2.

source Jabber format is an excellent choice for corporate servers. GAIM works with Jabber, so we can set up a corporate server and allow clients to access it, AOL, and so on from the same clients.

5.5   Complex Web Publishing

Complex Web publishing includes content management and portal servers. Portals consolidate information and tools from a variety of sources and present them in a single user interface. A portal is a collection of applications and infrastructure, not a distinct application in itself. These are then targeted at a set of customers, internal or external. Portals include some content management as a core function, but this is often offered as a separate product.

Content management servers are often derived from professional organizations, such as newsrooms or magazine publishing systems, with syndication as a core competence. They offer powerful control over document management, workflow such as approval processes, and content distribution. Unlike portals, they are often sold to nontechnical management, who like the control features.

This category is on the borderline between build and buy. In any organization, but especially in a large one, information is stored on a variety of devices or software. So portal selection is really the process of selecting a vendor, or vendors, for a set of infrastructure and development tools and components.

The ready-made portal software is most useful to smaller companies and those that are new; others will have too many existing assets and processes for these offerings to fit, and will do more custom development over time. In either case, the portal is a sample that serves as a jump-start.

The following are examples of portal offerings:

- Plumtree Studio Server
- IBM WebSphere Portal Server
- Sun iPlanet Portal Server
- Red Hat Portal Server
- Microsoft Sharepoint Portal Server
- PHP-Nuke
- eGroupWare

The following are content management servers:

- Vignette
- Red Hat Content Management Server
- Microsoft Content Management Server
- Plone
- Bricolage

These are overlapping categories, since a substantial portal includes content management. They will be treated as one requirement here. The goal of a content management solution is to allow business users to be able to easily create, retrieve, and share content for intranets, extranets, and ebusiness/ egovernment. The organization and structure of the content must be determined by and be relevant to the people who create and use it.

5.5.1   Portal Components

Any content management portal is going to need all or most of these technologies, either included or integrated: a directory, Web server, application development tools for creating additional custom components, indexing and search, and mail and calendaring. Usually a product will use the vendor (or its partners) strategic technology for most of these. Microsoft and IBM products use their own directory, database, Web server, development tools, and mail. The Plumtree portal uses the BEA WebLogic application server.

In most cases, the product can be configured to use at least some external products. A commitment to interoperability is really needed, so that other ways of developing are not locked out in the future. In the case of an open source portal, we will expect to be able to use open source components, such as OpenLDAP, Apache, MySQL, and an open source development language. We would also want access to legacy databases, other systems through Web services, and shared authentication.

There is no clear line between the simple Web publishing discussed in the previous section and the more powerful products discussed here. A requirements process is going to be needed to determine the right product.

Authentication and Personalization

Almost all customers will need an authentication system, or a system to determine who can perform which functions with which content. Generally, this will need to work with existing infrastructure, whether LDAP (including Active Directory), a proprietary or embedded directory (such as NT or Exchange 5.5), or one that is database based.

Forms-based login uses an authentication system to personalize content display and to control access to all functions. Role-based display of components supports multiple roles for an identity.

Content Management

Composition and presentation of files in various formats, including Office, PDF, HTML, XML, links (both internal and external), and composed articles with dynamic content, are needed. This includes information delivered in consistent user-defined hierarchies and other easy-to-navigate structures appropriate to the business. The system specifies how new content gets in. A process must be defined for each type of content to ensure that content can be captured and entered correctly.

Authors must be able to compose and edit content with any browser, without special technical knowledge, and tag it or profile it. They should also be able to use their preferred tools for content development, and the portal product for markup only. Content should be templatable, so new material can be quickly incorporated in defined styles.

Managers must be able to edit and delete content, and define and edit page and template layout, quickly and on a per role basis. Expired and deleted content should be handled correctly.

The product may need to allow comparison and reversion, so a user can view all versions of some page(s) and can revert back to those if needed. Some canned reports on content state and use would be helpful.

Some content management users need extensive workflow features. This includes delegation of content management to users with appropriate roles, and a process for review of content before display if appropriate. One of the critical process tasks is to determine not just what content will be captured, but what format it needs to be in to meet business needs.

Web sites with fresh content provide a compelling reason for return visits. Designing a content management solution should also incorporate the design of business processes to ensure that the content is current, fresh, and reliable. Some content may need to be updated hourly, others annually. Processes need to be established for each type of content cycle.

Indexing and Search

Search can be free-text or structured (based on a classification schema), but it should probably be both. For most organizations, a specific search should be offered for internal people and locations, and often for products and services.

It is important to define the right classification schema for content. Defining this metadata is very user and content specific. Some users may be willing to define an unlimited number of "tags" on content as they enter it. Other users may only have patience or time for a small number of tags. This must be analyzed and determined for each type of content and content source.

All documents available from the portal need to be indexed for searching, including content internal and external to the product in several formats. Ideally, an internal search should work like well-known engines, such as Google. Unlike Web engines, there may be authentication issues with documents you are allowed to see.

Component Integration

As with a daily newspaper, a portal needs both headlines and a rich set of content. The headline item is often some kind of balanced scorecard, preferably personalized, such as an analysis report comparing personal and district sales with others. The content often includes a variety of legacy applications. The portal product needs to allow development and integration of this type of material, whether internal or third party, in a rapid and flexible way.

Internationalization

Many organizations will need support for multiple portals with different languages from one or several servers, so that all content is displayed in the appropriate language while using a common database/server configuration.

Migration

Direct migration is not usually viable because of the differences between product features and architectures. Of course, most data and applications should be accessible using purpose-built migration scripts with appropriate planning.

5.5.2 Open Source Content Portals

There are a number of products in this area, depending on definition, and in another year it may have changed. I will select three open source products, which I know to have many users, significant growth and buzz, and architectures that allow rapid deployment of functional applications but scale to support complex custom development when needed. These are:

- Plone
- PHP-Nuke
- eGroupWare

Plone is developed in Python, using the Content Management Framework and the Zope engine. Python can be used to extend the application. PHP-Nuke and eGroupWare are both developed in PHP and can be extended with that language.

Figure 5.8
Plone home page.

Both Plone and PHP-Nuke can be used internationally, and their case studies include many examples of this. Figures 5.8 through 5.10 show the Plone and PHP-Nuke home pages (written in their respective software).

5.6   Manage User Desktops

Linux desktop deployment to a new group of users without existing systems is as simple as any such activity could be. The problem, as usual, is migration. The only situation that is considered here is that an organization has Windows desktops. UNIX migration is mentioned elsewhere. The very small group that has anything else at this stage must have its own special circumstances.

Migration of user desktops is a hard thing to do successfully. First, it involves touching every system, and possibly completely rebuilding it, and this will incur great cost. Second, users have some say in configuring their systems and have strong likes and dislikes. There is a high risk of user dissatisfaction with this type of change.

For most of us, an early large-scale migration of user desktops is not something to contemplate. However, we do want to plan, since we know this will happen eventually one way or another, whether it involves an

Figure 5.9
Plone example.

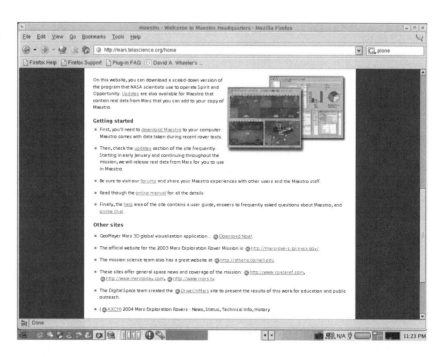

Figure 5.10
PHP-Nuke.

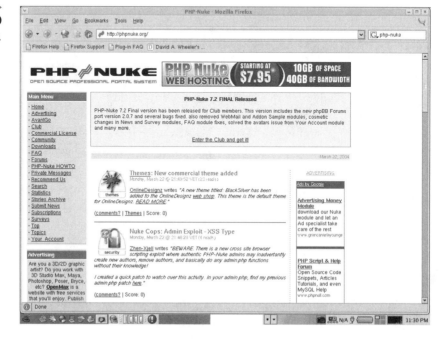

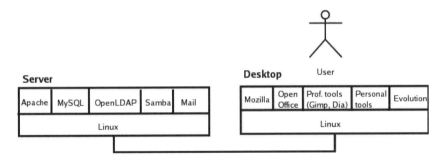

Figure 5.11
Desktop use.

upgrade to a newer version of Windows or a change. There is a potential return of hundreds of dollars per desktop in licensing fees from this migration, so if we could remove the licensing costs of Windows and Office from thousands of desktops we could save millions. The first step is to analyze and control desktop use with eventual migration in mind. See Figure 5.11.

Windows desktops could include any combination of Windows 95, 98, ME, Windows NT, Windows 2000, or Windows XP. They may have Office, again any of several versions, and a great variety of other software. Migration choices from Windows include:

- Introduction of some open source programs on Windows

- Total replacement of Windows with Linux and open source

- Use of software to make Windows programs available on Linux

- Any combination of these

If we want to move in an open source direction, the simplest first step is to run some open source programs on the existing Windows desktops. A good example is the Mozilla browser. This should work in almost all cases except for a few Microsoft Web sites, which are worth shaking out anyway, and can run side by side with Internet Explorer. Mozilla is standards based, open source, and cross-platform. It is not necessary to achieve complete adoption of Mozilla, or any browser. An organization can run more than one browser without interoperability problems, although there could be a support cost. Migration from another browser to Mozilla is not difficult. Users can typically switch browsers in a few minutes, the biggest issue being making their favorites/bookmarks available.

It is also possible to run OpenOffice and many open source mail programs on Windows. Switching mail can get us off Exchange CALs and also helps to manage the persistent virus and worm problems with Outlook.

We should analyze our office suite use to determine how many users could be switched to OpenOffice without disruption, and what the cost savings could be. There may be some users who can start using OpenOffice now—for instance, call centers, those using one or two dedicated applications, or browser-only users. Many others will be not be able to migrate now, but we can prepare for a possible move in the future. If appropriate policies are put in place now to simplify a future move, we will be prepared if licensing changes or other events encourage us to move later.

Depending on the status of license agreements and the feasibility, this is potentially a significant saving. Over 3,000 users at $300 per user is $1 million. This can be done across an entire organization if it is highly integrated. In many organizations, smaller business units may have different patterns of use, and this may be the right level to approach it.

At this time, we can consider other office suites or portal-based thin clients in the mix, since the analysis is the same. Desktop application management is regarded as expensive by many IT organizations. So although portal-based (browser-only) plans seem unattractive when you can give OpenOffice to everyone who doesn't have a suite and has a 10G drive, for some organizations the cost of maintaining software at those clients will make the portal attractive.

Any plan for a two-tier system with open source (or portal) and legacy users is going to face interoperability costs as a serious issue. So while all these ideas can save money, they will need careful analysis of the organization and its patterns of use.

5.6.1   Analyze Desktop Use and Licensing

We should review software use on the desktop with eventual migration in mind. This certainly includes Microsoft Office (Word, Excel, and Power-Point). Use should be measured for each product separately even if Office is licensed as one. Mail, whether Outlook or another, is also an important function to consider. We can also look at use of Access, Project, or Visio if it is significant, and, of course, third-party applications. The essential data to collect on product use—for instance, for the Office products—varies by organization but includes:

- What is the number of licensed users of the product?

- Which version(s) is in use (95, 97, 2000, 2002/XP, 2003)?

- How many users are complex authors, simple authors, primarily readers, or nonusers?

- Are Office documents circulated as part of essential business flows?

- Are documents authored with VBA macros, complex charts, Smart-Tags, or AutoShapes?

- How have prior migrations of desktop software played out in the organization?

This data should be enough to support some preliminary estimates of potential cost saving and migration feasibility. Given this, some organizations may be able to go further and make some decisions discouraging Microsoft Office use. For example, we could mandate OpenOffice use as a default unless MS Office features are required, and create a simple form that allows users to specify those features.

We can enforce standards on use—for instance, to prevent new proprietary features or to make later migration simpler. If possible, we can identify some groups whose use allows them to adopt open source products, such as OpenOffice, Gnumeric, Evolution, Dia, or GIMP, early.

5.7   Other Possibilities

We can review complex applications for their fitness for open source software over the long haul. In many cases, we can plan now for systems that will be installed on open source platforms in one or two years from now. These could be packages, such as an enterprise requirements planning (ERP) or customer requirements management (CRM) system, or a custom-developed system.

In other cases, we may be looking at opportunities that are farther afield, which could pay back in huge financial savings in the long run and establish a leadership position within your industry. This might involve beginning industry discussions on open source collaboration opportunities or working with startup companies to establish potential products for the future.

One possibility is takeover of a moribund commercial application. One way a new open source package could come about is the conversion of a commercial operation that succeeded as software but failed as a business.

OpenOffice is an example of a system that was not a particularly successful business on a global scale until adopted by Sun. There could be similar opportunities in other commercial businesses that could be revitalized through an open source strategy. For example, global standardization has reduced the field of ERP and CRM systems. They may be candidates for release to open source. Initiatives such as this could be:

- Horizontal (e.g., ERP, CRM)

- Industry (e.g., education, electronics)

- Niche (e.g., telecommunications billing, cruise ship reservations)

Many years ago, I did some work with a company out of Stanford that sold a financial package specifically for foreign exchange trading. The company had started by conducting a survey on needs in this industry for a number of the major financial institutions that were leaders in international currency trading; it then transformed over a period of years into a company selling software that supported this activity, while retaining most of the original customers. A similar transition from research project on needs to software product could work in many industries, where cooperation has rewards, in order to create an open source product.

The Open Software Application Foundation (OSAF) is building a horizontal product for personal information management, while also receiving sponsorship from educational organizations, that will ensure that an early delivery is an education-vertical variant of the product. Another possibility is that something like a pharmaceutical model can work, with code going to open source after a certain period.

Industries that can most easily sponsor new applications include finance, telecommunications, energy, and defense/aerospace.

Financial organizations can easily fund new developments; they have a tradition of custom development and are interested in maintaining a competitive advantage rather than sharing intellectual property with vendors. There is a long UNIX tradition on Wall Street that makes it potentially very friendly to open systems.

Many banks operate thousands of retail stores and call centers, as well as a vast network of automated kiosks (automated teller machines). They have very large numbers of tightly controlled desktops with long acquisition cycles. Banks do not have to run Windows; they were the last customers to run OS/2, years after it was unavailable as a retail product.

Telecommunications operates on an extremely large scale. The billing, rating, and provisioning systems of telecom companies are the largest systems in operation. Much of the work occurs in near real time, while others are some of the largest batch and paper printing operations around. The wire-line business is generally conservative, with systems that are 30 years old, but the new mobile businesses have been created more recently and grown at astonishing rates. Many of these systems are mainframe based, because that was the only way they could be built when designed. There is also a heavy UNIX influence, since most of these companies used to be part of AT&T.

In the energy business, electric/gas utilities are very mainframe focused at the center, and there is also a great deal of Oracle installed. The SCADA systems are all UNIX and generally need replacement. Costs historically are not as important, but may become so with more open markets. These businesses are major employers. Many employees in utility companies have Office and Windows systems with high licensing costs. Others have no systems, or systems with limited software available, and may represent opportunities for OpenOffice where there is nothing now.

5.8   Summary

Open source software offers several business opportunities. One thing to decide is whether we want to implement open source applications or applications on an open source platform, since the costs and benefits are very different in the two cases. The following is a summary of this chapter, with the ideas that will work for most people simply stated. Some ideas are of each type.

A directory is a very good candidate to be a vendor-independent, standards-based product, since it must integrate with everything else you have or acquire later. The open source directory choice is OpenLDAP. It is standards based, reliable, scalable, and very inexpensive compared with closed code products.

Migrate email if you can do it easily. Review your current use of traditional mail and calendar systems to see if open source products can fit. This is either easy, such as migration from UNIX or Groupwise, or difficult if there are high switching costs caused by existing users who will not accept change.

Start using open source groupware and collaboration tools such as a wiki. This can produce some quick benefits, and prepare for a big reduction of license fees in the future. Also look at the new open source products for information sharing, social software, and blogs.

Look at adopting an open source content management portal, such as Plone or PHP-Nuke, for complex Web site development and management. This can eliminate potential big costs such as proprietary content management software. These products have fast payback and easy management, and over time can be extended as necessary into large applications using standard development tools.

Analyze and control desktops to see what products people are using, which level of complexity they are employing, and how that matches to the licensing in place. This puts you in place for big license savings later on.

Finally, there are areas where open source applications are missing. There may be opportunities to sponsor such products, to discover closed code applications that could be converted, or at least to take part in initiatives to search for and sponsor such solutions.

6

Operating Systems

This chapter looks at what is in the operating system, open source alternative to Linux, how Linux is being enhanced, and the various distributions from which we can choose.

6.1   Contents of the Operating System

In this section, we will look at Linux and other open source operating systems, and then examine what goes into an operating system distribution and how to choose one.

An operating system (OS) contains a kernel, a base operating system, and a considerable number of other packages, where a package is like a product but not sold separately. Whether these additional packages are "included in the operating system" is a commercial and to some extent a political question. In the Linux community, the question of what is included is answered by the distribution and the installer. A distribution packages a Linux kernel, patches, other components, and other packages that are clearly applications. The installer generally has some control over the packages included, as well as other issues such as default Windows manager and look and feel.

The Linux kernel is managed by a single project team. Other packages are run by other project teams with no or little formal connection to the kernel or each other. Several core packages are part of the GNU overall project. Linux distributions generally perform integration testing and incorporate a means for online updating of packages.

In a closed code system, this resolves into a kernel, a base operating system, and a platform and ecosystem. Closed code systems include Microsoft Windows and Apple Mac OS X, and also server systems such as Sun Solaris and Novell NetWare.

In closed code systems, the vendor decides what is included in the operating system. The vendor performs integration testing and provides a means for online update. Further, the packages in the operating system are distributed and supported by the vendor. They may have been licensed or purchased from third parties originally, such as DoubleSpace or Internet Explorer in Windows, but they are from the vendor now. There is an incentive for this set of packages to grow, since this encourages users of the closed code system to purchase upgrades from time to time. The vendor generally provides indemnification (against the code not being theirs to license) and any other warranties, which are usually disclaimers of warranty.

In closed code systems, there are two additional categories. First, there are applications sold by the vendor for an additional fee, such as Office and SQL Server on Windows, iLife and Keynote on the Mac, or Zen on NetWare. Microsoft calls this "the platform," and I'll use that term. These can be very important sources of profit. Office is the major engine of profit for Microsoft.

Second, there are applications sold or distributed by third parties. Novell calls this the "ecosystem," and I'll use that term also. It is usually the existence of this ecosystem that makes the operating system attractive. Over time, the closed code vendors will attempt to expand their "platform" at the expense of their "ecosystem." The launch of a new version of Windows or the Mac is an opportunity to showcase a set of packages that was previously part of the ecosystem and is now part of the platform. Although this is usually presented as "innovation," as something new that was not included previously, it is really incorporation. The selling of Windows Media Player by Microsoft, or iTunes by Apple, is an example of this. Hopefully, in a healthy economy, the ecosystem can grow outward through innovation, by solving new problems.

The distinctions between operating system, platform, and ecosystem arguably do not exist with open source, at least not as strongly. There are some cases where the distribution vendor develops additional code (platform). This may be distributed exclusively, as SuSE Yast2 has been until now, or nonexclusively, such as Red Hat RPM or Tux. They may also be sold, probably not exclusively, such as Ximian Desktop 2 (XD2). Linux distributors do not earn significant revenue from such enhancements now, but that may change. Both Novell and Red Hat have plans to do more of this.

The expectation in open source is that packages come from third parties. There is a distinction maintained by Debian, and perhaps others, between "free" and "nonfree"—that is, between packages whose licensing terms are similar to those of Debian and packages that have licensing restrictions or fees.

In Linux, the kernel is quite small and common to all distributions. It is upgraded continuously. Major kernel upgrades are happening every year or so, with minor updates flowing regularly, every few days. In the Linux numbering scheme, even-numbered kernels are stable; odd numbers are for developers and testers only. Last year, 2.4 was stable and 2.5 was the development code. Now, the 2.5 development code has become the 2.6 stable kernel. Users can upgrade the kernel without waiting for the distribution. In March 2004, over 20 percent of users reporting were running 2.6. In May 2004, SuSE 9.1 and Fedora Core 2 will be the first major distributions to ship with the 2.6 kernel. Red Hat Enterprise Linux is operating on a slower upgrade cycle, but has the major enhancements (threading and scheduler) in a custom 2.4 kernel. The threading improvements in the kernel are very significant. Because of them, Linux performs many common tasks much more efficiently. Testing shows that the 2.6 kernel brings improvements in performance of as much as 50 percent in common tasks, including Web serving, file serving, and database.

Offering more packages is one way that Linux distributions compete with each other (and with Windows), so there is an incentive for Linux distributions to grow. In fact, Linux distributions can be quite large. Linux distributions range from one CD (e.g., Knoppix) to four (e.g., Fedora Core 2 and RHEL3 WS), five (e.g., SuSE Professional 9), or seven (e.g., Debian Woody 3r1) and are tending to get larger.

There is a potential trade-off in the more enterprise-focused distributions, since they are expected to offer support and more packages will increase support costs. It seems that this loses out to user desire for a wide variety of packages to choose from. The result is that the major distributions generally offer both KDE and Gnome, MySQL and PostgreSQL, OpenOffice and its competitors, all the scripting languages, and all the utilities and games.

All the vendors bundle versions for home, professional, smaller businesses, and larger businesses but in a different way. Open source vendors provide all the same features but vary the support. Closed code vendors limit the functionality of less expensive versions (and typically charge extra for enterprise support). Generally in Linux and other open source software there are no limited or "crippled" versions. Someone could put the missing functions back in, after all. Differences between Linux versions are usually in the support contracts. Because of this, smaller businesses that need rich products typically get a better deal with open source.

Linux in practice ships with a great deal of usable software, which is included in added-cost "platform" code in other systems. This is often ignored in reviews and comparisons. Every version of Red Hat ships with the Gnome tools Evolution and Gnumeric, an Outlook clone and Excel clone, respectively. Each of these includes sophisticated tools for managing tasks. Calendaring and spreadsheets are both valuable business functions that most small (and larger) businesses want to use. But because they match components of Microsoft Office and not Windows, you typically won't see them brought up in reviews of the operating system.

6.1.1   FreeBSD

The FreeBSD operating system, whose history was covered previously, is certainly not in widespread use compared with Linux, but it is a stable and powerful operating system. Although there are less software products available for FreeBSD than for Linux, the most important server products, including Apache and database servers, are available for it. So FreeBSD is a good basis for a server, particularly a dedicated one. It is used by Yahoo! and by many organizations that need a platform for custom development or manageable Web or database servers.

As a client system, FreeBSD is most used today as a component of Mac OS X. The Mac OS X operating system is now the #3 desktop operating system by current sales, after Windows and now Linux (which just overtook it). Over the last few years, the Macintosh operating system has been rewritten and is now based on UNIX, specifically FreeBSD.

The Apple base operating system is available as the free system Darwin, which is a solid free operating system but with no GUI. By running X11 and applications obtained from Fink on OS X, you have a solid operating system that supports the Mac hardware well and can run most Linux software.

So Mac OS X is a hybrid. It has some of the benefits of an open source system. It is a robust, solid system and has enjoyed the open source testing process up to a point. Of course, it is not open source. You cannot see the API implementation, and you are at the mercy of Apple, as with any closed code system, if it should go broke, decide to raise the price, or make other changes in licensing. The elegant Mac GUI, and most of the applications that run on it, is closed code.

6.1.2 **The Value of Alternative Operating Systems?**

It may not be clear why it is valuable to have other operating systems that are not based on Linux. Linux is stable and successful, is improving rapidly, and is widely used, and I am not advocating that you even consider the open source alternatives. Consider it disaster insurance. There has already been one disaster in the open source community: GNU Hurd. Hurd was supposed to be the kernel of the GNU operating system. It is about 15 years late and still not ready. Fortunately, the Linux kernel was developed. If the Linux kernel had not been developed, then a BSD kernel would probably have been adopted instead, and life would have gone on.

Suppose you are concerned about a lawsuit against Linux. You probably should not be, since any claim that some lines of Linux code are lifted from someone's copyrighted code would be simply remedied by replacing that code (once it had been identified). The previous major lawsuit, between Novell and UC Berkeley, was settled like this in 1994. But take the worst imaginable result: that the Linux kernel was somehow removed from open source and either unavailable or only available with unreasonably high license fees. The entire Linux kernel could be replaced if necessary by FreeBSD, or even Hurd. This would be unpleasant, but less disruptive than some of the remedies that were proposed during the Windows monopoly case would have been to Windows.

This possibility, of wholesale substitution of any major component, is part of the value of open source software. FreeBSD, or another system, can run Linux software, because the developers have access to the code that implements the interfaces, and they are entitled to use it. So if there is a market need for a better package, and if there are developers willing to provide one, nobody can prevent it from being made available in a way you can easily use.

6.1.3 **Using the Shell . . .**

. . . or why does Linux have so many files to configure?

The latest Enterprise Linux versions have a GUI interface for almost everything, and it often looks very much like the Windows Control Panel. If all goes well, you can get a lot done on the system without opening a terminal these days, certainly more than a couple of years ago. But you very quickly find that it is not the way of the Linux community to use these GUIs much. Old habits die hard, of course, but there is more to it than that. One practical reason is that the GUIs are different, while the underlying files are not, so it can be easier to describe an edit to the file /etc/hosts, which has not changed in 20 years and will work on any version of Linux, than to explain the different ways to enter an IP address in SuSE's Yast2 or Red Hat's Network Device Control and whatever GUI you are running on Debian. That reason alone could explain why discussions on mailing lists and user groups that cover multiple distributions are usually in terms of the configuration files. Actually, even vendor-specific support databases and mail responses (e.g., Red Hat) are very often couched in file editing terms. The Red Hat GUIs have changed too, and the support people may use other systems outside work. This is only partly a Linux issue; every Windows release has changed the system interfaces for network configuration.

Many GUI interfaces abstract the simpler aspects of configuration but cannot cope with all possibilities. This is not a Linux issue but a consequence of designing the GUI to simplify choices. The result can be a great "demo" of an interface that can support, say, the top available wireless PC cards on release date but then is defeated by a new manufacturer or an enhancement such as WEP. If you are going to need to drop through to the underlying system sometimes, the Linux user argues, you may want to do it all the time and stay in practice.

Finally, because everything in Linux can be done on the command line, everything can be scripted. This can be very powerful, since most things need to be done repetitively, often unattended. It is a simple transition from entering commands on the command line or into a file to creating scripts that can be moved around the network and executed automatically at the right time. The equivalent for a GUI is quite awkward. There are utilities in the Windows OS, platform (Systems Management Server), and ecosystem (ScriptIT) that allow you to force GUI conversations in unattended scripts, but none is generally satisfactory. This argument, in particular, is so important that it is a major goal for the next Windows version, Longhorn, to be completely scriptable from the command line.

Why are they flat files? UNIX flat files go back to the original UNIX philosophy. There are many good tools for working with flat files, so it becomes easy to access them from scripts, analyze them, and so on. As on other platforms, there has never been a single SQL database that you can rely on being present.

6.1.4 **Recent Linux Improvements**

If you've used any version of UNIX, Linux will be similar enough to be familiar. However, if your UNIX experience was a while ago, Linux is probably more up-to-date than you expect. Compared with Windows, it is functionally similar. Many things are done differently, but you should be able to do anything you could do on Windows. A week will get most people over the hump using a GUI, but modifying config files, writing scripts, and so on, if necessary, will take longer.

In Figure 6.1 we see a Fedora desktop on a 1,600 × 1,200 display with four windows visible. The windows are chosen to illustrate Windows and Office compatibility. They show (clockwise from top left):

- OpenOffice with a PowerPoint file

- OpenOffice with an OpenOffice document file, which I will convert to a Word .doc before sending to the publisher

- Evolution with a three-pane view similar to Microsoft Outlook

- Gnumeric with an Excel file

Figure 6.1
Fedora and Office files.

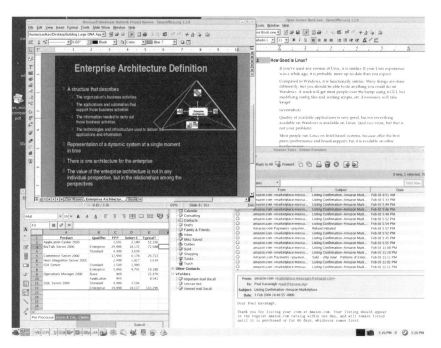

You can also see clickable icons on the desktop and the Red Hat symbol, which works like the Windows "Start" button.

The quality of available applications is very good. Not everything available on Windows is available on Linux, but, of course, this cuts both ways.

Most people run Linux on Intel-based systems, because they offer the best price/performance and broad support. It is available on other hardware too, such as PowerPC (e.g., Apple, IBM RISC systems), and most recent UNIX hardware (as used by HP-UX, AIX, Solaris). Linux currently supports 64-way multiprocessing and 64-bit processors.

The speed of development in Linux can be quite surprising. In the last half of 2003 there have been improvements in at least these three important areas:

- Ease of installation

- Quality of graphical desktop

- Performance and scalability improvements in the kernel

In ease of installation, both Red Hat 9 and SuSE 9 have reduced the amount of manual effort by adding wizard-like GUI programs. They are more likely to correctly set up graphics, find file and printer shares, and to configure network cards, without manual intervention, than previous versions. Red Hat Enterprise Linux 3 is a large improvement over its forerunner, 2.1, which was more like Red Hat 7.

Graphical desktops have been improved by closer attention to fonts and integration and by newer versions of OpenOffice and Evolution.

6.1.5   Scaling Linux up and Down

Figure 6.2 illustrates the scaling dimensions that open source software, and particularly Linux, faces and handles. Systems can scale up or out from the "classic" PC form, or they can scale down. Some of these systems represent breakthroughs as the first or largest of their kind.

Some of the open source systems in place are very large by any measure. There are systems that have very high transaction rates, data volumes, and numbers of users. Some of these systems scale out by using many small systems, in many cases providing reliability through redundancy. These may use new hardware of "blades" and other small form factors. Some scale up

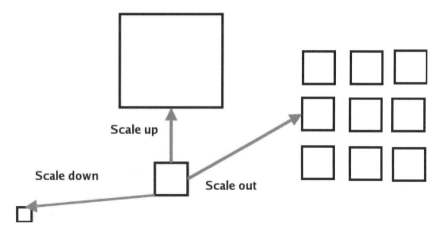

Figure 6.2
*Scaling the
operating system.*

by using "big iron" symmetric multiprocessor systems, which were formerly running single-vendor UNIX systems. There are systems that use thousands of processors and many terabytes of data, as well as systems that are distributed around the world. Some of these are world famous, such as Google, eBay, and Amazon. Others may be more discreet, such as National Security Agency use or the new army supercomputer.

Systems also scale down. Some are consumer appliances, which test extremes at the other end—of cost, small footprint, and time between failures. There are over a million TiVo systems in consumer use, for example. Other systems run in cellular phones, PDAs, and are embedded in automobiles. Some of these systems can be very inexpensive; Linksys and Netgear systems for routing are sold profitably for a few dollars each. The reliability requirement for these systems is extreme; there is no reasonable possibility of manual repair.

As a server, Linux can scale very high. Versions of Linux are commonly deployed with sixteen or thirty two processors and support up to 1,024-way symmetric multiprocessing. Clustering using Beowolf is common and has been done for years. High-performance clusters have reached very high performance in research labs such as Lawrence Livermore and Las Alamos.

Having a common operating system between client and server is not necessary but has advantages—for instance, in the common API, which means code can be developed with one set of skills and also moved between platforms, and the common GUI. Servers that are not also desktops will not generally invest in as good an interface (e.g., Novell NetWare).

6.1.6 Security

Here I will make a few brief comments, and then leave security as a topic for another book—for instance, the Becker book *Linux Security for Large-Scale Enterprise Networks*.

The general feeling in the open source community is that open source is simply going to prove over time to be a more secure development method than closed code. This is derived from the beliefs of the security community as articulated by experts such as Bruce Schneier.

Recent attacks on Microsoft systems have not been replicated as widely on Linux and BSD-based systems. The reason for that is not clear. Some claim it is just that Microsoft is the dominant system, so more likely to be attacked, or that it is a "monoculture" with the risk that entails (Linux systems vary more among themselves in configuration and programs installed more than Windows systems).

Viruses and worms can be written to run on Linux systems, as any other, and the CERN reporting shows that Linux gets its share of attacks. Some specific Microsoft decisions for ease of use over security have caused problems, such as running executables from Office and the mail client, but I believe those are mostly fixed now.

6.2   Linux Distribution Vendors

A distribution vendor does several things, such as:

- Select the kernel version and apply (and perhaps create) patches.
- Select a collection of packages with its own versions and patches.
- Coordinate bug reports and feed them back to package maintainers.
- Select (and perhaps create) installation and deployment tools.
- Test and certify the collection and combine onto media for distribution (e.g., physical CDs, ISO CD images, DVD).
- Market the distribution, and provide other services such as training.

6.2.1 The Many Versions of Linux

In adopting Linux, one key decision is the distribution to use. As so often in open source, there are many choices, perhaps more than you would like to deal with. Several of the distributions offer different editions, such as

Professional or Server. Also, of course, there are different versions over time. In a general sense, the differences are not large, but it can be difficult to make specific statements about exactly how anything works. For example, take Red Hat. In the last couple of years it has offered Red Hat Linux versions 7.0, 7.1, 7.2, 7.3, 8.0, and 9 plus Red Hat Enterprise Linux 2.1 and 3 and Fedora Core 1 and 2. All of these are in use and you could, for instance, find books on any of these in a bookstore today. Most of these were available in multiple editions.

Red Hat is undergoing a big one-time transition, and this will resolve to RHEL3 and Fedora. There are similar issues with SuSE, which moved in a few months from 8.2 to 9 and now 9.1 while being acquired by Novell, whose Ximian acquisition offers some overlapping functions. Among smaller distributions, different forms of instability may occur, since there has been a continuing shakeout in distributions in the last couple of years.

It is a good thing to have choices available if they are significant to you. You may want, for example, to make a small stable core OS for your retail stores without consumer applications, or adopt a new window manager, windowing system, or even kernel as soon as it is available, rather than waiting for a vendor to integrate it.

These same choices may be meaningless noise, or frightening, to other users. Other choices, such as between KDE and Gnome, or the various utilities for configuring networks and printers, just lead into a frustrating rehash of historical details not interesting to most users.

There are many versions of Windows also. The following versions of Windows were all sold during the last four years, are in widespread use, and are officially supported by Microsoft:

- Windows 98 and 98SE

- Windows ME

- Windows NT4

- Windows CE (several versions, including SmartPhone, Pocket PC)

- Windows 2000 (various editions)

- Windows XP (Professional, Home, Tablet)

- Windows 2003 Server (various editions)

Table 6.1 *Linux Most Often Identified under Apache (Netcraft)*

Distribution	January 2004 (in thousands)	Six-month Growth (%)	January 2005?
Red Hat	1,232	18	1,430
Cobalt	549	2	400
Debian	443	25	550
SuSE	296	23	400
Mandrake	53	2	55
Gentoo	24	20	30

This actually represents three wholly different operating systems: Windows 98SE/ME, the mobile system Windows CE, and the others, which are all based on Windows NT. A task such as installing a network card is done differently in each of these systems. This proliferation of versions is something most people commonly complain about with Windows. It is reasonable to think they will like this aspect of Linux even less.

Most-Used Distribution Vendors

As we do elsewhere in the book, we will survey the field and then attempt to focus on a few most likely choices.

D. H. Brown, in *Linux Function Review 2003*, selected Red Hat, SuSE, and Debian as the three leading distributions of Linux, in that order. The D. H. Brown review compares functionality and vendor support mostly, with functionality strong for all three and vendor support being strongest for Red Hat and SuSE.

The most important single use of Linux is for Web servers. There is a Netscape report on the most-identified Linux under Apache. See Table 6.1. Unfortunately, this report needs careful interpretation. Distribution is known in only 25 percent of Apache Linux sites, and there may be systematic reasons why it is missing. Cobalt seems to be reporting itself disproportionately and thus getting overcounted relative to the others. Cobalt appliances are no longer sold, having been replaced by Sunfire systems running Red Hat or SuSE, so they will be quickly overtaken. Leaving aside Cobalt, the top three distributions in this table are Red Hat, Debian, and SuSE, in that order. Debian and SuSE are faster growing, but at these rates will not together match Red Hat in the next few years.

At my local users group, Florida Linux Users Exchange (FLUX), a survey is maintained of "favorite" distributions. Among 233 responses were seven distributions, with five over 10 percent, as follows:

- Red Hat   28%
- Debian   21%
- Slackware   15%
- SuSE   14%
- Gentoo   10%

This group favors the smaller "free" distributions, Debian and Slackware, preferred by many enthusiasts. People may report Slackware or Debian as a "favorite" but use Red Hat when working at their place of employment.

Managing Distributions and Packages

The first choice for an organization to make is whether to purchase an "enterprise distribution" with support or to "roll their own" with a system. Many organizations may do both, depending on the environment. You can choose among:

- Outsourcing distribution (Red Hat, Ximian Red Carpet)
- Roll your own but use a package distribution mechanism (Debian)
- Outsource your custom package creation (Progeny Platform Services)
- Modifying a distribution to suit, and then distribute it as you wish

Today, whether you run a Linux distribution, Mac OS X, or Windows, you can (and should) choose a software update system from the vendor that will distribute updates and patches automatically. Package formats include RPM, used by Red Hat and SuSE, and DEB, used by Debian (and derivatives) and also optionally by Red Hat Fedora. The package formats are used with front-end commands for application. RPM is used with the front ends up2date and YUM, while DEB is usually used with APT.

Unlike Windows, you do not have to license every desktop. Of course, if you are buying support for some desktops and not others, there will be measures to prevent abuse.

6.3   Enterprise Distribution Vendors

The two enterprise distributions that are likely to be the choices of larger organizations, particularly those moving to Linux from elsewhere, and particularly in the United States, are Red Hat Enterprise Linux and SuSE Linux (Enterprise and Standard). These are the premier offerings of the two largest corporations offering Linux distributions to the enterprise. Red Hat has been the leading Linux distributor for years, has a high reputation, and has been profitable and growing for several years. SuSE has long been the second major distribution, as well as the leader in some European countries, including Germany. It was recently acquired by Novell, and the new financial strength and combination with Linux development powerhouse Ximian, also acquired by Novell, can only strengthen it.

These two are the likely choice of the organization that is willing to pay for a supported distribution and does not want to build its own.

6.4   Community-Supported Distribution Vendors

Debian and Fedora are two major community-supported distribution vendors.

6.4.1   Debian

There are more choices for organizations that want to "roll their own." The third major distribution is Debian GNU/Linux. It has a very different style: community supported and always free. Debian is a large distribution that offers a wider set of software choices than any other.

Unfortunately, the timing of this book does not work well with Debian releases. The version that will be available ("stable") by publication will be Sarge. The software mix will be more up-to-date, and the new installer should bring that aspect of Debian up to (or close to) the standard of Red Hat and SuSE. The current "stable" (Woody 3.0r2) is known to be a difficult Linux to "cut your teeth on." It is difficult to install and contains old versions of much important software.

Debian is often chosen by other distributions as a basis, because it is solid and has in APT a powerful distribution mechanism. The consumer products Lindows, Xandros, and Knoppix, for instance, are all Debian based. Two Debian-based projects of interest to business are Progeny and UserLinux. Progeny, a new company founded by Debian cofounder Ian Murdock, supports companies that want to develop their own custom Linux installations. UserLinux is a new initiative that plans to appeal to the business community by simplifying the choices and allowing business users to move to a standardized user desktop based on Gnome and OpenOffice. For an explanation in detail, see http://userlinux.com/white_paper.html.

6.4.2 Fedora

Another alternative to the enterprise-branded distributions is the new community-supported version of Red Hat: Fedora Core. Using Fedora, you will pay essentially nothing to get the distribution but may have to make decisions about support more explicitly than with Red Hat and SuSE. Fedora is the follow-up to Red Hat 9, and looks similar, but can be set up to use either the YUM or Debian APT distribution management system. It is available not directly from Red Hat but through a new channel of users and inexpensive distributors. Fedora is more "cutting edge" than Red Hat Enterprise Linux, on a faster development cycle. Over time, Fedora may diverge from its origins, but now it is clearly administratively affiliated with Red Hat and technically not very different from Red Hat 9 and Red Hat Enterprise 3.

Where this book specifically references a distribution, as with screenshots, it uses Red Hat (Fedora and Enterprise) and SuSE. Selecting these choices enables me to get the book written in a reasonably explicit style and hopefully helps you to read it, without limiting choices unduly.

6.5 International Alternatives

Outside the United States there are alternatives in certain areas, notably:

- Mandrake   Europe
- TurboLinux   Asia
- Conectiva   Latin America
- Red Flag   China

These have strengths for particular languages and cultures. SuSE, which is based in Germany, is also strong in Europe.

6.5.1 Consumer Linux Choices

For consumers, Linux distributions to consider, in addition to versions of Red Hat and SuSE, include Lindows and Xandros. Xandros, formerly Corel Linux, is based on Debian with the KDE desktop. It installs easily and offers an automatic dual-boot version on a machine with Windows installed. Lindows, also Debian based, is available preinstalled on some systems. Mandrake is another strong choice.

6.5.2 Booting from a CD

One more very useful Linux distribution to mention is Knoppix. Knoppix is based on Debian and the KDE desktop with OpenOffice and a powerful set of programs. It comes on a single bootable CD, so you have nothing to install. It recognizes devices, including the network.

Knoppix is great for evaluations or loaner machines, because it just works. It is also a good base from which to fix up Windows or nonbooting boxes. This is very useful for system repair or to provide Linux tools to work with on non-Linux systems. For example, you could use the Linux "parted" utility to alter partitions on a system that boots in Windows.

Knoppix is easy and attractive to use. You can get a good look at a working Linux system and get some work done on it. Knoppix is at 3.3 and is well tested and popular. Figure 6.3 shows Knoppix in the process of booting from a CD. Figure 6.4 shows the Knoppix screen after booting with the KDE desktop visible, Konqueror open, and Mozilla and OpenOffice available on the menu bar.

There are alternative "live" (bootable) CDs, including some on business-card-sized CDs or that can boot from USB devices. SuSE Linux 9.1 Professional is self-booting, so eventually I expect all distributions will be. Until then, Knoppix is the best known and most mature, so for most people it is the one to try first. For those who prefer Gnome, there is a similar product called Gnoppix, but this is in beta and I would advise waiting for it to reach 1.0 and sticking with Knoppix for now.

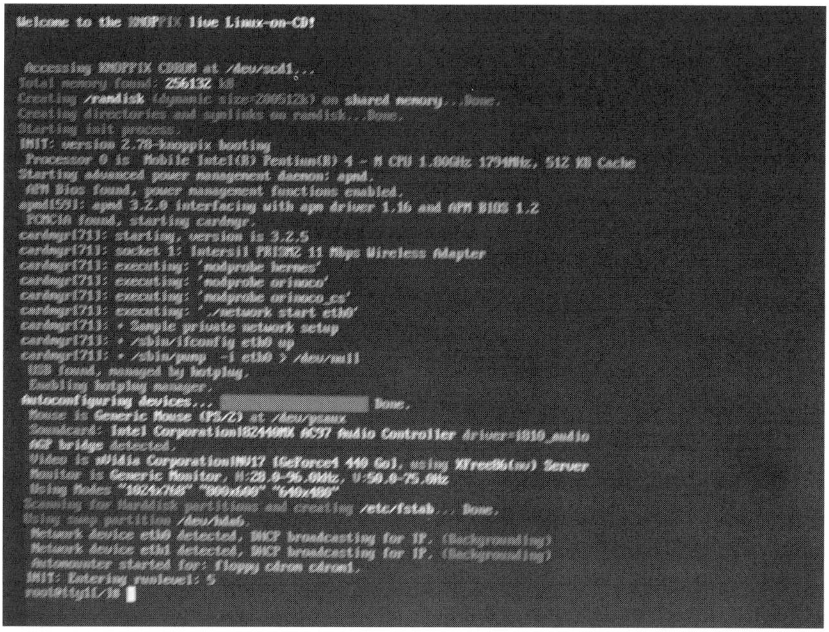

Figure 6.3
Knoppix booting.

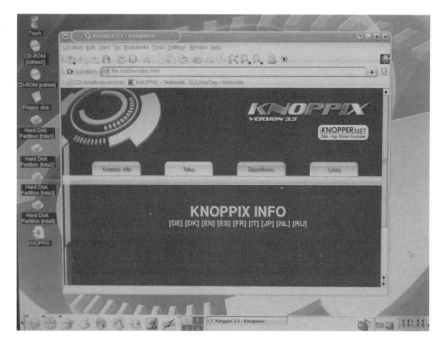

Figure 6.4
Knoppix desktop.

6.6   **Summary**

The ecosystem around the Linux operating system is dynamic, with many companies and rapidly changing versions, but stable in important ways. Applications developed for Linux run on all the distributions and versions without change. A Linux vendor could discontinue distribution, but systems it distributed could be migrated to other Linux versions without a large disruption. This issue is actually more of a concern for closed code products. Many times, closed code vendors have gone bankrupt, been acquired, or just discontinued a product, and their customers were into migration to a replacement at an inopportune time. This happened with the DEC TOPS-20 and OS/2 operating systems, for example.

Unlike closed code systems, Linux does not rely on having a single successful vendor. The open source model means that another company can always pick up the code base and continue. Some Linux distributors, as with some closed source companies, have gone into bankruptcy organization or out of business, but this has not had a serious impact on their customers. Other Linux distributors, such as Red Hat, have been consistently successful.

It may be that in the future, Linux will consolidate around one or two major vendors. Perhaps, in the worst case, we'll be back where we've been in the past, with those vendors calling the shots, as in the 1980s with IBM or, more recently, with Microsoft. But open source is different in that you will always have choices. Any company can set up to distribute, support, or sell training in Red Hat Linux. You may make a decision to consolidate buying from IBM Global Services, but you are still going to be able to get other components that you need (hardware, other software, support, consulting) from other vendors.

Linux distributions are sufficiently similar that a customer can always select another distributor. Applications and custom solutions developed for one distribution will work with another. There might be some dislocation, but less than involved in a closed source situation of the same type.

The Linux operating system has developed over the past ten years at an extraordinarily fast rate and is now the operating system of choice for new systems—from the very largest supercomputer clusters to the very smallest appliances and hand-held systems, as well as for typical uses of business server computers of all sizes.

In this book, we repeatedly make the point that open source systems are good enough for many purposes. Linux is more than that. It is simply the best operating system in many respects and for most purposes. It is more secure than other general-purpose operating systems, has the fastest networking stack of any system, scales to the smallest appliances and the largest clusters, and is constantly improving.

7

Open Source Server Applications

The important open source server applications, which will be discussed in the following sections include:

- Infrastructure services
- Web servers
- Database servers
- Mail servers
- Systems management services

7.1   Infrastructure Services

Infrastructure services consist of basic network services, security services, and file, print, and directory services.

Basic network services include DHCP, DNS, and WINS plus caching services, and routing where that is not done by an appliance. It is typically very inexpensive to provide these services, on the order of $100 per user per year, and this is a commodity activity that any server should be able to perform.

Security services include firewalls, virtual private networking, intrusion detection, antivirus services, authentication, and authorization. These services are difficult to distinguish at times from basic network services and directory services, which support them, or even mail services, such as the case of antivirus and antispam services. Active Directory, for example, provides directory and security services through the same product and the same interface. Sometimes, indeed increasingly often, these are provided by appliances.

A major difference between open source and Windows in this area is that Linux is usually the operating system of dedicated appliances. Security is actually the most common single use of Linux in the enterprise, and this is mostly in appliances. Appliance vendors prefer Linux (or FreeBSD) for two reasons:

- They pay no licensing fees.
- They can tune the system precisely for their needs.

As a result, these appliances are inexpensive because of the custom footprint and low license fee. Linux networking appliances are also generally very fast. Linux (along with FreeBSD) is generally recognized to have the fastest networking stack, and the code can be further tuned for particular dedicated purposes. Microsoft offers support for appliances also but usually prefers a more integrated approach, where Windows systems run a mix of services on a larger server.

7.1.1 File and Print Services

In a mixed environment, we will generally use Samba for file and print services. Linux systems also support file sharing very efficiently and easily using NFS and FTP, and this is a good choice in existing UNIX environments. Another choice is the Novell iFolders technology, which was recently open sourced. Given the current distribution of servers and clients, most organizations are currently using Windows networking, and adopting Samba will be the simplest choice.

Samba allows non-Windows systems to share file and print services with Windows systems. Samba clients function like Windows clients, but for Linux, Mac, or other operating systems, so they see file shares and printers published by Windows or Samba servers. Samba servers function like Windows servers, but on Linux or other systems, so they can publish file and printer shares and also authenticate users in a way similar to a Windows server. The current version of Samba can authenticate by acting as a Windows NT primary or backup domain controller, by accessing Windows NT domain controllers, or by accessing the Windows 2000 Active Directory.

Samba is an efficient program and scales well. Companies such as Bank of America and Hewlett-Packard use Samba to support many thousands of clients. The program, written by Andrew Trumbull while at SGI, is an implementation of the Windows Networking facility called Server Message Block (SMB). The name Samba is a play on SMB. The protocol traces back to the period when IBM, 3Com, and Microsoft were working together; is also used in OS/2; and is also known as the Common Internet File System (CIFS).

We may be able to arrange file sharing within an organization (inside a firewall) by implementing one of a few simple approaches. If information is usually either private or enterprise wide (public), then we don't need a directory system. We can create and share public shares on file sharing systems and teach users to move information for sharing to those shares. On Novell systems, these were usually set up as virtual drives. Once we get beyond public/private into allowing groups or individuals access to specific information, we will probably need a directory of some sort, although not necessarily LDAP. Using Samba, at least since version 3, the choices are:

- Use Samba to manage users. Samba can act as a client to an NT server for authentication or work like an NT primary domain server for NT4 replacement, in which case users are migrated from the NT4 server to Samba.

- Use Active Directory. Samba can act as a client for authentication to a Windows 2000/2003 Server running Active Directory (but not as a server).

- Set up OpenLDAP or another LDAP server and use that as the directory for managing file sharing.

There are several dependent components for Samba. Samba shares printers by using the local printing facility (generally CUPS today on Linux). It also relies on WINS for naming services by default. Originally, SMB was based on NetBIOS, later on NetBIOS over TCP/IP (with the NetBEUI stack removed). It can now run without NetBIOS, which many organizations require. To see and work with Samba files—for instance, to create file shares or access them—you will need a GUI tool such as Nautilus or Konqueror that supports SMB.

7.1.2   Directory Services

OpenLDAP is based on the original LDAP server, written at the University of Michigan. It takes a little more work to set up than the commercial alternatives, but it is open source, solid, scalable, and provides authentication that is configurable for many of the services we will want to use:

- Samba file and print sharing
- Apache Web server
- Courier and Postfix mail servers

The Mozilla browser and other client programs can read user information from OpenLDAP. In addition, we can program access to OpenLDAP from the command line or from our own applications.

7.2   Web Servers

There are really no other general-purpose open source Web servers to consider than Apache. It has a high share and is the reference standard for a Web server. It is easy to administer and has low overhead, so it works for small sites and systems. The largest Web sites in the world use it. It can be tuned to perform extremely well, and for specific needs. Support for Apache is the gold standard for open source support. The Apache organization is so successful that it has spawned a family of related projects.

7.2.1   Apache

Apache is by most measures the most successful single open source software project. It is the most commonly used Web server in the world, constituting about two-thirds of all Web servers. A recent Netcraft survey (November 2003) shows Apache with 67 percent of top Web servers and 69 percent of active, against Microsoft's 21 percent and 24 percent, respectively. See www.netcraft.com. Active Web servers are usually regarded as the most useful measure of Web server activity, since names reserved but not used are eliminated. Apache has similar shares worldwide across large and small servers including those used for ecommerce.

Apache is based on the original Web server written at the National Center for Supercomputing Applications (NCSA) at the University of Illinois in 1993. The first Apache beta was released in 1995. The name originally stood for "a patchy Web server."

Apache runs on many operating systems, including Linux, most versions of UNIX, Windows, and Novell NetWare. Apache is currently available in two series: 2.0.x, which has been available as a production release for two years since early 2002, and 1.3.x. At the time of writing, the 1.3 series is still significantly more used than 2.0, reflecting apparently a conservatism among Apache users. The Apache license allows its inclusion in commercial products, and it is included in IBM WebSphere among others.

Apache is structured into a kernel and a number of modules, which includes both statically and dynamically loaded modules supporting extension tools such as Front Page and WebDAV; languages such as PHP, Perl, Python, and Java servlets; and authentication against Samba/NT, LDAP, and various databases.

If you are migrating from the Microsoft Web server Internet Information Server (IIS), CGI programs can be migrated without change because Apache and IIS support the same CGI standard. If your Windows programs were developed with ISAPI, ASP, or Cold Fusion, your simplest option is to run Apache on Windows. Programs that use ISAPI require Windows to function, but if you have Cold Fusion or ASP programs and you really want to migrate off IIS, you can purchase modules, from Allaire and Sun, respectively, that allow these products to run on Apache on Linux. For ASP, you can also consider a product called ASP-to-PHP, which does the one-time conversion implied by its name.

Web servers are inexpensive to buy and maintain. Another option is to let Windows and Linux Web servers work side by side for a period.

Apache sites install modules to communicate with development languages, typically called mod_X for language X. Over half of Apache sites run mod_php, a little under 20 percent run mod_perl, and a little over 1 percent run mod_python. Further sites may run programs with CGI. Plainly, PHP is the most common development tool for Apache Web sites. In fact, PHP is the most commonly used language on the Web (Microsoft ASP is second) and its use is growing.

7.2.2 Other Web Servers

Alternative general Web servers are the commercial products iPlanet (formerly Netscape) server on various operating systems and, of course, Microsoft IIS, on Windows only.

There are some niche products in special markets, such as the Red Hat Stronghold Secure Web Server. Some tools or applications—for instance, Plone and Tomcat—come bundled with a Web server, but this is usually as a convenience. They generally allow you to use Apache.

Tux is a kernel-based Web server developed by Red Hat. It is combined with Apache to improve the performance for straight HTTP display. It can improve performance of such pages a lot; in the right circumstances by an order of magnitude or more. This is similar to the caching products offered by IBM and Microsoft.

Other Web servers include Zeus and servers included with development products such as Jetty, which is included with Tomcat, but the share of these products is not over 1 percent.

As far as which operating system the Web server runs on, approximately 50 percent of sites run on Windows, 30 percent on Linux, 6 percent on BSD, and 9 percent on UNIX, mostly Solaris, with other or unknown 5 percent, according to Netscape data in 2001. Quite a lot of Apache servers run on Windows.

7.3   Database Servers

Most major databases are available on Linux, and have been for years—Oracle since 1998, for instance. The only major modern database that is not sold to run on Linux is SQL Server. The benchmarks and references are there, and the vendors are quite enthusiastic. Running Oracle, DB2, Sybase, CA-Ingres, or Informix on Linux is clearly a safe conservative choice, and any issues or limitations specific to the platform can be discussed with the vendors. This is essentially migration from UNIX to Linux in almost all cases, since the version of DB2 on Linux is the UNIX version. As with any UNIX to Linux migration, switching costs are reasonably low, as access to these databases from other systems is the same.

You can choose to run an open source database, such as MySQL. The open source choice is more likely to deliver significant savings. It is a more adventurous choice than closed code on open source, but there are many organizations already doing this.

Many organizations will be able to use a mixed strategy, combining MySQL and Oracle, for instance, depending on the scale and risk of the application. While open source databases can be used anywhere, they are a particularly good fit where many small databases run, as in a distributed or embedded situation. So, an organization might use a few large Oracle database systems combined with many smaller open source databases.

7.3.1 Classes of Database Servers

We are going to cover all databases here, even desktop ones. We will treat desktop servers as a small class of database server, and some elements of desktop systems as client tools. For example, Microsoft Access can be regarded as a desktop application that administers and updates a database server. The server for Access can be an Access database, which can be local or remote, or it can be a SQL Server, upgraded using the wizard provided by Microsoft, built directly using Access tools, or another database accessed with ODBC.

So these types of database products need to be looked at separately:

- Online transaction processing (OLTP) servers
- Data warehouse servers
- Embedded databases
- Client access tools including decision support systems

There are open source choices in all of these areas, but some are stronger than others.

7.3.2 Analysis of Database System Sizes

Research into large transaction processing systems published by Microsoft in 1999 found that, at that time, the following were numbers of transactions per day at the largest commercial organizations processing transactions (not necessarily automated in all cases):

NYSE:	1M
All card and check processing:	20M
Citibank, Bank of America, Wal-Mart:	10–40M
All airline reservations:	220M
AT&T calls worldwide:	200M

Visa did 30M transactions for 400M customers at 250,000 automated teller machines worldwide. That is about as big as it gets. There are a few new technology and ecommerce applications on the Amazon and Google scale that may run higher volumes than these, but most business systems are orders of magnitude smaller.

The TPC Benchmark

TPC stems from a debit-credit benchmark for banking transactions that originated at Bank of America in 1972. The Transaction Processing Council (TPC) was set up to manage an evolving series of benchmarks starting from TP1 in an independent manner. TPC-C, which was introduced in 1992, is the major published transactional benchmark and has evolved to respond to limitations discovered in earlier such benchmarks. The benchmark supports a mix of five transaction types and requires all elements of the database, such as numbers of customers, to scale along with transaction measurements. TPC numbers are published with the relevant cost data so price/performance can be considered, and there are clear rules on how cost is calculated. The benchmark is only for hardware and software that can be ordered by customers and is shipping now or will be available within a few months. In reviewing the actions of various competitors, the TPC has learned many methods of enhancing the results by bending the rules. It has met this continual challenge by developing methods to control and eventually prevent this. The TPC is as good an organization for publishing benchmarks measuring business database transaction performance as we have or are likely to have.

Limitations of the TPC-C Benchmark

The TPC-C benchmark is expensive to run. Because of the way it scales, and the precision needed to meet the standards correctly, it takes significant time and money to run a benchmark (some say $1M). So only a limited number of these are run, depending on the vendors that choose to spend this money. We can only use the data to approximate a solution we are considering, usually by interpolation. Our chosen hardware and software are not likely to have been specifically tested, and we will look for something similar.

The cost also means that running our own TPC-C benchmark is almost certainly prohibitive, but it is generally desirable to do this. Another method is needed to allow us to get really specific in addressing our needs.

TPC cannot enforce that the methods used for the benchmark are the methods actually used in the real world. One reason the benchmark is expensive is that the skills to set it up are unusual, because it is now usually run on quite specialized software that ordinary organizations would not use, as follows:

- Most vendors use custom C++ code and the Tuxedo application server, while recommending Java application servers.

- Big database measurements use tricks such as distributed partitioned views, which customers don't like to maintain, and materialized views, which customers do not benefit from.

- TPC-C prohibits methods such as queuing that allow smaller databases to manage high-peak workloads.

The highest-performance TPC-C numbers are now so big that they dwarf normal business needs by orders of magnitude. Compared with what most people are doing, this is like comparing a jet fighter to a crop-sprayer. Most customer database needs are nothing like the top end of the TPC-C performance table, and most customers would probably be better off with something much less expensive and fast, but easier to use.

What we can say about TPC-C is that if a database/platform combination appears high in the performance table, that combination is capable of tremendous potential performance beyond almost all practical customer database needs. If a system is in there, it can do the job.

The TPC-C price/performance table shows a very different set of platforms. The very largest systems (compared with a jet fighter) turn out to be much more expensive per transaction than mid-sized and mid-priced systems, so the price/performance table is dominated by these mid-sized systems. Given the difficulty of building large high-performance databases, this suggests that a good choice for most businesses is to avoid these larger, more complex, and more expensive systems where possible and go with systems in the better price/performance range. And these are the systems that are the volume sellers. Organizations typically do not like too many small databases, because they are hard to administer and plan for, so they generally consolidate to a smaller number of larger systems, but not the exotic types that win the TPC-C performance table.

The Winter Top Ten Lists

Winter Corporation publishes Top Ten lists of large production databases, both OLTP and DSS. The statistics are self-reported by customers, sponsored by database vendors, so it is a little bit of a "bragging contest." There

Table 7.1 *Big Production Databases (Source: Winter)*

Measurement	Range
OLTP Database Size	2.9–18 terabytes
OLTP Number of Rows	8–42 billion
OLTP Peak Workload	155–450 (UNIX), 113–3,630 (Windows)
DSS Database Size	9–29 terabytes
DSS Number of Rows	65–496 billion

may be larger systems that choose to remain anonymous. However, the data reported appears to be accurate and includes some of the largest systems, so it is very useful for my purposes here, which is to get a sense of how big databases really are and what platforms people really use.

Table 7.1 shows the size by various measurements of the databases in the annual Winter Top Ten tables published at the end of 2003. These are the very largest systems.

These are large databases. However, the workloads are not all particularly high. In particular, the real-world Winter measurements, like the real-world research numbers, are much lower transaction rates than the TPC-C high performers. So this confirms that the best (and most expensive) systems being measured today are substantially outperforming the requirement.

So we have a theoretical measurement and some practical measurements. Table 7.2 combines these two measurements and shows leading databases, whether they run Linux, the status of their TPC-C benchmark (a measurement of high potential performance), and their status in the Winter Top Ten (a measurement of largest deployed transactional systems in the real world) at the beginning of 2004.

From Table 7.2, we see that Linux is not in the Winter tables yet, but that is not surprising. Winter is, by its nature, a very conservative data source, since it takes years to get such big systems built, and it is unusual to migrate them once created. Winter has several IBM mainframes in it, for example. In the largest production systems, we actually see only three platform combinations: IBM mainframes, SQL Server on Windows 2000, and Oracle on UNIX.

In the TPC data, we see Oracle on Linux with a couple of very high numbers. This is an important breakthrough for Linux, which is in the TPC measurement for the first time, and on top. The Oracle measure-

Table 7.2   *Leading Databases, January 2004 (Source: Winter)*

Database	Linux	OS for TPC	OS for OLTP	OS for DSS
Oracle	Yes	Linux, HP-UX, AIX	HP-UX and other UNIX	HP-UX
DB2	Yes	AIX, OS/400	Z/OS	AIX
SQL Server	No	Windows 2000/3	Windows 2K	Windows 2K
CA-IDMS	No	None	Z/OS	None
CA-Datacom	No	None	Z/OS	None
Sybase	Yes	HP-UX, Solaris, Compaq Tru64	None	HP-UX
Informix	Yes	None	None	None
CA-Ingres	Yes	None	None	None

ments, done on HP systems, show that with vendor support Linux can match proprietary UNIX on the same hardware. We already know that Oracle on UNIX systems can run very large production systems, and so we are confident that we can build the largest systems with Oracle on Linux. Only Oracle has demonstrated this today. However, we are probably confident given the vendor commitment that DB2 and Sybase, which have demonstrated high performance on UNIX versions (IBM for DB2, Sun and HP for Sybase), can run with high performance on Linux also. Ingres and Informix are not in these measurements. This is probably mostly a matter of not having money to spend or a corporate parent who is very bothered about them, but that is something for customers to take into account, after all. So, I resolve Table 7.2 as follows when considering very large databases.

Mainframe systems, including DB2, CA-IDMS, and CA-Datacom, can support very large, high-transaction databases, but they are legacy systems, too expensive and complex to consider for new applications—except that for organizations that already have DB2 deployed on a mainframe, it represents a practical choice.

Oracle on UNIX supports very large fast databases on several hardware platforms and has many reference cases including the majority of large Internet systems. This specifically includes Linux.

SQL Server on Windows 2000 works with some large reference cases and has the best price/performance by a substantial margin in the size range most customers deploy.

Table 7.3   *Database Categories*

Category	GB	Typical Hardware	Rows	Development Method	DB Requests/ Second	Cost
Very big	1,000s	Big (e.g., 8x) SMP box, cluster, or mainframe	10B	Custom complex	100K+	$5M +
Big	100s?	One big 4-way SMP	1B	Often complex	10–100K	$500K
Medium	10s?	Commodity 4-way	100M	Simple to moderate	1–10K	$50K
Small	Fractional	Small 2-way server	Few million	Simple	100s	$5K
Tiny, embedded	0.01	Desktop, notebook, server	Small	Embedded	Few	Fractional

Sybase and DB2 on UNIX work and clearly should work on Linux. Informix and Ingres work on UNIX and presumably on Linux but are basically in maintenance mode.

With this information about large databases, and some common-sense knowledge about the needs of typical businesses, we can create Table 7.3 to use for categorizing database servers by performance category. We can use the categories defined in this table to look at the various choices, and select the two or three best in each category.

We will do that in the following pages. Note that no single database is the right choice across all categories. SQL Server comes closest, since there is a small royalty-free version available. Unfortunately, there is a big licensing restriction. The versions of SQL Server (MSDE) for small and embedded systems are only available if we use Visual Studio or Office as development tools or use SQL Server as a centralized database.

Berkeley DB is a special case. It is not a general-purpose SQL database, and it is broadly distributed, since it is embedded in many essential open source tools.

Table 7.3 assumes conventional database development. With enough custom development, anything can be made to work on any platform. Later, we will discuss design choices that will allow us to push past these limits under the right circumstances with custom development. These would tend to allow smaller and less expensive choices to do the job.

Very Big Databases

The very big systems discussed here are custom developed and cost many millions. Only a few dozen are built in a typical year. The practical choices in this area are DB2 on a mainframe, Oracle on UNIX, or SQL Server on Win2K.

Oracle is the only database with a Linux TPC-C published benchmark; it is the highest ever database performance as I write, achieved in December 2003 with a 16-box cluster of 4-way Intel systems. See www.tpc.org for the latest. The very high cluster scores on this benchmark are quite different from most normal commercial practices. Who uses Tuxedo? The numbers do show something about vendor commitment to the platform and about theoretical feasibility. For instance, it is remarkable that the 64-processor Linux result on a 16-way Beowulf cluster beats the 64-processor HP-UX result with the same number of processors on more integrated machines.

There is no Linux database in the Winter Top Ten data. Winter publishes a general and a UNIX Top Ten. Databases in the top ten included five on mainframes, three on Windows, and two on UNIX; DB2, CA-IDMS, and CA-Datacom, all on zOS; SQL Server on Windows; and Oracle on UNIX. Oracle had the entire Top Ten Winter UNIX list, with none on Linux. The DB2 code base for zOS and AS/400 are different from UNIX (and each other) and cannot be usefully compared; DB2 has an AIX benchmark, which is the same code base as Linux, but the hardware is probably not the same as you would run DB2 for Linux on so it is still hard to compare. Sybase has some UNIX benchmarks, although not too impressive. Sybase and DB2 have had Linux products for several years, and they use the same code base and should have similar characteristics to the UNIX products. Informix is a legacy product at this stage.

When looking at database on Linux case studies, they do not yet appear to be very large systems. The large database business is, reasonably enough, very conservative. It takes years to deploy most large systems, then they stay on the deployed architecture forever after. My conclusion is that if you plan to run very large databases on Linux, you are in the area of "technically feasible but bleeding edge" and will need good-quality support from the database vendor. If you do this, you should probably look first to Oracle as the vendor committed to Linux and the leader on UNIX. Second would be DB2, and then Sybase in special circumstances such as the financial industry.

Best choices for very big databases:

- Oracle/Linux
- SQL/Win2K

- DB2/zOS

Big Databases

The choice of database servers in this category comes down to DB2, Oracle, Sybase, and SQL Server on UNIX or Windows. This is a stable category. It was true in 1994 and is still true today.

What has changed in ten years is that SQL Server can now scale larger and has more share, and open source databases are beginning to be a possible choice. Because database pricing is per processor, buyers tend to go for big machines with fast processors in this range. A cheaper, say $150K, box would cost as much as the big one for the database, so price/performance goes off.

The obvious choice in this category is Oracle, with most share and most references. IT is also usually the most expensive. SQL Server will often have better price/performance, as will DB2. Of course, MySQL has the best price/performance. It is often helpful when negotiating with a database vendor to have other choices, particularly less expensive ones, so these should be considered.

Systems in this class may have a large batch component, or tight integration with legacy systems, and are often mission critical, such as line of business, ecommerce, or enterprise application, all of which can make them more complex and expensive.

Here is a revealing irony. What I call a big database here, Oracle calls "entry level" in its marketing. In a Linux TPC-C benchmark performed in September 2003, Oracle achieved over 136,000 tpmC at a cost of under $4/tpmC. This was being publicized by Oracle in early 2004, as the system became commercially available. Compared with a Microsoft benchmark done a couple of months earlier on the same hardware, an HP Integrity rx5670, Oracle was faster and cheaper. The Oracle headline was: "Oracle Database 10*g* on Linux Faster and Cheaper than Microsoft SQL Server 2000 on Windows." The Microsoft result was 121,000 tpmC at $4.49/tpmC. Oracle refers to these systems in the article as entry level. These are half-million-dollar systems at the high end of my "big database" category, and far bigger than most customers need. Oracle wants to see this as entry level because in the smaller categories they are not as competitive, and they want customers to look here and upward.

Best choices for big databases:

- Oracle/Linux
- SQL/Win2K

- MySQL or PostgreSQL

Medium Databases

The medium database category is typically run on a good four-way Intel system with RAID. This is the commodity database server at this time, or the "meat and potatoes" of databases installed in organizations.

It is a practical fact that this category is dominated by SQL Server in a price range from $30K to $60K.

For most reasonable-sized databases, Oracle or DB2 on Linux should be a reasonable choice over the next year or two, something to evaluate. The challenge, where performance is not the overriding challenge, is expressed by examination of the TPC-C results by price/performance. This category is dominated by Microsoft SQL Server at about $2/tpmC. Oracle has one moderate benchmark with 10*g* on RHEL on an HP, with 136K tpmC at $4.09.

This is not an area in which to use proprietary UNIX systems or less usual databases such as Sybase, unless you already have them in house. So the set of choices here comes down to SQL Server on Windows, Oracle or DB2 on Linux, and MySQL or another open source database.

You could, of course, run Oracle on Windows, but that's not recommended anymore, and we are looking at Linux here. The issue in this space is that SQL Server is only available on Windows and offers better price/performance than the alternatives. Fortunately, MySQL is available and has the best price/performance.

If you are looking at new systems in this area and for some reason are not considering open source databases, you should evaluate Oracle and DB2 on Linux against Microsoft SQL on Windows for price/performance. There is not much lock-in if you run SQL on Windows and avoid integrated login. I suppose you could consider porting SQL Server systems to Sybase, which is very similar, and Sybase offers this service, but given the higher price of Sybase and its legacy status, I should not think anyone would want to do that.

The Meta Group (March 2003) considers MySQL able to handle comfortably 300–2,000 database requests/second and 2–12 GB of data, which puts it squarely in the competition for the medium-sized databases. Meta also states that MySQL is "comparable to Oracle 9i on a well-known bookstore benchmark." The well-known bookstore test would be Nile, loosely based on Amazon.com. (Amazon.com runs Oracle and is not, of course, in any way medium sized.) There are many production MySQL databases in the 40-50GB range.

Many organizations will find that this is the perfect space to introduce MySQL to an organization. It is well inside the database's performance envelope and offers a big payoff in price.

Best choices for medium databases:

- SQL/Win2K

- MySQL or PostgreSQL

- Oracle/Linux

Small Databases

The category of database being considered here is a two-way processor, two-disk box or rack server typically costing from $2K to $20K. However small the database, if it is managed with separate tools it is in this category.

These small databases are an excellent fit for open source at this time. While the platform is inexpensive, the relative prices of the databases come to the forefront. Small open source databases also remain full-function, while the big closed code vendors have a tendency to remove functionality and add restrictions to their inexpensive versions. In an extreme case, there is a royalty-free version of SQL Server, but it has no management tools, only supports about five users, and has other restrictions.

A two-way system with five users costs $1,000 for Oracle and $1,500 for Microsoft SQL Server; PostgreSQL and MySQL are free. Yet these small systems can often service up to 100 users quite easily. An unlimited user license for a two-processor system is $10,000 for Oracle and SQL Server. Under a commercial license, MySQL Pro (which has row-level locking and transactions) is $500 for unlimited processors and users.

Best choices for small databases:

- MySQL or PostgreSQL

Embedded Databases

This category includes databases for desktop systems, appliances, and application-specific systems that may run on servers or desktops. The performance that matters here is usually fast loading and small memory and disk use rather than transaction rate.

Simple and fast is more important than high functionality, so many of these systems may not use SQL. However, there is a case for small databases that support SQL, because that allows larger applications, which always use SQL, to scale down without rewrite.

The Microsoft version of this is Microsoft Database Engine (MSDE), which replaced Jet (the Access database engine). This is SQL Server without the tools, but unfortunately it is seriously restricted. The performance restriction (a thread limiter preventing more than a few concurrent accesses) is not a concern in this application, but the licensing restriction is.

MySQL offers an embedded version, and if SQL is needed, MySQL is the database of choice here. If SQL is not needed, this category totally belongs to Berkeley DB.

Best choices for embedded databases:

- MySQL
- Berkeley DB

Figure 7.1 plots the database products against size and cost to summarize these choices.

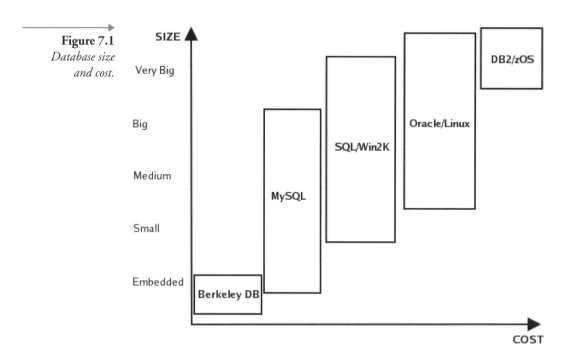

Figure 7.1
Database size and cost.

7.3.3 Open Source Database Choices

There are three open source databases to consider seriously for general use, in my view. These are Berkeley DB, PostgreSQL, and MySQL. They are all widely used.

Two more systems play in niches. MaxDB was formerly known as SAP DB and before that Adabas-G or Supra. It has some major clients, mostly in Europe, but has never caught on in the United States even with the pull of its integration with SAP. Its role will probably be to bring technologies for incorporation into future large-scale versions of MySQL. Despite being a solid product that has been around for some time, Firebird, formerly Borland Interbase, has not grown beyond a small niche.

Berkeley DB

Berkeley DB is a core tool under several important open source products, and apparently has 200 million deployments. Berkeley DB (BDB) is a high-performance derivative of the old "DBM" databases, which have been part of UNIX and UNIX-like operating systems from the beginning.

As an embedded, or application-specific, database, BDB is included with products, often without the user being aware. This is like Btrieve or Microsoft Jet and MSDE engines. It is a flat-file database, not SQL.

BDB has a dual licensing model. It is open source (GPL license) when used in open source products or at a single site. When distributed with a commercial product, there is a commercial license.

Berkeley DB is used by Sendmail, Apache, and OpenLDAP servers, the Netscape and Mozilla browsers, and the Python and Perl programming languages. Commercial customers include Sun, Google, Veritas, TIBCO, Cisco, Amazon, and HP.

PostgreSQL

PostgreSQL is an open source database, available under the BSD license/copyright regime. It is based on the Postgres product designed at Berkeley in the 1980s, and before that on work performed on the Ingres database by Michael Stonebraker since 1974. It was not a SQL-based product until 1995. Ingres and Postgres were developed on BSD UNIX. It is available now on Linux and UNIX, including the Mac, but is not native on Windows, running in the Cygwin emulation.

Postgres has historically offered better support than MySQL for standard SQL behavior, although MySQL seems to be catching up. Currently,

Postgres supports stored procedures, triggers, and views, which MySQL 4.1 does not. This is a strong argument for Postgres with experienced database developers, who are used to having these functions.

Postgres is a good database server with a strong following in the open source community, but in business use it is perceived as lagging MySQL in adoption, marketing, and support arrangements. Support arrangements offered by Great Bridge and Red Hat (the Red Hat database was based on Postgres) did not make much headway.

MySQL

The MySQL database server is robust, fast, and a very good cross-platform product on clients, including Windows and the Mac and a variety of UNIX servers. It has a small footprint and good management tools. The product is distributed by the Swedish company, MySQL AB. MySQL is used much more than PostgreSQL; the company estimates about 4M users worldwide. The product has momentum, with considerable enhancement happening, and last year's acquisition of MaxDB will likely lead to more enterprise-scale features later.

MySQL is dual-licensed, meaning it is available under a commercial license or the GPL. Because linking with the GPL-based libraries requires your code to go GPL, commercial developers who are not open source will want to pay for the commercial license. Also, the MySQL company asks commercial users to buy an unlimited commercial license. That commercial license is $500 for the product, including InnoDB, which is transactional—that is, unlimited processors and users. With this licensing model, MySQL is powerful and inexpensive for commercial users and it is open source for government, education, and personal users.

Historically, MySQL has missed some SQL standard features that many users regard as essential. This was originally a set of design decisions, as the product was intended to be fast above all. There is now a published plan to catch up on these, which is in progress. Transactions (ACID) were released in Version 4.0, when the previously distinct InnoDB engine was incorporated in the main product. Subqueries are in Version 4.1, which is close to production as I write. Stored procedures will be in Version 5.0 and triggers in 5.1.

MySQL is powerful enough for most purposes and easy to install and use. It is widely used in business organizations, including large systems such as Sabre. It powers the OSDN sites, including Slashdot, Freshmeat, and SourceForge, and is used by Google and Yahoo!.

7.3.4 **Database Performance Is Good Enough**

Table 7.4 shows some Microsoft SQL Server results on the TPC-C benchmark since 1996. The data was taken from TPC (www.tpc.org) in July 1999 and later.

Table 7.4   *Selected SQL Server TPC-C Results*

Date	tpmC	$/tpmC
December 1996	5,000	70
August 1999	40,000	20
January 2002	500,000	2.2

In mid-1999, an eight-way Microsoft SQL Server 7.0 reached 40,000 tpmC on one server with a then five-year cost of $.75 million. Because of the way the TPC-C benchmark is scaled, the 40,000 transactions in August 1999 represent 90M customers, 300M stock items, 120M transactions per day, 32,000 simultaneous users, and 5 terabytes of storage. At that time, SQL Server was good enough by transactional measures for almost all actual business database uses.

Improvement has continued at this pace. By 2002, the fastest SQL Server benchmark was ten times quicker than that. Price/performance on many typical systems is now below $2/tpmC, which is ten times better. Put another way, the tenfold improvement of the last two and a half years can be taken as better performance or lower price.

Databases are used as a component in a complex system. Most databases in organizations sit behind Web sites. Others are behind client/server applications or distributed. Their performance is constrained by the front-end systems and the end-user needs. Most are in the medium or large categories, but not very large like the TPC-C record breakers.

During these years, Oracle has usually held the highest performance benchmark, with SQL Server catching up periodically. So over this period, approaching ten years, we have the "disruptive technologies" situation shown in Figure 7.2, with first Oracle and then SQL Server outperforming most customer needs. Just as SQL Server was ready for most customer needs by 1999, MySQL is good enough in 2004 for most applications.

The publication *Eweek* published a benchmark in February 2002 comparing Oracle and MySQL. This is available on the Web at

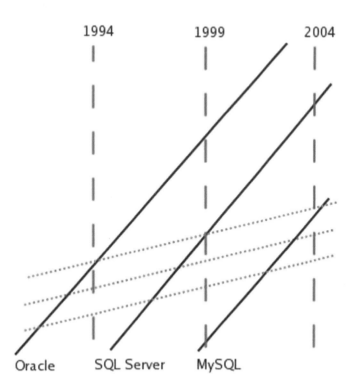

Figure 7.2
*Database
performance
over time.*

www.eweek.com/article2/0,3939,293,00.asp. The SQL Server testing is flawed by a poor JDBC driver, since fixed, but the numbers show that at the time MySQL was quite comparable to Oracle in this test.

We should, of course, do our own benchmarking. However, this is a potentially very complex subject. A good treatment in depth is Jim Gray's *Benchmark Handbook*, which is out of print but can be purchased used on Amazon or read online at http://www.benchmarkresources.com/handbook.

It can be expensive and time consuming to run the big and heavily defined industry-standard benchmark, and get it audited. Just getting the hardware is a big deal for a large system.

OSDB Benchmark

There is an open source implementation of Gray's, AS3AP Benchmark available on Freshmeat as the Open Source Database Benchmark (OSDB). AS3AP is the ANSI SQL standard scalable and portable benchmark for relational systems. According to the *Benchmark Handbook* (Chapter 5, p. 2), it is designed to:

- Provide a comprehensive but tractable set of tests for database processing power

- Have built-in scalability and portability, so that it can be used to test a broad range of systems

- Minimize human effort in implementing and running the benchmarks

- Provide a uniform metric, the equivalent database ratio, for a straightforward and unambiguous interpretation of the benchmark results

AS3AP determines a performance metric, the equivalent database size, and a price/performance metric, which is the cost per megabyte over the equivalent database size. OSDB provides more metrics than this benchmark requires. It has also been relaxed to better support databases with less than complete ANSI SQL capabilities. This is already set up to run against MySQL and/or PostgreSQL. It will take work to get it to run against, say, Oracle, but the Oracle code should be in the repository by the time you read this.

Benchmark code should be open source. We want to know what is being measured, and it is often useful to customize a benchmark to make it simulate some concern of our own. This benchmark is written in C++, so knowledge of C++ is needed to maintain or extend the benchmark, but this does lead to good performance. If a "back of the envelope" OSDB run looks good, I would recommend following up by running the test on the hardware you plan to use, or similar, tuned in the way you plan to deploy it and with data volumes close to your predictions.

7.3.5　Competing with Closed Code Databases

You cannot install a large database in any organization without having to compete with sales pitches from Oracle, Microsoft, and IBM. Salespeople from any of these companies will try to treat open source databases as toys. If they are forced to admit that the open source database could do the job under discussion, they know they will lose on price, so they will move the debate elsewhere. They will talk about theoretical large databases and grid computing, their results at the TPC-C racetrack, or the idea of consolidating all your databases into one big system.

Oracle will emphasize its market leadership, making it seem like the only safe choice and emphasizing the risk of anything else. Oracle will also talk about grids. Microsoft will emphasize price/performance and ease of management. Microsoft also pushes its extensions, such as DTS and Analysis Services, Web-based access, and XML everything. IBM in particular goes for integration; DB2 is usually sold on IBM platforms along with WebSphere.

Oracle and IBM run their UNIX database benchmarks on the Tuxedo application server. They use this platform because it is much faster and less expensive than their standard application servers. However, Tuxedo is an old system that is difficult to develop for, and it is almost never used for real business databases. When IBM and Oracle are selling systems to business customers, they recommend IBM WebSphere and Oracle Application Server, respectively.

When benchmarking, Oracle always looks at large databases and compares performance. Microsoft has some large performance numbers, but prefers to look at small to medium databases and compare price/performance. Oracle runs its mid-market benchmark on the same box as Microsoft and gets a slightly better result. It is not going to do that on the smaller boxes, where the cost of the database dominates the numbers.

7.4 Mail Servers

In the UNIX and open source world, mail servers are split between message transfer agents (MTA), which are senders, and receivers/message stores.

Mail is usually sent with the SMTP protocol and accessed with the POP3 or IMAP protocol. This works about the same with closed code mail servers such as Exchange, but both sending and receiving programs are called Exchange (or Groupwise or Notes).

We have already mentioned Sendmail, the venerable program that may be the oldest open source program in widespread use. After paying it due respect, it is time to admit that Sendmail is an old program and may not be the best mail server to choose today. It has a reputation for being difficult to configure and a history of security problems. The consensus these days is that you should choose Postfix instead to avoid these issues. There are other alternatives, such as Exim and Qmail, but we will look at Postfix here.

Postfix is fast, scales well, and is reasonably self-evident to configure. It can use different formats for the message store (Maildir or Mbox). We usually prefer the Maildir format, which stores each message in a single file. This makes message processing with external tools much simpler.

The alternatives for message receivers and stores are POP3 and IMAP. IMAP is richer and generally preferable. Exchange supports either protocol. The native Exchange store appears to be IMAP-like but differs slightly, so that Outlook IMAP support can be quirky. Sometimes we may choose to use POP3 with Outlook for that reason. Choices for IMAP servers include Courier-IMAP and Cyrus IMAPD.

For a directory server, we prefer OpenLDAP for this. Postfix and Courier-IMAP or Cyrus IMAPD can access OpenLDAP for authentication.

Many organizations like to have a browser-based mail client option. Horde is an example of a server that supports browser-based email. Horde looks similar to Outlook Web Access and provides similar functions. It can access OpenLDAP for authentication, address lookups, and contacts.

7.5   Systems Management

The basic choice for open source systems management, as in other areas such as database, is whether to adopt open source tools and methods completely, which will involve getting or developing administrators with UNIX administration skill sets, or whether to adopt closed code system management tools, which are generally cross-platform and may already be in place in the organization. Both approaches will probably be needed. However attractive the graphical tools, system administrators usually need a thorough understanding of the platforms they are using.

The next level, if needed, of systems administration is programming using a cross-platform scripting language. This will allow us to develop more flexible and automated approaches to, for instance, backing up or managing the size of user files. The good news is that there is a long tradition of scripting in UNIX, and the work to do this is well understood and available. The bad news is that although it is compatible with Windows systems, it is not compatible with the approaches that have generally been used in Windows.

The closed code tools are comprehensive and graphical, so they look wonderful in use. The open source tools are generally targeted to a more experienced administrator, and lean more to the UNIX philosophy of "doing one thing well." There is no reason not to use tools of both types. Many organizations that use Tivoli or Unicenter also employ open source tools such as Snort for intrusion detection and write shell or Perl scripts to manage their own applications.

Closed code tools available for Linux include:

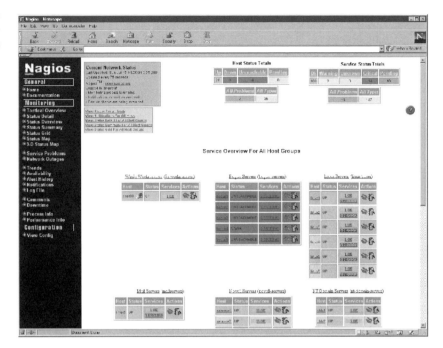

Figure 7.3
Nagios status overview.

- BMC Patrol
- CA Unicenter
- HP OpenView
- IBM Tivoli
- Novell ZENworks

The leading integrated graphical open source system monitoring tool is Nagios. This is being used in production by organizations with up to 5,000 hosts. As Figures 7.3 and 7.4 illustrate, it is comprehensive and graphical. An online demonstration of Nagios is available at http://nagios.square-box.com.

Open source administration tools include a huge selection of specific tools for particular purposes. Most existing larger organizations will have a multiplatform administration solution in place and will simply extend it to include the open source systems.

Figure 7.4
Nagios status map.

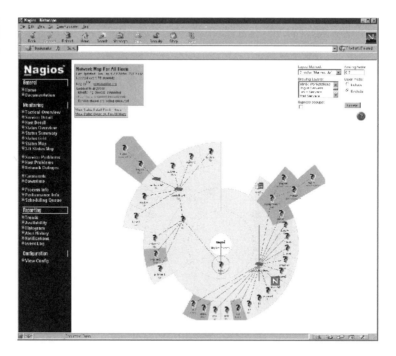

Systems need to be monitored at all levels. Open source applications are easier to instrument to support event logging into system management tools. Other great open source tools include TCPdump, Snort, and Ethereal.

7.6   Summary

Open source choices for these important server applications include Samba and OpenLDAP for infrastructure services, Apache for Web servers, MySQL and PostgreSQL for database servers, and a variety of programs for mail servers.

There are also good closed code programs with commercial support available on Linux in most of these categories, such as iPlanet for directory services, Oracle and DB2 for database servers, Scalix and Contact for mail servers, CA-Unicenter and HP OpenView for systems management, and many people will choose to employ them.

If your organization is not ready for the different sales models of open source, and not prepared for the integration of components that is usually needed, then selection of some closed products and support services from major vendors may be the best way to go.

If your organization is prepared for the open source sales model and for some integration, then a selection of open source software is available for infrastructure, Web, mail, and database services at almost any scale. By running open source servers, you can reduce licensing and hardware costs while increasing flexibility.

8

Open Source Desktop Applications

8.1 Introduction

8.1.1 The Open Source Desktop

A complete open source desktop with applications can be easily installed and demonstrated on a typical personal computer using Linux. Most people would agree that such desktops are attractive, powerful, and as easy to learn from scratch as Windows. Such desktops can be significantly less expensive than closed code systems, since they can save the operating system cost plus the cost of applications such as Microsoft Office.

It is also possible to build a desktop on Windows, where all the applications are open source. Again, this can be attractive, powerful, and easy to learn. In many situations where the operating system is already installed, such as on home computers, there is no savings to replace it with Linux, but there are huge cost savings from replacing applications such as Office with open source.

The important open source desktop applications, which will be discussed in turn, are:

- Graphical desktops
- Web browsers
- Office programs (word processing, spreadsheet, presentation software)
- Professional applications (graphics, database front ends, Web designers)
- Personal applications (media players, games)

8.1.2 Linux Desktop Share

Linux has come a long way in power and ease of use, but it is still not widely used on the desktop. Linux has now overtaken since 1994 the Mac in sales to become the #2 operating system on the desktop. IDC reports that Linux grew from 2.8 percent in 2002 to 3.2 percent in 2003, while the Mac remained at 3 percent. This is significant, but is still has only a small share. Windows has a 94 percent share. IDC forecasts growth to 6 percent for Linux in 2007, but Windows would still be over 90 percent by then.

These figures probably undercount Linux presence on desktops now and in the future. Linux is underreported, because it is very often not purchased. Windows ships on essentially every new PC, and where users are replacing Windows with Linux they are probably not getting measured effectively. It is also used in concentrated niches, some of which are very high growth, such as some new Asian installations involving millions of desktops. The major computer companies—IBM, HP, and Sun—all have programs to encourage Linux desktop adoption now, and some major corporate announcements have been made. Linux has exceeded expectations in the past, and may grow on the desktop much faster than currently predicted.

8.1.3 Limitations to Desktop Linux Adoption

Whatever Linux growth may be, in the next three or four years we know that there will continue to be an order of magnitude more Windows users than Linux users. This has an effect on the availability of hardware, applications, and support services. Each of these limits the possibilities of Linux desktop deployment significantly.

Hardware

Approximately half of corporate personal computers are now notebooks rather than desktops. It is this group that is least likely to adopt Linux quickly. Setting up Linux on a notebook system is still likely to need some custom work, and there are hardware limitations, including wireless support, such as Intel Centrino wireless and most 802.11g cards; some graphics cards; and advanced power management. Notebook users may have to accept some loss of functionality to run Linux. Notebook users are typically professional users, and are not likely to accept compromises like this unless they are developers or are committed to open source for some other reason.

Applications

Given the disparity in installation share, it is perhaps surprising that there are many applications available for Linux desktops, and there are generally several good choices in the major categories. Smaller niche applications are more of a problem. There are many thousands of applications in the Windows "ecosystem," usually written to the Windows tools and interfaces, often addressing specific vertical industries.

In a migration situation, any specific application may be a "must-have" for a group of users Microsoft Office is just the biggest, best-known example of this. Section 8.6.1 has some tactics for this situation, such as emulation, but often this will necessitate Windows on some systems.

Support Services

There are thousands of corporate employees, and many more people in outsourced services, working with users of Windows desktops in support and training roles. Some of these have qualifications such as MCSEs, others do not; but most have a significant investment in the skills needed to support Windows systems and the common applications deployed on them. There is little incentive for these people to relearn their jobs using a new technology, and in some areas the skills to support activities such as solving issues with Linux systems that won't boot or training users in OpenOffice may not be available yet. It will be several years until this situation is resolved entirely.

8.2   Graphical Desktops

It is possible to start and run Linux in a character mode, but this is reserved for installation and debugging situations nowadays. Linux is usually installed to start in a graphical mode, running a windowing system, and a desktop system will usually run a desktop manager with a set of integrated utilities. If you want to work in the shell using a command line and typing commands, as you probably did sometimes in Windows, you can open a terminal. Linux users tend to use the command line more than Windows users, partly because it is more powerful.

Essentially all Linux systems use the X Windows system (X11) as the graphical user interface (GUI)—generally XFree86, which is the most used port of X11 on Intel. This is the underlying code of Linux graphical user interface systems. Exceptions include some servers that may not need a GUI and run in character mode, and some embedded systems that use other GUI systems not based on X11 to get better performance, such as Qtopia, which is used on the Sharp Zaurus.

X11 was written at MIT in the early 1980s and made available under an open source license similar to Berkeley. There had been several previous X versions but X11 became widely adopted and the numbering stopped there. There were alternative windowing systems, such as Sun's Network-extensible Windowing System (NeWS), but X11 won out and became the de facto standard for windowing on UNIX and similar systems. X11 was innovative in important ways. Unlike its rivals, the Windows and Mac GUI, it is portable across many systems and is not hooked to a particular operating system. It separates the display component (or X server) from the client application, so that applications can be operated across a network. It supports virtual desktops, so you can scroll across a much larger space than the physical display. And it is much more customizable than other systems.

X11 by design was not prescriptive on window management or look and feel. The intention was that different organizations could innovate and enhance these areas, rather than enforcing a standard. For some time, UNIX vendors attempted to distinguish themselves from each other, so it became customary to develop different window managers and style guides. Eventually, there was a movement toward adoption of a set of standards for the UNIX desktop. This became the Common Desktop Environment (CDE), which adopted standards based around Motif, which was Windows-like. Unfortunately, Motif/CDE was not open source at that time, which slowed the effort.

The X11 toolkit is written in the C language and accessed at quite a low level, so it is not easy to program for. "Widget sets" were developed to make this development more consistent and less low level; these evolved into object-oriented APIs, and there are several of these. From time to time there are proposals to replace this layer with new code, but it is not likely to happen soon.

So Linux systems have a common graphical code base, but alternative sets of window managers, look and feel, and development toolkits. As with other areas, we get the double-edged benefits and costs of choice here. There are some really interesting customization opportunities. For unusual systems, such as very large or small or some custom areas, this separation of interface from technology allows great flexibility. Any application can create its own look. So embedded systems can have a simple proprietary look like a TiVo or a high-performance interface like the Sharp Zaurus. We can use this to make a retail or call center application look exactly the way we want. Also, power users can configure their systems as they wish. There are a variety of windowing managers for specialized uses, such as for system administrators or developers.

For general business systems, we will usually prefer a standard desktop, such as we get with Windows or the Mac, since this can reduce costs of training and support. Standard desktops provide a combination of useful components:

- Window manager, which organizes windows, menus, and scroll bars in a coherent manner

- Desktop arrangement, or a place to launch programs, organize and find things

- File manager, similar to Windows Explorer or Mac Finder, which may be integrated with a Web browser

- Standard look and feel, including a consistent set of menus and dialogs, and choice of fonts, themes, effects and general "eye candy"

- Set of applets for utility functions such as printer setup or appearance control, similar to Windows Control Panel or Mac System Preferences

- Useful applications

- Games

This is the type of package of components that is offered by Windows or the Macintosh. Of the many desktops available for Linux, two are of major importance. They are the Gnome and KDE projects, which both started around 1997, with the goal of introducing a richly featured desktop, and have released new versions regularly since. These systems now compete with Windows for consistency and ease of use and learning, but they are perhaps not so close to OS X yet.

The Gnome and KDE interfaces can run on the same computer, even both together on a user desktop, and applications can run within each other's desktops. But they look different and are built using competing development platforms; KDE is built with the Qt toolkit, while Gnome is built with the GTK+ toolkit. While each has strengths, they are largely redundant, duplicating most of each other's functions. So they are really competitors. As a developer, you would have to choose which toolkit to develop an application with. As a user, you will probably lean toward one or the other most of the time.

This issue leaves Linux desktops free to be more innovative than Windows, but also often a little harder to learn. Everyone in the Linux community understands that it would be simpler in many ways if there were a single desktop standard, but this is not going to happen in the near future. A recent proposal to standardize UserLinux on Gnome rather than KDE revealed the depth of feeling around this. These two projects are powerful, ongoing, and both have strong support.

In the long run, there may be a form of convergence driven by the major distributions. Red Hat has worked to make the differences between KDE and Gnome largely hidden in their newer "Bluecurve" versions. Novell, which owns both Ximian, a major Gnome driver, and SuSE, a large KDE sponsor, has announced a plan to converge the desktops over time.

Figures 8.1 and 8.2 show screenshots from Gnome and KDE desktops. These are both very configurable, so your desktop could vary.

The Gnome desktop shows:

- A graphic saved as background
- The Home folder at the top left
- Trash at the bottom right
- Other folders and links on the desktop
- The Nautilus file manager looking at some network file shares
- The Gnome menu at the bottom, including the following from left to right:
  - The main menu (Red Hat) button
  - Application launchers for several applications
  - A screenshot utility
  - Wireless and battery information
  - The virtual desktop manager
  - System manager utilities
  - Clock

The KDE desktop is similar, but has a different graphic background and is running the Konqueror file manager, not Nautilus. The menu bar is similar. It happens to be configured a little larger and with some items placed differently. Again, the Red Hat button and launchers are to the left, and other utilities to the right. The screenshot, battery life, and clock utilities are programs different from those in Gnome but serve a similar purpose.

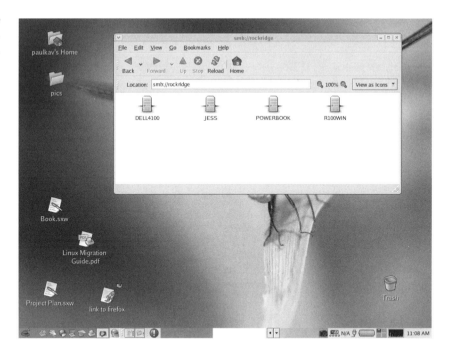

Figure 8.1
Gnome screenshot.

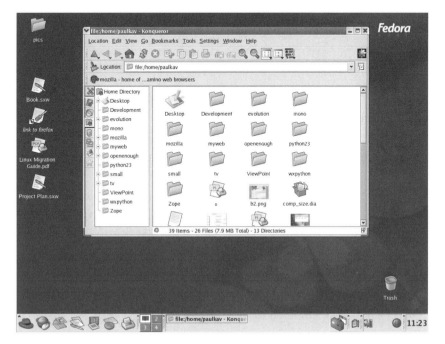

Figure 8.2
KDE screenshot.

Table 8.1   *Choosing a Browser*

Browser	Platform	Status	Comment
Mozilla, Navigator	Windows, Linux, Mac	Open source	Navigator is based on Mozilla 1.6; Mozilla Firefox is new code, much smaller.
Internet Explorer	Windows	Included with OS	On older Macs but now discontinued. AOL uses IE.
Konqueror	Linux	Open source	Uses Qt libraries, works well with KDE.
Epiphany, Galeon	Linux	Open source	Both these browsers use the Gnome toolkit and the Mozilla rendering engine.
Safari	Mac	Included with OS	Based on the Konqueror rendering engine (Qt runs native on the Mac).
Opera	Windows, Linux, Mac	Free with advertising, or fee	Small, fast, but not open source.

8.3   Web Browsers

When developing applications, we do not usually want to require a particular Web browser and operating system. In many cases, we cannot know which browser an application user will be using. Even if we can determine this, as in a customer or business partner situation, it is probably an unreasonable restriction to impose. So when developing, we will usually plan to support a choice of browsers.

In principle, we know that if too many people write to a specific browser, that could destroy one of the best features of the Web, its independence from particular hardware and software platforms. Generally, the best plan is to write for several browsers. Of course, we do not want too much of a testing burden. Table 8.1 has some good choices for browsers available on different platforms. We should probably plan to test on Mozilla, IE, and one other, probably Konqueror or Opera.

8.3.1   Deploying Browsers

Although we may want to support several browsers when developing, when deploying desktops we will probably want to use a single standard to lower the support and training burden. Most Windows shops use Internet Explorer (IE) for obvious reasons: It is good enough and is already installed. The limitations of IE, such as its lack of control over pop-ups, can be addressed with third-party add-ins or managed from the firewall.

Organizations that would like a single browser across multiple platforms can select the open source Mozilla, either Firefox or the older integrated versions, Netscape or Opera. The other browsers are specific to their platforms: Safari on the Mac, Konqueror on KDE, and Epiphany and Galeon on Gnome.

Figure 8.3 is a screenshot of Mozilla Firefox pointed at the Mozilla home page.

Once a browser is installed, the common plug-ins need to be installed. The four most commonly used are Adobe Reader, the Real Audio Media Player, Macromedia Flash, and the Java 2 run time. On Linux systems, Flash is available but there is no Macromedia Director plug-in, so Cartoon Network games, for example, don't work. If Windows plug-ins are needed, we can look at the CodeWeavers product Crossover, which supports these on Linux.

Figure 8.3
Mozilla Firefox.

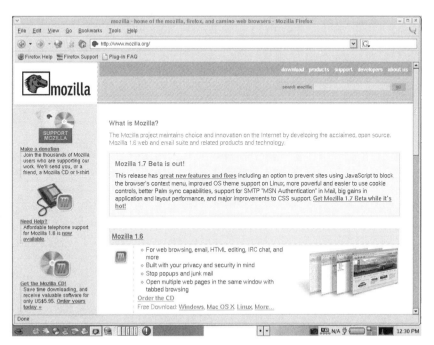

8.4   **The Office Suite**

In considering the office suite, we will consider the word processing, spreadsheet, and presentation programs, although the open source suites, such as Microsoft, include other programs, such as drawing and image management. In terms of Microsoft Office, then, we are looking at replacements for Word, Excel, and PowerPoint. We will discuss database front-end programs and mail front-end programs such as Access and Outlook elsewhere under separate headings. There are excellent open source equivalents of these and of other Office programs, such as drawing, organizational charts, spell checking, and so on, but the core components are usually seen as these three.

There are several alternative open source office suites:

- OpenOffice
- KOffice
- Gnome Office

KOffice and Gnome Office contain some good products, and many individuals may find them to be exactly what they need, particularly when working with other programs from those desktops (KDE and Gnome). But OpenOffice is clearly the strongest. It has three very powerful constituent programs, and is the best office suite for working with Microsoft formats. OpenOffice has a great deal of momentum, with millions of users, far more than the others. OpenOffice has been adopted as part of the standard desktops of Red Hat, SuSE, Ximian, Sun, and UserLinux. OpenOffice works well on Windows and Linux. Anyone recommending an office suite as a standard to an organization really has to recommend OpenOffice. An alternative might be not using a suite, but allowing individual programs to be selected. So in my view there are three practical methods that can be combined within a population to approach the office issue:

- Install OpenOffice as the default standard desktop on Linux and/or Windows.
- Leave Microsoft Office on desktops of satisfied users, and allow users to specify Microsoft Office on new installs if they need it for a reason.

- Allow users to use individual programs such as Gnumeric or Abi Word if they choose instead of a suite.

8.4.1 **OpenOffice.org**

OpenOffice.org (abbreviated here to OpenOffice) is the leading open source office suite. Sun purchased StarDivision, the German developers of StarOffice, in 1999, then established OpenOffice.org to manage the open source process and distribution while continuing to offer StarOffice on a commercial basis. StarOffice and OpenOffice share the same code base and file formats; OpenOffice is open source while StarOffice is sold commercially and contains additional features.

At the time of writing, OpenOffice is at Version 1.1 and StarOffice is at 7.0. The main programs are identical, but StarOffice includes additional products in the distribution, including TrueType fonts, spell checking and thesaurus utilities, additional templates and pictures, and a desktop version of the Adabas database, called Base. Sun also offers commercial support for StarOffice. In this book, we will from now on refer to OpenOffice to include StarOffice as a possible choice.

Fonts and spell checking are weak in OpenOffice as shipped. An organization adopting OpenOffice should look at options for these functions. Another example of OpenOffice integration is Ximian. The Ximian edition of OpenOffice makes changes to ease Office migration, using Microsoft file formats by default and shipping Microsoft-compatible fonts. It also makes changes to improve integration with the Gnome programs Galeon and Evolution and to recognize Gnome desktop theme and font settings.

File formats are identical between OpenOffice and StarOffice and with the previous versions (1.0 and 6.0). OpenOffice 1.1 is available for Linux and Windows. These versions are essentially identical. The Mac OS X version of OpenOffice is 1.0 as I write. File sharing is still possible, but some functions of the program are a level back. The Mac version is not native but based on X11. Between the back level and the nonnative issues, I have found the Mac version of OpenOffice to be too slow and with a poor on-screen format. This will be fixed in a few months. At the moment, there is a version called NeoOffice/J, using a Java front end, that is fast and presents very well.

Figures 8.4 through 8.6 are three screenshots of OpenOffice on Linux: a document, a spreadsheet, and a presentation.

Figure 8.4
OpenOffice write.

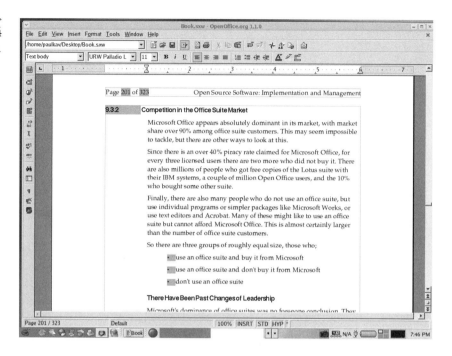

Figure 8.5
OpenOffice calc.

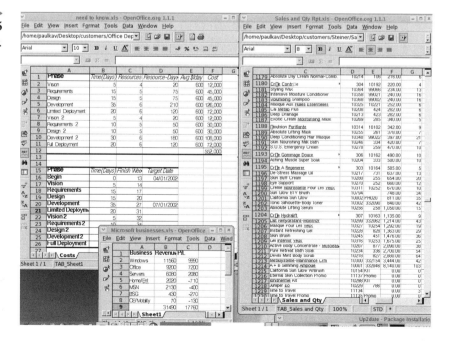

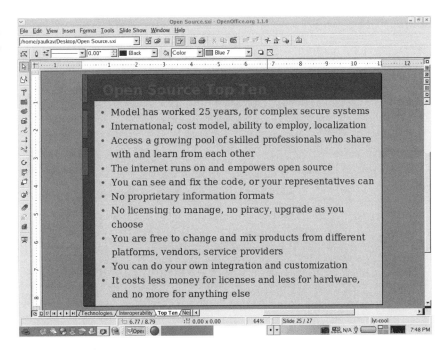

Figure 8.6
*OpenOffice
presentation.*

8.4.2 Competition in the Office Suite Market

Microsoft Office appears absolutely dominant in its market, with market share over 90 percent among office suite customers. This may seem impossible to tackle, but there are other ways to look at this.

Since there is over a 40 percent piracy rate claimed for Microsoft Office, for every three licensed users there are two more who did not buy it. There are also millions of people who got free copies of the Lotus suite with their IBM systems, a few million OpenOffice users, and the 10 percent who bought some other suite.

Finally, there are also many people who do not use an office suite, but use individual programs or simpler packages such as Microsoft Works, or use text editors and Acrobat. Many of these might like to use an office suite but cannot afford Microsoft Office.

So, there are three groups of roughly equal size—those who:

- Use an office suite and buy it from Microsoft
- Use an office suite and don't buy it from Microsoft
- Don't use an office suite

The second and third groups are immediate candidates for OpenOffice, as are some of the first.

There Have Been Past Changes of Leadership

Microsoft's dominance of office suites was no foregone conclusion. It was not the leader in any office category originally, or for many years. The first personal computers in business were the CP/M-based machines of the 1970s. Top-selling programs were WordStar, VisiCalc, and dBASE II, offering word processing, spreadsheet, and database functions, respectively. On MS-DOS, WordStar and VisiCalc were replaced by WordPerfect and Lotus 1-2-3, respectively. They were better products.

Microsoft's products, Word and Multiplan, were mediocre sellers. Microsoft products did better on the Apple. With the introduction of Windows 3.1, the Microsoft products (now Excel, Word, and the purchased PowerPoint) proved technically superior and pulled into the lead. Office rose to its high share on the basis of steadily improving performance and falling prices over a period of years, from the mid-1980s to the mid-1990s.

So the standard office programs have changed a couple of times in the past. When there were clear technical differences, new programs gained dominance. These changes have been very painful, in use and in file formats, even inside Microsoft Office. Spreadsheet moves from VisiCalc to Lotus 1-2-3 to Excel involved reimplementation of most of the programming. The move from Microsoft Office 95 to Office 97 replaced all the macro languages (WordBASIC, Excel VBA, AccessBASIC) with VBA 5 and changed all the file storage formats, as had the previous move from Office 4.2 to Office 95. But the products had more room for improvement then, and many of the early users were more technology-oriented early adopters, often single-product users. Expectations for support were lower, and there was a base of new users to spread to. It is going to be more difficult today to find a large group of office suite users with any desire to switch products.

There Are Other Formats Now

The leading format for exchanging precisely formatted documents is not Word but Adobe Portable Document Format (PDF). PDF retains all formatting so it can perfectly match the look of paper documents. PDF readers, such as Acrobat Reader, are widely available and are free.

The leading format for exchanging presentations (persuasive material presented on computer screens) is HTML, with Acrobat again or Flash if certain precise effects are desired. PowerPoint and its competitors originally date back to a time before the Web, when presentations were done with slides accompanied by paper handouts.

In contrast, I do not believe there is a good alternative to the spreadsheet, and so there is no effective competition to the Excel .xls format. XML is good for data representation, but interesting spreadsheets are much more than the data they contain.

If the need is not the precision of Acrobat or the reach of the Web, but the exchange of editable information, then XML formats hold the most promise, as everyone recognizes, and those formats need to be public and open to all to access.

It Is Hard for Microsoft to Improve Office

One problem faced by Office today is the difficulty of making any useful improvement. It is not that Microsoft does not innovate, but users regularly report that they don't use many features of the product, and are happy with the ones they do use. Microsoft considers its biggest competitor to be its own installed base; people don't upgrade because they are satisfied. This is perhaps not surprising, since products originally aimed at professional writers, accountants, and presenters are now sold to a much less demanding audience, who don't need the features. One survey found that half of Excel users did nothing but manage data lists, so Microsoft added the "autofill" feature to simplify this task. It is as if a camera user had a professional SLR with a full kit of lenses but wanted an autofocus point-and-shoot. Office is open to replacement by a less expensive competitor and Microsoft cannot offer functional improvement as a solution to this.

The direction Microsoft has taken includes innovation—offering new and extended features such as SmartTags, new wizards, new XML formats, and so on. Some of this is a genuine attempt to improve the product. But most innovation is an attempt to increase:

- Reliance on proprietary features that are specific to Microsoft Office
- Related sales by tying Office use more closely with other Microsoft products such as Exchange and Sharepoint Servers

Some of the innovation is an attempt to encourage custom development, which will lock users into the macro and form languages or proprietary XML features, making it more difficult to replace Office later. But the largest move strategically is to attempt to tie in Office with other Microsoft products in order to increase sales of those products. That is also why Office is sold as a suite. Because people pass editable documents around networks to share them, they rely on the format being interchangeable. Microsoft Office formats are unpublished and have been changed several times, so it was not easy to interoperate with Office programs.

Microsoft will lower effective prices when it needs to, but will do it quietly. It is reluctant to publicize that prices may be coming down, partly because many users have signed long-term license deals and it is attempting to sign more. Recently, Microsoft began selling a low-priced "Student and Teacher" edition. It can also choose to make changes to international pricing, volume discounts, or tighten or loosen licensing and upgrade restrictions. One benefit all users of office suites may see from increased competition will be a lowering of prices for all products, including Microsoft Office.

Problems with Licensing

Concurrent licensing is a scheme where use is tracked and the organization pays for use, generally for the "high-water mark" of use. The idea is theoretically attractive to a customer organization; after all, of a few thousand Excel users, how many are actually using it at any one time, particularly if you make readers available? It is very unattractive to the selling company. As the cost of a concurrent license is pushed higher, some users balk at purchases, since the price seems excessive, although even at 10 or 50 times, it still brings less revenue to the vendor than licensing everyone. The information on use that is essential to a concurrent scheme provides feedback that can be used to lower use further—for instance, by spreading out a period of peak use. But that issue cuts through to the problem at the heart of Microsoft Office. Most people don't use most of it.

8.4.3　Comparison of Microsoft Office to OpenOffice

Bundling

OpenOffice does not include an email client like Outlook, but most people will use Evolution, which is powerful, similar to Outlook, integrates well with OpenOffice, and is open source. Similarly, OpenOffice does not include a database program, but most people will consider MySQL if they need a SQL database program. MySQL is more powerful and scalable as a database than Access, but has no equivalent integrated front end. Possible front ends include Mergeant, the Gnome database front end, OpenOffice, and database tools such as MySQL administrator and Quest. Star Office includes a database. OpenOffice does include a drawing program, but for most purposes I would recommend the more powerful GIMP instead.

Integration

OpenOffice can connect to databases using the access methods ADO, JDBC, or ODBC. It can for instance connect to Access using ADO, MySQL using JDBC, and SQL Server using ODBC.

OpenOffice formats are XML based and published, so integration with other systems is simpler than for Microsoft Office. It is not necessary with OpenOffice to buy more expensive editions to manage XML formatting. There is a software development kit for extending OpenOffice using Java.

Formats

There are some serious problems with using the Microsoft office formats. They are proprietary, subject to change, and not documented. It is quite difficult for third parties to access them, although some good programs are available. Using these formats in correspondence, for instance, is implicitly requiring others to acquire the Office programs when they may not own them or need them.

OpenOffice uses a zipped set of XML files. In practical use, the OpenOffice format is generally no more than half the size of the MS Office files (unless bit maps or other uncompressible attachments dominate the size). The OpenOffice format is also simple to read using standard tools, because the XML format is published.

It has often been pointed out that Microsoft Office documents keep earlier versions of documents and author information history in the file in ways their owners do not expect. Authors have been caught by data discovered in their Microsoft Office files that they did not know was there. New digital rights formats in Microsoft Office 2003 are likely to cause more problems in accessing data from older or less expensive versions of Office.

Microsoft Office cannot read OpenOffice formats at all, while OpenOffice reads Microsoft formats quite well. OpenOffice can create PDF files directly, while Microsoft Office has to use a third-party tool.

8.4.4 **Migration from Microsoft Office to OpenOffice**

The Microsoft installed base is Office 97 and Office 2000. There is very little Office XP or Office 2003 yet. This immediately highlights the main problem with Office migration today, which is that nobody wants to do it.

Microsoft is having difficulty achieving upgrades, even though it now makes these very easy and attractive. People will not change without a reason, which is usually significant improvement. It is extremely difficult to deliver significant improvement in office suites as perceived by the users. Microsoft has trouble moving Office 97 users to a new version because they are fairly satisfied with what they have. They are not prepared to learn and adopt the new features. The problem with changing for cost saving is that the people who have to change don't recover the saving, so they are not motivated.

If integration of Access or Outlook with other office products is regarded as particularly important, migration to open source is probably not practical. There are many small applications included with Microsoft Office, such as Chart, Query, and so on. Most of these have some match in open source; Math and Draw are included in OpenOffice. But again, if these are regarded as particularly important, migration is probably not practical.

Importing/Exporting between MS Office and OpenOffice

First off, Microsoft Office cannot read OpenOffice files at all. Any OpenOffice files must be converted to Microsoft formats in OpenOffice. OpenOffice-specific features will be lost in these formats.

OpenOffice is very good at reading Microsoft Office formats, but not perfect. There are several formats to consider, such as Office 95, 97, XP (2002), or 2003. Microsoft Office since Office 97 uses an OLE format of structured storage, typically containing several "streams" of information. Office 97, 2000, and XP use the same formats (for these three programs). The earlier Office versions, 4.2 and 95, used different incompatible formats, but are unlikely to be met in corporate environments today, partly for that reason. Every version has a different macro language—for example, WordBASIC, VBA 5, VBA 6, and VBA 6.3.

OpenOffice can read and write Office documents and templates in the 97/2000/XP format. Last year, I translated all the documents I had in my possession, which had been developed over several years, from Microsoft Office into OpenOffice as a one-time operation. There were a lot of these documents, but I was able to convert them in a batch process. There were no problems in Word or Excel, by my criterion, which was no loss of data. I did relink attached documents, and it was necessary to do some minor formatting of presentations and some Word documents. Font size differences and some line and spacing had pushed a few words off their pages.

But there were some reasons for this success. I already knew that the documents worked in different versions of Office, including the limited Pocket PC version. While the spreadsheets used many formulas and multiple worksheets and simple charts, I had never used macros (VBA) or forms. The documents I used had no pivot tables. The Word documents were large and used tables, styles, headers, and tables of contents, but did not use them in especially complex ways and did not use many other popular features. Again, there were no macros or forms. I did not use multimedia in PowerPoint.

8.4.5 Lock-in and Complexity

Not all organizations will be able to migrate away from Office now. It depends on the way they use it. Users will be slower to change if they are locked in, because they use Microsoft Office features that do not migrate. How seriously your organization is locked in needs to be evaluated for each group of users in the organization. It is a function of:

- Advanced or professional users authoring documents
- Use of technical features (macros, shared components, etc.)
- The overall pattern of collaboration over documents

Table 8.2 lists some features in Microsoft Office that can cause migration issues.

Macros cannot work because they address the Microsoft Office object model and are written in VBA. OpenOffice has macros but a different language and object model. All macros must be translated by hand if needed. The macro information is retained in the document so it can be used again in MS Office in a pass-through situation.

Documents will change in many small ways during conversion, and need to be fixed up. Document pagination will almost certainly differ. Fonts may differ and character spacing is calculated in a different manner. Fonts are a particular problem to be aware of. Linux systems often have fonts different from those in Windows, and OpenOffice seems to handle some font sizing a little differently, so pagination may vary. Tables and multicolumn formatting may differ, and while data is not lost, it may disappear off the page and fail to print. Documents that are not simple and contain many of these issues will need to be hand-converted. If there are many of these, a migration will be very difficult.

Table 8.2   *Office Features with Migration Issues*

Feature	Program
AutoShapes	All programs
Macros	All programs
OLE objects	All programs
Revision marks	Word
Tables and multicolumn formats	Word
Form fields	Word, Excel
Pivot charts and tables	Excel
Some charts	Excel
Some formulas, functions, control fields	Excel
Background master	PowerPoint
Grouped objects	PowerPoint

Whether you can migrate from Office depends greatly on whether your users have developed custom programming that has dependencies on Office. If you have users who program extensively in VBA, developing custom forms, you will find moving to another product expensive or even impossible.

If some of your office suite users are professional creators of documents as opposed to primarily consumers, they will be unwilling to switch to a product that is in any way inferior, or even different: It is just too important to them. If there is a shared library of common documents, it is harder. The last hold-outs against Microsoft Office, for example, were legal offices, because they had custom libraries of WordPerfect documents. In that situation, more sophisticated features get developed by skilled authors and then used by others, which locks the organization into the implementation of those features.

These sophisticated users could be a single department, such as financial analysts using Excel or legal secretaries using word processing macros. In some situations, those groups can be left alone and the rest of the company migrated. This works, depending on the pattern of collaboration. If you are currently using Office for collaborative document production with other groups, in or out of the organization, that are not in the open source transition, you may not have the option of migration.

One-Time Migration

If you plan a one-time migration versus continuing interoperability, you can handle most of the problems in a reasonable way. If your intention is to stop using Office and migrate all documents to OpenOffice, you will find that most documents will transfer with minor format changes that will not bother users on a one-time basis. Hundreds of documents may be transferred with a few hours clean-up work. For example, page numbering may be slightly off, some fonts may be replaced in a way you don't like, and some complex references to external files may need to be checked. In this situation you can test as many documents as you need, and also arrange for some expertise to be available to support the migration.

Two-Way Interoperability

If you intend to continue transferring documents back and forth on a daily basis, the hours spent "fixing up" documents will add up indefinitely and become an impossible burden. That is why patterns of use need to be analyzed. Any plan that involves a regular exchange of complex documents back and forth between the different office products will need to be reviewed carefully, and preferably altered to eliminate this.

The Effect of Switching Costs

OpenOffice is a good product that meets the needs of most poeple in most organizations for an office suite. It is good enough. Most people can install OpenOffice and gain a system that does everything they need. However, most organizations already have Microsoft Office in place, and that changes everything. Unlike server products where switching is easy or even undetectable, changing the desktop is a big deal.

As discussed, migration of documents is not a small task. For some very productive people, this is going to represent months of work having to be revisited and possibly lost. For the average person, it means some inconvenience without compensation. Retraining is also an issue, as OpenOffice is similar but certainly not identical to Microsoft Office. Depending on the organization, this can cause high costs and some dissatisfaction.

The effect of switching costs such as migration of documents and retraining of users makes this unattractive for many organizations. Figure 8.7 shows the effect of these switching costs using the disruptive innovation diagram reviewed previously. These costs can delay economic adoption for years or indefinitely. If, for example, each user needs a day or two of training, that could wipe out the saving in licensing costs. This is why we will first see OpenOffice adopted where users have not already invested

Figure 8.7
Switching costs and OpenOffice adoption.

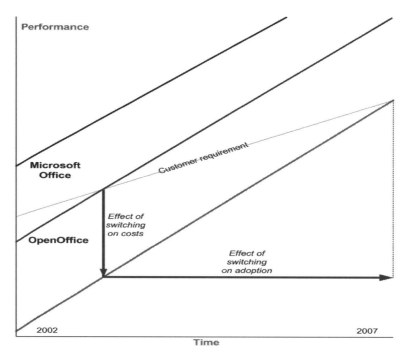

time in learning to use Microsoft Office and built up stores of documents using those formats.

8.4.6 When You Don't Need an Office Suite

Individuals and organizations that don't need to pick a suite can look at individual products such as the AbiWord word processor and the Gnumeric spreadsheet as possible "best of breed" choices. The idea of an office suite for everyone is a relatively new idea and not particularly natural. Originally, PowerPoint was used by marketing and sales departments, and spreadsheets were used by accounting. Many corporate writers only need an email program. In a company that licenses thousands of copies of Office, it could be that there are only a few hundred (or a few dozen) who create original Word, Excel, or PowerPoint documents. Many of these use only a fraction of the available functions.

There are free readers available for these documents. In a Windows environment, you could use Word or Excel for creation where appropriate. Finished documents would either be rendered as PDF files, or Word/Excel viewers would be made available. So for many people, it is possible to consider not using an Office suite at all—perhaps for most people at most companies.

In an open source environment, you could make OpenOffice your standard suite but perhaps an elective rather than part of your standard install. Finished documents would be rendered as PDF files and spreadsheet data as CSV files.

A real-world example of a successful system that is generally used effectively without an office suite is the Apple Mac. The Mac as sold includes TextEdit (which can read/write Word documents), AppleWorks (which can read/write Excel documents), and Mail/iCal/Address Book, which work together, similar to Outlook or Evolution, and serve as a client to Microsoft Exchange. Keynote, which can read and write PowerPoint documents, is sold separately. Apple applications are well integrated and consistent without being a "suite." Apple users can choose to buy Microsoft Office, or can install OpenOffice, but most do neither.

Before GUIs, horizontal integration (which is really look and feel, such as Word to Excel) was not seen as a necessity. Most users selected "best of breed" applications such as Lotus 1-2-3 and WordPerfect. Horizontal integration is surely not needed if the GUI toolkit and Windows management style are consistent, so that functions such as cut and paste work correctly. That is in fact what the GUI provides and why we have style guides. If total consistency needed applications from the same vendor, there could only be one vendor for all applications.

8.5   Mail and Calendar Clients

There are several good email open source clients available. This includes browsers that also do mail, such as Mozilla and Opera, and dedicated email clients, such as Eudora.

A big question with mail programs is the extent to which you want to replicate Outlook. If you want the Outlook features, including the bundling of calendar, email, and small-scale personal databases, you will probably want to use Evolution, which matches the look of Outlook very well. Evolution includes mail, calendar, task list, and contacts and offers screens that combine all these. You can use Evolution as a front end to Microsoft Exchange, using a connector available (for a fee) from Novell/Ximian, or use Evolution with other mail servers that support POP, IMAP, or MAPI.

Figure 8.8 has a screenshot of Evolution with several open panes. Clockwise from top left, it shows the start panel, mail summary, an open mail

Figure 8.8
Evolution.

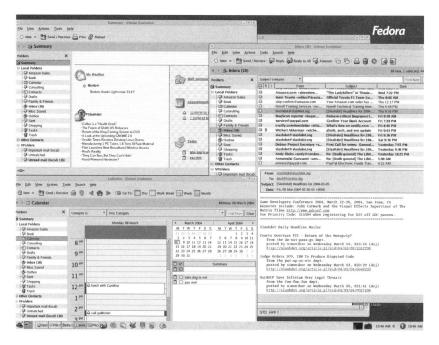

item, and the calendar pane. The appearance is customizable and can certainly be made very similar to Outlook if you wish.

Another option is to use a pure browser-based email, options to support this include Outlook Web Access, the open source program Horde, or services such as Hotmail and Yahoo!.

A big reason why many organizations move away from Outlook is to control problems with attachments. Mail programs that do not allow executable attachments will not automatically run viruses.

8.5.1   Professional Applications

This includes applications for project management, drawing and image management, and other professional work. In some ways the situation is similar to that with Office. There are good open source programs available, but they may not match feature for feature, and migration raises problems of data formats and user training. An application inventory is going to be necessary.

8.5.2 **Drawing and Image Management**

The open source programs GIMP, Dia, and Sodipodi compare favorably for general users with PhotoShop, Visio, and Illustrator. As with Office, the most demanding professional users will not switch because of their time invested and high-end neeeds. Most people will find these programs more than sufficient. GIMP is available on Windows also and is a very good image program for professional and home use on that platform as well as Linux. Dia is similar to Microsoft Visio. It does not have a comparable array of stencils available, but it is good enough immediately for simple work, and for custom work the format for creating shapes is open and reasonably easy to use. Most of the diagrams in this book are created with Dia.

Figures 8.9 and 8.10 are screenshots of GIMP (GNU Image Manipulation Program) and Dia. These two programs make extensive use of floating panels. The image is one panel, and the various tools are in separate floating windows, which can be moved or closed. This style, which originated with GIMP, is unusual when first met but very powerful. Fortunately, GIMP has an excellent tutorial available.

Figure 8.9
GIMP.

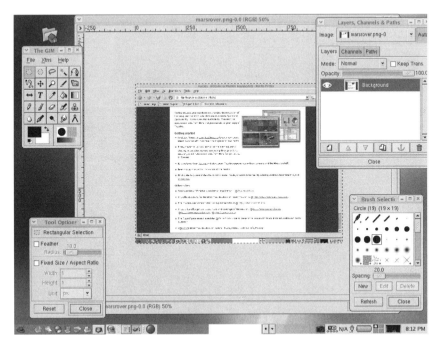

Figure 8.10
Dia.

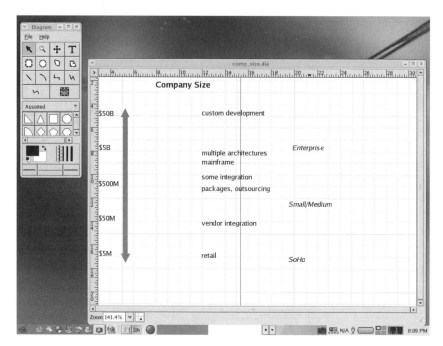

8.6   Personal Software

This area is one where Linux is catching up quickly. I still think that today if you simply want to choose the best machine for performing multimedia functions or games, no other considerations, you should look at the Macintosh or Windows XP. Mac OS X is the leader in graphical user interface and multimedia tools, particularly tools that are integrated and easy to use, while Windows XP is the leader in PC gaming, with far more games available and specialized hardware, which is easy to install and support. The Sony Playstation is another good gaming choice. Linux cannot match the PC or Playstation for variety and currency of games.

That said, many of us choose a machine primarily for work or communications and then play games or media as secondary activities, so we want to know that these functions are possible. If you need to play a few games or watch a movie when you take a break while traveling, you'll be fine with the choices available on Linux. There are several instant messaging programs. GAIM, which is the best known, can support AIM, Yahoo!, MSN, and ICQ. There are many media players. Xine can play Windows Media formats. There is software for making movies and burning CDs, such as

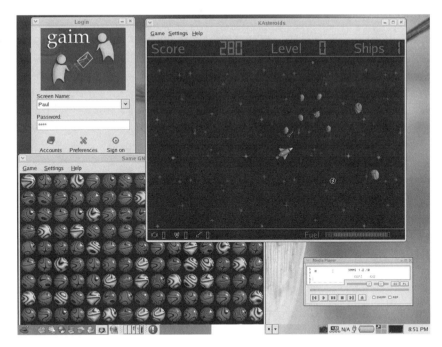

Figure 8.11
Some personal applications.

GnomeToaster, and DVDs. The Ogg Vorbis, Mplayer, and Xmms media players are powerful and support several formats.

Figure 8.11 is a screenshot of some personal applications, including a media player, GAIM instant messaging, and two games.

There are several programs to connect to Palm-based PDAs and allow synchronization, such as Gnome-pilot. Another option is to consider a Linux PDA, such as the Sharp Zaurus. This runs a full standard Linux system, has a Qtopia-based GUI, connects to the PC using Samba, and includes emulation software that can read and write Office formats. Figure 8.12 shows a Sharp Zaurus C700, close to actual size, open to its main menu. The tiny Zaurus C700/800 series systems measure 4" × 3" when closed.

8.6.1 Running Windows Applications

Sometimes we have to run an application that is not available on Linux. Most needs can be met in a general way, but there are quite often particular programs that are not available. If it is necessary to run a particular program that is not available on Linux, this can be met with a variety of techniques. First, we can check against a Web site such as the table of Windows equivalents at http://linuxshop.ru/linuxbegin/win-lin-soft-en/table.shtml to see if

Figure 8.12
*Sharp Zaurus, a
very small Linux
computer.*

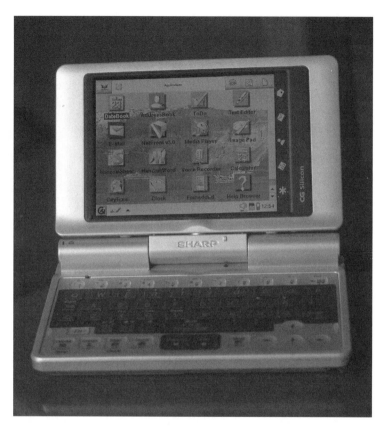

there is a Linux equivalent. If there is not, and we cannot match it or migrate it, we can host Windows programs on Linux using the emulation program Wine. This program is also packaged with additional material as CrossoverOffice to run Microsoft Office. Using Conexant drivers, we can access hardware that requires Windows drivers. With VMware, we can even run a complete Windows operating system on Linux. Of course, these options are not inexpensive, since they involve the emulator and the licensed Windows programs.

Another choice to consider in some cases is a "thin client" running a browser combined with a portal that offers remote programs, either Web based or using Citrix. The experience is not a complete match for desktop software, but this can reduce licensing costs and make desktops easier to manage operationally.

Finally, some people will run "dual boot" systems so they can run an essential Windows program when they need it.

8.7 Summary

You can run Linux on the desktop or Windows or a mix (Windows, Linux, Mac) and still use open source desktop software.

If you choose to run Linux, you should be able to deploy a powerful and manageable desktop to new users. Hardware will need to be tested, since not all components in PCs that support Windows will support Linux. Notebook computers need particular care. Software needs have to be evaluated and planned.

Users of mail, the Web, and dedicated applications can be very satisfied with new desktops. The most difficult thing to do is to migrate Office and Windows users. This is being done successfully, and the barriers are mostly not technical. There is no motivation among the users to switch, and while the programs are functionally equivalent they are not identical in use. The extra work that users will have to do to get over the differences will not be recognized or rewarded.

Users who could not afford programs such as Office, Visio, and Photo-Shop should be delighted with OpenOffice, Dia, and GIMP. Many professionals will find them suitable also. In some areas, such as video editing and high-end publishing, where UNIX programs are being brought to Linux, the professional programs are better on Linux. In other cases, they are not competitive with Windows. This has to be evaluated.

There is a variety of personal software available that will meet many needs, but of course there are some areas where Windows offers more choices or better hardware support.

9

How Open Source Software Is Developed

The methods of development used for open source software are often discussed. From the famous essay by Eric Raymond, "The Cathedral and the Bazaar," to recent press articles, anecdotes suggest that there is something new, different, and better about the open source model. But usually we have no consistent picture of how open source is generally developed or of the alternative development models to which it should be compared.

9.1   Methodology

As far as open source is concerned, there appear to be several models that are in use. These include:

- An individual working largely alone
- A "bazaar," or large loosely knit dispersed group
- A conventional collocated product team

Commonly, products transition between these structures over time, and they also merge these ideas. Most often, a product starts with an individual or a product team and later moves toward the bazaar, often retaining strong central ownership.

Some open source software has been built on the bazaar model, where a loosely structured, large network of people with little formal organization cooperates. To be clear, there has to be a seed product first, that can be run, distributed, and tested to get the process going, and that is generally created by an individual. Also, all accounts suggest that Apache, Linux, and BSD were all tightly structured around a small central leadership team. The first example of the bazaar could be the Berkeley effort to get AT&T

files out of BSD, which was led by Eric Bostic in 1990. Others could include Linux, starting from around 1992 and Apache, starting around 1995, led by Brian Behrendorf.

Some open source software is built by tightly structured teams that are modeled in a way similar to conventional software development organizations. Examples include Gnome and MySQL. Some open source software was built by conventional software companies, which have then converted the product to open source. Examples include OpenOffice, Mozilla, Eclipse, and Firebird SQL. These organizations have changed more or less gradually but have retained elements of their original structure.

Some open source was built by individuals working alone, but is now maintained by a loose team. Examples, which date back to the earliest open source still in use, include Sendmail, GNU Emacs and C, Samba, and Perl. Since the open source model requires some code that works and some belief that a solution has potential, it generally begins this way. Apache and BSD started from an existing code base rather than an individual's work, but Linux and GNU clearly began with an individual, as most new ideas do.

9.1.1　Open Source Compared with Closed Code

If we compare successful open source development to the successful development of similar closed code software packages—for example, at Microsoft—the similarities appear to be larger than the differences. There are some reasons this is not surprising. Estimates on the number of open source developers vary, but cluster around a million. Most of them work some (usually most) of the time in closed code development. So we are talking about the same people.

Perhaps this is partly because what they have in common is success. For example, great open source and great open source projects usually have great developers in charge, and other projects generally do not. Certainly in closed code software companies, these three methods (giant group, product team, individual) all have their counterparts.

In general, individuals stay longer with open source projects, often transitioning to some sort of consulting or honerary role but not leaving completely. Individuals do not seem to last as long in closed code software, tending to move on to other projects. Anders Heljberg has done Delphi, C#, and moved on again, while Guido Van Rossum is still working on Python (among other things) and Larry Wall on Perl. Dave Cutler left the Windows

NT team before Linus left his operating system. From the name alone, surely Linux is more individualistic than other operating systems, not less.

Comparing similar product development efforts such as Linux to Windows NT, MySQL to SQL Server, PHP to ASP, or Python to Delphi/C# we usually see similar project structures, time frames, and leadership. Operating system development, for example, has always been a massive effort, and an evolutionary one, that has drawn in large teams for testing and related development. This was true of OS/2 and Windows NT, and of MVS and VMS before that, and is true of Linux. Database and development tool projects are tighter and generally led by one or a few. SQL Server had a small core team. MySQL database code is checked in by one of two individuals.

There is a question sometimes raised of open source "following tail lights"—that is, copying existing designs rather than creating new ideas. This does not seem historically accurate. Most early programs, some of which were highly innovative, were open source. Open source programs with no obvious precursor include Apache, Sendmail, BIND, and the BSD networking code. These have been copied in closed code but not improved.

This point does apply to some open source programs, in particular GNU, where it was an explicit goal, and the later BSD file replacement work, but not the earlier code including networking. It could also be applied up to a point to Linux, following UNIX and Windows, and OpenOffice, following Microsoft Office. However, as these products catch up they begin to branch out in their own directions. Linux window managers offer features such as tabbed browsing, multiple desktops, and extensive UI customization that are not available in Microsoft products. OpenOffice creates PDF and Flash files directly and has a more powerful and flexible development kit than Microsoft Office.

Newer open source products such as Plone and Twisted can be hard to grasp at first, because they are blazing a new trail and do not have equivalents on other platforms. The database product MySQL has clearly made its own choices in the past, emphasizing performance instead of following features in the standard, and has often been criticized for that.

The "following tail lights" accusation is also commonly leveled at Microsoft and others and probably can be applied to most commercial activity, since complex working systems always have simpler research predecessors. It certainly applies equally to many closed code products. Examples include Windows NT following VAX/VMS and UNIX, the Windows user interface following the Mac and Xerox Star, and Microsoft Excel and Word following Lotus 1-2-3 and WordPerfect, which themselves followed Visi-Calc and WordStar.

To refer ahead to a methodology framework, the earlier vision and planning phases are not exposed in open source, which only speaks to the development and testing activity. This resolves much of the tension. Vision and planning are done by an individual or small team, development and testing by a larger one. Also, much open source software is infrastructure, and in infrastructure software (and all mature software) most changes are defined by bug lists, not ideas for new use.

It appears that every successful open source project has a very modular structure. This supports parallel development, that is, many people can work on separate parts at the same time because they are separate. Online support for change roll in (and back) and repeated automatic testing is also needed.

Open code follows an incremental model, in which small changes accumulate over time, but so does Microsoft much of the time. If you compare the Microsoft position on daily builds with open source, it is very similar. Of course, in all such systems there must sometimes be architectural breaks, and they are very difficult and are often the cause of major forks. Such a break occurred between OS/2 and Windows leading to the Microsoft/IBM split, and between Windows 95 and Windows NT as Microsoft ran a ten-year plan to get rid of the old DOS-based 16-bit architecture. There is a similar architectural shift going on in the Apache world between 1.3 and 2, and in Perl as it moves to its new Parrot virtual machine.

Successful closed code companies are often located in one or a few actual places. A major strength of Microsoft is its single location in the state of Washington, although in recent years other labs, including those in Canada, Israel, the United Kingdom, and India, have sprung up. In the 1990s, Microsoft was able to reorganize massively and quickly several times on its Redmond campus without layoffs or geographic moves. Geographic clusters, such as those around northern California and Boston, clearly matter to closed code and open source equally and are in fact the same places in each case. Open code developers are often more distributed than that, but there are some that are collocated: Red Hat, Gnome, and Mozilla, for example. The importance of geography is also indicated when European developers such as Guido Van Rossum and Linus Torvalds are living in the United States.

Much of open source is released and tested using a large network of volunteers. This is a very effective method, but it is not unique to open source;

Microsoft has done this for years. What is unique to open source is that the large pool can see the code, a method known as "with enough eyeballs." Elsewhere I have argued other advantages to this approach, but it is not clear that this is essential to user testing. Eric Raymond argues that software that requires high reliability should be open source. However, Windows 2000 is a very successful and fairly reliable product despite the belief of many in the open source community at one time (including Raymond) that it would never get done.

9.1.2 Open Source Compared with Corporate Development

Comparing open source development to corporate development, we do see much bigger variations. First, both open source and closed code software developers pay a very high price for failure; they disappear as organizations and are not actually being considered here. Corporate developers can fail and live again, and analysis shows that most corporate systems do fail on measures of time, cost, and quality. So we are really measuring successful software products against all corporate practices, mostly not successful.

Second, corporate development is not usually maintained over the same time frames and with the same levels of staffing and consistency as open source. Where it is, as with the reservation system Sabre or with some financial systems, it often approaches the software product in style and sometimes even in formal structure.

Third, while the software house toolkit is similar to open source (mostly C/C++ with other languages used for peripheral development and front-end scripting), the corporate developer favors proprietary toolkits that have shifted over time, currently usually Java based, and as a result has no substantial consistent track record of tools or practices.

9.1.3 Open Source Development Tools

The open source community is conservative and frugal in tool use. Open source tools include CVS; Emacs and other text editors; GNU Make, debugger, and other tools; and Jakarta ANT. All these tools have a long tradition and are very effective. They have crude but robust features and are often ugly when first approached, but are well understood in the community. In other words, they are like Ken Olsen's old remark about UNIX as the "Russian truck."

9.1.4 Managing People

Some articles, particularly introductory ones, make open source development seem like altruism, or communism, or something else unrealistic and unlikely to survive, but we should dismiss this. History shows that this approach to software development is about as old as software itself and grows out of earlier models for academic and scientific work that are much older.

We find very similar motivations in open source as anywhere else when we look in detail. One obvious similarity is to the research scientist. Many scientists don't get rich (although a few do), but they make a living and see a clear career and skill progression. They often don't care what kind of car they drive anyway. They really enjoy the work they do, both for its results and its intrinsic nature. And they enjoy publication and recognition, such as the occasional conference where they get together with their peers. As with the research scientist, the software engineer in a commercial world often has a culture conflict with the salespeople and others in the corporate end of the business.

Motivation in the software community includes:

- Playing with technologies and experiencing the sheer fun of writing code

- Getting something done that an individual needs, such as inventing the Perl language, or a peer-to-peer music sharing system

- Earning money, or enhancing career and skill development (which is deferred money)

- Ego gratification, such as publishing, leadership, or belonging to a community and helping others

Managing people in closed source software development has always involved pulling all of these levers. Technology developers are not as directly motivated by money as salespeople. In open source product development, the money motivation is probably not as high as in some other places. The ego factor seems to be higher in many cases and, of course, the ability to select what to work on. This is an age-old story of handling creative people.

Although the developers of open source products need to be managed differently in some ways, the people who are implementing and managing open source products in organizations should be little different from the people who are doing similar work with closed code. They are paid in a similar way; in fact, they are us. The place where it is necessary to deal with a different kind of person is when negotiating with open source product developers.

9.2 Languages Used to Develop Open Source Products

It is interesting to analyze the languages used to create open source software. I did this in three ways:

- Analysis of data on language on SourceForge (http://sourceforge.net), which is by far the largest repository for open source projects

- Review of the best-known open source programs, such as Apache

- Anecdotal review of developers at open source conferences and user groups

SourceForge contains all the best-known projects, and there is no reason I know of to think that the projects on it are not typical. It is very easy to query this database for statistics by using Freshmeat. Figure 9.1 shows open

Figure 9.1
Open source language use.

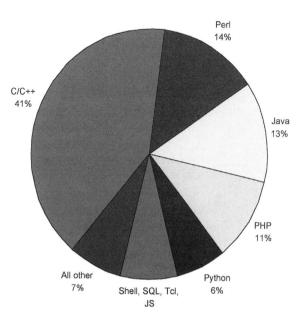

Table 9.1   *Open Source Language Use*

Language	Number of Projects
C/C++ (C 5639, C++ 2550)	8,189
Perl	2,806
Java	2,473
PHP	2,124
Python	1,238

source language use, based on the data in Table 9.1, which contains analysis that was done on Freshmeat in November 2003 and January 2004.

9.2.1   C and C++

Half of the projects on Freshmeat are C or C++, with the rest split fairly evenly among the higher-level languages: Perl, Java, PHP, and Python. Most of the successful open source products so far are written in C/C++. Table 9.2 shows the top 20 most popular Freshmeat projects and the language of development. Out of 20, 15 are wholly C/C++; three combine C/C++ with another language (Java, PHP, JavaScript) used for front-end scripting; one is in PHP; one is in Perl.

Table 9.2   *Most Popular Projects*

Project	Language	Function
Mplayer	C	Movie player
Linux	C/C++	Operating system kernel
cdrtools	C	CD burner tools
Gaim	C	Instant messaging
xine	C	Movie player
MySQL	C	Database
gcc	C	Compilers
TightVNC	C/C++, Java	Remote desktop
PHP	C, PHP	High-level language
Apache	C	Web server

Table 9.2   *Most Popular Projects (continued)*

Project	Language	Function
phpMyAdmin	PHP	Database administration
Nmap	C	Network security
zlib	C	Compression library
GKrellM	C	System monitor
Webmin	Perl	Web administration
Mozilla	C++, JavaScript	Browser
Samba	C/C++	File/print sharing
OpenSSL	C/C++	Cryptography
libjpeg	C	Graphics library
XMMS	C	Multimedia player

To put it simply, C/C++ is the language of choice of the open source community. Actually, it is mostly C.

Table 9.3 is an attempt to throw the net wider in an unscientific and somewhat arbitrary attempt to find a representative sample of programs written in languages other than C/C++. It shows that there are many useful programs written in other languages, but these are not on the scale of popularity or use of the top 20.

PHP, Perl, Java, and Python are the language choices of the open source community for projects other than C/C++.

Table 9.3   *Projects Not in C/C++*

Project	Function	Language	Comment
Movable Type	Weblog publishing	Perl	OSDir.com choice
Webmin	Web administration	Perl	Heavily used program
SpamAssassin	Mail filtering	Perl	Heavily used, popular program, OSDir.com choice
Slash	Content management/feedback	Perl	Runs the heavily used Slashdot site

Table 9.3   *Projects Not in C/C++ (continued)*

Project	Function	Language	Comment
The Gallery	Image management	PHP	In Freshmeat top-rated 20
Moodle	Learning management	PHP	In Freshmeat top-rated 20
Nova	Gaming framework	PHP	In Freshmeat top-rated 20
PHP-Nuke	Content management portal	PHP	Popular program
b2	Weblogging software	PHP	Popular program
Exchange4-Linux	Exchange replacement	Python	—
BitTorrent	Peer-to-peer data delivery	Python	OSDir.com choice, 10 million users
Mailman	Mailing list management	Python	Linux Magazine and Source-Forge projects of the month
Chandler	Personal information manager	Python	OSAF
Plone (includes CMF, Zope)	Content management	Python	O'Reilly open source winner
Anaconda	Red Hat installer	Python	Very visible project seen by every Red Hat user
Twisted	Network programming framework	Python	Innovative project with broad potential
Lucene	Text search engine	Java	From Jakarta project
Compiere	Enterprise requirements and customer relationship software	Java	Rare example of open source enterprise application software
Eclipse	Integrated development environment	Java	Massive product, originally IBM internal

Table 9.3   *Projects Not in C/C++ (continued)*

Project	Function	Language	Comment
Cocoon/ Lenya	Content manage-ment system	Java	Apache project

9.2.2   Perl

Perl has an enthusiastic community and a well-respected leader, Larry Wall. It is a practical, portable language. A major asset of Perl is its database of reusable code, CPAN. Using CPAN, it is possible for Perl users to quickly find solutions to problems that are new to them but have been met and solved by others. Other languages have built similar systems modeled on CPAN, but perhaps not so effectively.

Referring to Table 9.1, we see that Perl is somewhat more widely used than PHP or Python, perhaps because it is the oldest of the three. Perl is best known for scripting, such as by system administrators, and also as a Web language (e.g., Apache mod_perl). Perl is a good language for sophisticated scripting. IT is criticized for being hard to understand and is probably a better choice for individuals than teams.

Perl applications include several system administration tools, including Webmin, the very popular SpamAssassin tool, and the Movable Type Weblog tool. Perl code runs the high-volume Slashdot and Kuro5hin content sites.

9.2.3   PHP

PHP is a Web development language similar to Active Server Pages and Java Server Pages. PHP originally stood for Personal Home Page; it was more like Front Page originally but has evolved into an object-oriented language.

PHP is primarily a Web language, but it can be used for scripting, and there is a version of PHP for GUI development called PHP-GTK.

PHP is the newest of the languages in Table 9.1, with a young community that is growing fast (about 50 percent annually), whereas Perl and Python are stable or shrinking. Because of this, it seems likely that PHP will be the #2 language in the open source community, overtaking Perl and Java, within a year or two. It is already the leading language for Web development (most of which is not open source).

PHP is powerful, an easy language to learn, and there are several well-rated open source applications written in it. PHP appears to be the leading language for developing Web applications.

9.2.4 Python

Python is an object-oriented language that is easy to learn and use. It has extensive libraries available to allow development of pretty much any kind of application, including games, OpenGL graphics, cross-platform GUI, and network programming. As a general-purpose language Python is powerful, balanced, and well organized.

One unusual feature of Python is the version called Jython. Although Python is usually implemented in C, there is a version written all in Java called Jython. Jython has the same syntax as Python, so that Jython 2.2 is equivalent to Python 2.2. It can call equivalents of most Python classes but is additionally able to call any Java classes. Jython is a good scripting tool for Java applications and an excellent integration tool between Java and other systems.

Python is used to develop complex client applications such as OSAF's Chandler and Red Hat's Anaconda, as well as server-based applications such as Mailman and BitTorrent.

9.2.5 Java

Java is a popular language, but is used less for open source development than you might expect. It seems caught in the middle between C, which is the best performer, and scripting languages, which are more productive. Java is less of a general-purpose scripting language with built-in functions for common tasks like Perl or Python, but it does have a strong available set of classes.

The most important exception, Eclipse, is a system that single-handedly demonstrates the feasibility of developing a successful large system in Java. It is not, however, a typical open source project but began as an internal IBM corporate effort that was "open sourced" after development. Also, as a desktop system, it demonstrates capacity for complexity and response time but not high throughput.

There may be more Java projects in widespread use over time, particularly in complex higher-level application areas. Java is still new, and the table of big projects mostly contains code started ten years ago that could not really be in Java. However, new projects such as Gaim and Xine are still written in C, and the primary uses of Java are as front ends to C core code, not wholesale replacement of C. Mozilla was once planned to be in Java but is in C++ and JavaScript for performance reasons.

The Java language itself is not an open source project. There are open source Java implementations available, but none has much share. But many crucial tools used with Java, such as Java Server Pages, Tomcat from the Jakarta project, and the JBoss application server, are open source. Java is a reasonable development tool for open source software, but not the first choice in practice.

9.2.6 Other Languages

The next most used language after those listed in Table 9.1 is UNIX shell. This, of course, is a good choice for simple tasks, most of which probably don't get loaded to SourceForge, but shell scripting does not scale well to larger applications. Large applications are not written entirely in shell scripts. Perl and Python were designed to be more integrated and portable than shell.

JavaScript is most commonly used for client-side coding in browsers. It has a unique role in this, since it is the only language supported by the two major browsers, Microsoft Internet Explorer and Mozilla/Netscape. There is little relationship between JavaScript and Java.

Other languages, including Ruby, Scheme, and C#, have their admirers but are not used in significant numbers.

9.3   Cross-Platform Code

Most servers today run Windows, Linux, or another form of UNIX, and most larger organizations have a mix of those. Those servers today are split fairly evenly between the UNIX-like systems (including Linux) and Windows. Linux is growing faster mostly at the expense of UNIX, so this will be an even split for still some time. Windows' share of desktop PCs is still over 90 percent, with Linux second but still only 3 percent. However, if clients are defined more broadly to include other small appliances, Linux (and other systems such as Palm and the Japanese embedded system Tron) has much more share.

Since there will be a long period where most organizations will have Windows and Linux servers, it is not necessary for server software to run on both systems as long as it can interoperate. Software for PCs may not need to run on anything but Windows for most markets. So it is not necessary for all open source software to be cross-platform.

However, in servers CIOs are very interested in "commodity computing," which will enable them to host applications without regard to the operating system beneath them. It will certainly be helpful if we can make application selections without platform constraints. This ability to run software on a variety of platforms is, other things being equal, plainly an advantage in flexibility and cost. More freedom to run applications on available servers is better. Organizations over time need to balance loads and repurpose systems, and this is simpler to do if you are not restricted on which applications are deployed on which infrastructure.

On desktops, most organizations have standardized on Windows desktops, but three things may change that. The Web provides a simple standard for cross-platform applications and a class of user outside the organization whose choices cannot be controlled. Linux and the Mac are viable alternatives for the general desktop in some markets, particularly international and youth. And new appliances, including phones and music players, which probably do not run Windows, begin to play an acknowledged role in organizations.

There is an opportunity cost to making applications run on multiple platforms. Microsoft, for example, states two issues: ability to focus on functional enhancement rather than porting, and ability to optimize for the chosen platform. This is all a matter of constrained resources, so it is true in practice except, ironically, for the largest companies and applications.

Table 9.4   *Cross-Platform Applications*

Product	Function	Competes with	Runs on
Apache	Web server	IIS	Windows, Linux, UNIX, others
Oracle	Database server (client tools)	SQL Server	Windows, Linux, UNIX, others
Notes	Calendar & groupware	Exchange	Windows, Linux, UNIX, Mac, others
Opera or Mozilla, Netscape	Browser (client)	Internet Explorer	Windows, Linux, Mac, others

Table 9.4 shows examples of cross-platform applications that are competitive functionally and performance-wise with Windows applications while also running on several other platforms.

Why Open Source Is Cross-Platform

Open code developers are able to develop cross-platform. The languages that are used for open source (C++, Perl, Java, PHP, Python) are all available on Linux, Windows, and other UNIX platforms, including the Mac. So are key elements of the development platform: shell, database, Web server, support tools. The most awkward area is GUI tools, and this is often the reason for otherwise surprising cross-platform limitations. There are three good GUI tools: Qt, wxWindows, and TCL. No one is the right choice across Linux, Mac OS X, and Windows when you consider performance, native support, and licensing. Qt is the only one for embedded systems, but is dual licensed and has to be purchased on Windows. wxWindows is fast and powerful but is not native on the Mac, where it runs in X11 with an Aqua-compatible window manager. TCL does not use native toolkits on any platform and is not very powerful. See Table 9.5.

Open source developers are motivated to develop cross-platform. They favor Linux much more than the general public but work in a mixed world. At OSCON 2003, which contained a broad set of open source users and developers, I observed a fairly even split among Linux, Mac, and Windows (30-30-40). Open source developers favor Linux even more, with most hardcore developers using Linux. But of course, in the general public, the market most programmers address, the distribution is strongly Windows (3-3-94).

The structure of open source projects allows for cross-platform development where there is a market. In a small closed code company, limited resources must be deployed making economic choices, and some skill sets

Table 9.5 *GUI Toolkits*

Tool	Linux	Windows	Mac OS X	Embedded Linux	Comments
Qt	++	+	++	++	C++ native on Mac, not Python
wxWindows	++	++	+	—	Not native on Mac (X11)
TCL	+	+	+	—	Not native anywhere, slow

may be lacking. In open source projects, there may be a group of volunteers prepared to develop a Mac or Windows version, or a company prepared to sponsor it. This need not impact the resources or budget of the original effort, or at least not much.

Open Source on Cross-Platform in Practice

Looking at open source products in actual practice shows that most of the more popular server products are available on Linux (all distributions), Windows, and some forms of UNIX, with a few on Linux/UNIX only— for example, Apache, MySQL, PHP, Perl. Popular client products (media players, instant messaging, office, mail) will mostly be Linux/Windows/ Mac but may be Linux/Mac or Linux only.

Sometimes the purpose of a project is to make functions available on Linux that are available on Windows or the Mac, so there may not be much point in making it cross-platform. Wine (Windows emulation) is the most obvious example here! The purpose of the Gnome and KDE desktop project is to improve Linux to meet and beat the Windows desktop, and Evolution specifically is a Linux replacement for Outlook, so they are Linux-only.

The Mac is a special case, because it is often supported only for the newer UNIX-based systems (OS X) and with an X11 version rather than native Mac (Carbon/Cocoa). This is simpler to do and these versions can look quite good (the Mac X11 window manager looks like Carbon) but are slower and require installation of the X11 software. OpenOffice, for example, is available for Linux, Windows, and Mac. The Mac version is 1.0, which is a level back and is not native but requires X11 installation.

There are some cases of Windows-only open source products, and even a few VB projects: open source software written in a closed code language for a closed code platform. It would not be unusual to develop a Perl program to manage Windows networks that runs only on the Windows platform, or a Python or Java driver to access SQL Server on Windows. At least one open source system is written in the language MUMPS.

9.4   **Summary**

The methodology of successful open source software projects is not really tremendously different from that of successful closed code software development practices in ways that can be proved. Open source developers tend to stay with the products longer, and the products tend to undergo smoother upgrade paths, presumably because they are less affected by corporate shifts. The advantages of many users reviewing and contributing are genuine, but closed code has evolved methods to get similar results.

Open source code projects do appear different from typical corporate practices in several respects. The problem space is different, more focused on tools and products. The language and tool choices are consistently different, probably because they are more geared to the problem.

The language of choice for open source development is C (including C++). The open source community very clearly prefers C. All of the famous open source projects are C/C++. This prevalence may be somewhat related to the type of software; encryption, compression, and portable libraries really have to be written in C, and other system software probably should be. It may be partly because open source development core teams are small and highly motivated. But the dominance continues into projects that could be written in other ways. Projects can be structured with front ends written in other languages, and while this is done, it is done less than possible. I think it comes down to the fact that C++ is an excellent choice for a motivated group of developers developing products, and this describes the environment of most successful open source software.

Application development in the open source community outside of C++ does take place. The languages chosen for successful projects most often appear to be the scripting languages Perl, PHP, and Python. If the application is large, the project may use a layered architecture with low-level functions written in C/C++ and higher-level functions in the scripting language. Perl, PHP, and Python all employ this architecture.

For large architected software systems, the consensus of the development community, open source and closed code, now is C++ or Java. The closed code development community can be separated into software companies and large corporate IT departments.

Software companies (Microsoft, IBM, Oracle, SAP, PeopleSoft, etc.) have mostly used C/C++ for their core products, with some use of scripting languages. Many have now mixed in some Java front ends, and some are attempting to write new products all in Java (or in Microsoft's case C#), but this transition takes a long time. Outside the open source community, we should expect software developers to continue as they have done before: using a mixture of C/C++ with scripting languages and Java, with Microsoft using C#. To the extent that open source gains a larger mind-share, the scripting languages will tilt toward LAMP.

10

Managing System Implementation

In this chapter, we will look at system deployment in the large organization and see how the current state of the art is affected by using open source tools and methods.

Contemporary system implementation in the organization is usually not a matter of custom development versus package deployment, but of both. A solution is established by assembling products and integrating them with custom components. The process consists of product selection, customization and integration, deployment, and then ongoing support.

To discuss the issues, we will fit the deployment effort into a framework with models for the implementation team and process and a set of principles. Then we will review issues of migration and support.

10.1 Implementation Roles

A software development or installation team is generally a very mixed team, regarding skill types and levels and often other factors, but it runs as a team of peers. There may be varying talent and experience, but good teams tend to be highly demanding of talent and work effort. Teams must also work well with other groups in the company, which may have different skills and motivations, and must interact externally with customers, suppliers (such as software component and tool vendors), competitors (to understand the market situation), and other external factors such as regulation and funding availability.

Teams vary in size, but some components are always present. One way to approach this is to define a set of roles. We can define six internal roles as follows:

- Customer management

- Program management

- Development

- Testing

- Communication

- Deployment

Figure 10.1 illustrates the implementation roles. The roles are seen as peers, although the program management role is central for coordination.

These roles can be viewed quite flexibly. In general, all of these roles will be present on each project, but not as one person. On smaller projects, one person may play several roles. However, there are certain roles that do not combine well. Program management should not usually combine with customer management, and testing should not combine with development, as there are conflicts of interest. A possible small team is one person doing customer management and testing, another doing development, and another doing the other roles.

On large projects, some roles will be played by teams and there may be a need for team leaders; we also may break large tasks into feature teams, par-

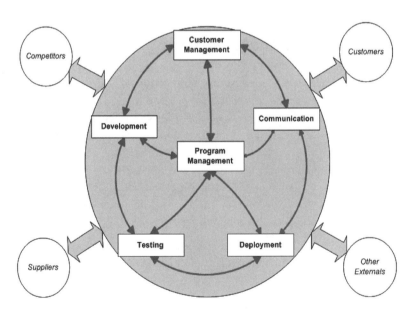

Figure 10.1
*Implementation
roles.*

ticularly in development. The roles are defined in the following text, and the part they play in each phase will be described phase by phase. The primary terms used (such as customer management) are not important. In some open source projects, quite informal or humorous terms (such as "benevolent dictator" and "lieutenants") may be used.

10.1.1   Customer Management

This role is one of sales and evangelism. The customer management role represents the customer and his or her needs to the project team, and the project team represents its product to the customer. This is the role that plans and predicts the market and its needs. When trade-offs are being made, this role will usually be an advocate for more features. The success of this role is measured by the product's ability to create satisfied customers.

10.1.2   Program Management

The program management role manages and maintains the project plan and schedule. It is responsible for managing activities in line with cost and personnel plans. It maintains and updates the risk estimates. The success of this role is measured by delivery of the product to specifications, within constraints.

10.1.3   Development

This role designs and builds the code and tests it at the unit level. The development role selects the tools used in development and the components incorporated into the product. The success of this role is measured by the delivery of working product and the rate of addressing reported issues.

10.1.4   Testing

This role involves translating the specification into functional test plans, selecting and creating automated tests, reporting and tracking problems, managing the testing community to ensure test coverage, and managing the product toward shipping.

10.1.5   Communication

This role manages communication with the user, including interface design, documentation, a help system, and training materials. Documents may be paper or interactive; these days they are often composed of HTML and may include multimedia elements. The success of this role is measured by user uptake, satisfaction, and level of complaints.

10.1.6   Deployment

This role manages system setup and delivery. This may involve researching particular problems with remote sites and special client situations. The success of this role is measured by issues at deployment and after. This is a key channel of communication with customers. This function can collect issues and feedback into the next phase design, such as user and support FAQs.

10.2   Open Source Impact on Team Issues

Development moves in increasingly rapid cycles, and this is continuing. This makes incremental development and use of rapid languages increasingly necessary. There is a trend to more types of outsourcing, so that teams are more virtual and probably have little in common except the specific project. Per project hires are more common, so transparency of work and rapid testing are more critical. Teams must work to industry-wide standards, because there is no time or system to create project-specific ones. Much more than in the past, we are now working with people outside our immediate organization, including customers, competitors, industry bodies, standards bodies, and the open source community.

It is useful to find ways of extending the team to bring in extra resources while maintaining coordination of efforts. Here, the work of the open source community can be directly applied to corporate development. Open source practices have demonstrated that virtual teams can extend the development and testing resources. There are limits to this, caused by the need to integrate code in development and to coordinate testing around a plan in the testing phase. Some products are highly constrained by these limits, as Fred Brooks pointed out in "The Mythical Man-Month." It is unlikely that core database servers can benefit from more developers, for example, since the integration is more critical than the extra features. On the other hand, a word processor can be extended from support for 40 languages to 100 by additional development and testing resources. Figure 10.2 shows the impact on team composition. Open source development teams are able to draw on developers outside their core team. They also leverage testing from a large group outside the core team. More resources are available, and some resources that would have been part of the core team can be "outsourced" to the virtual team in this way. These practices can be employed in some internal projects if the circumstances are right.

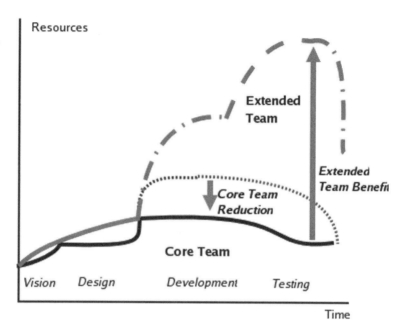

Figure 10.2
Effect of extended teams on resources.

In the open source process, a vision is often propagated and used as a rallying point. The vision should be simply stated, shared among all parties. The vision can change over time, but too much change may be a warning sign. The design phase does not appear to be exposed in as general a fashion. It is not clear how specifications will be gathered from the user, if that user is not on the development team. In the testing phase, open source style becomes similar to corporate testing or the best practice in corporate environments.

There are more international issues with a modern team. The use of Internet technology for development and testing has made it possible to bring together teams from all around the world. The first issue is time zone differences, which can sometimes be exploited positively to allow code hand-off around the world for 24-hour development on some projects. When developers and testers co-operate worldwide, language issues arise such as bug reporting or test data. International development can lead to misunderstandings of various kinds, as there may be cultural differences in methodology or communication styles. For example, many jokes translate poorly or offensively. There are differences in etiquette, as in levels of aggression, between different cultures.

There may be some opportunities to work in the open source style within organizations. We can assemble teams from different departments, encourage them to work together without regard for their position in the organization, and resort to unconventional methods of reward and motiva-

Figure 10.3
Development process model.

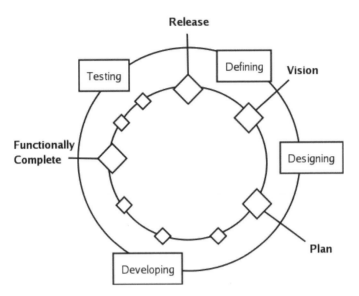

tion. This could apply to community processes within the organization, such as standards. This type of effort needs collaborative tools, usually needs to bring together people from different parts of the organization, and is not well rewarded in a conventional manner. Another example could be involving users in a migration project in an explicit way, in an attempt to convert potential hostile energy into a positive force.

10.3   Implementation Process

Figure 10.3 shows the implementation (or development) process model. This is cyclic, with a continuous series of releases. Each release contains four phases: defining, designing, developing, and testing. Table 10.1 lists the phase definitions.

10.3.1   Releases

There can be some overlap between phases, but generally this does not include coding, which needs special arrangements. Most commonly, the vision and plan for the next release can take place during testing of the current release.

Releases iterate at two levels. In addition to external releases, there will often be releases at an internal level. There are several benefits to scheduling internal releases. The trick to development is to get the product to a known state and then incrementally build on it, and this supports that by ensuring

Table 10.1   *Phase Definitions*

Defining	The team defines goals and determines scope.
	Interim milestones are team formation and drafts of the project definition components.
	End milestone is delivery of the project definition, complete and reviewed.
Designing	The team drafts a specification and plans a schedule.
	Interim milestones are design components, reduction of high risks, and more complete costs and schedule.
	End milestone is delivery of the functional and technical specs and updated project definition, complete and reviewed.
Developing	Interim milestones are partial releases and components.
	End milestone is a functionally complete system with managed source code and executables, user support and testing support materials, and updated functional and technical specs and project definition.
Testing	Interim milestones are typically preliminary releases. This is driven by problem reporting, until the number of acceptable severity bugs allows release.
	End milestone is release.

that components are complete and working together. To schedule releases, we break big systems into smaller systems that do known work and can be tested, revealing measurable progress (done or not done; not 80 percent done) and allowing correction. We can manage risks and priorities by putting risky features in early releases. Internal releases also allow a team to gain practice at releasing, which is a morale booster.

10.3.2   Team Roles during the Process

During the phases, team roles vary to some extent. Table 10.2 shows the focus of different roles during different phases.

Table 10.2   *Team Roles during the Process*

Role	Defining	Designing	Developing	Testing
Customer management	Owns process; vision document; concept	Communication plan; managing customer expectations	Manage customer expectations; communicate with customer	Communication; test site/result coordination; next release planning

Table 10.2   *Team Roles during the Process (continued)*

Role	Defining	Designing	Developing	Testing
Program management	Design goals; project risks and costs	Owns process; functional spec; project plan	Track project; communicate with team; plan testing	Project and bug tracking
Development	Prototypes; feasibility; approaches	Development plan; technical spec	Owns process; build and test	Bug resolution; optimization
Testing	Acceptance criteria; testing strategies	Evaluate design for testability; detailed test plan	Develop test cases and scripts; test components; begin testing releases	Owns process; bug finding and reporting
Communication	User performance and communication needs	Plan for user performance and education	Develop and test	Training; bug fixing
Deployment	Major deployment and support considerations	Evaluate design for deployment; deployment plan	Operational documentation; plan staging; support internal deployment	Test deployment; deployment planning; operations/support training

10.4   Implementation Principles

Many principles of system implementation that are relevant to all development are the same now as they have always been at successful software houses. Managers know that the future is uncertain and we can't control all of the developments in a significant project. Because of this, we should not commit to fixed schedules and prices. This uncertainty includes the competitive outlook and business context. Often, projects must change direction because of the actions of competitive or complementary systems. Our uncertainty also includes which code will get written. We cannot predict the completion date of any but the most trivial tasks, and significant pieces of code can have surprising effects or performance characteristics.

10.4.1   Resource Trade-offs

There is always a need for trade-offs between resources, features, and schedule. It is difficult to add resources effectively late in a project. Because of this, when a problem develops we usually have a choice between slipping features to maintain a schedule, or slipping a schedule to maintain features. The rule at software houses and in corporate life is generally that it is better to hold the date and slip features into future releases. Open source may be different, because the presence of volunteer workers and the community process for feature addition may make it hard to throw out features while providing additional resources to get them done. It may be possible to hold features and slip the date. This needs to be considered carefully, as the downside to this is the cost of integration. Plus, of course, if features don't get delivered, they don't ship.

10.4.2 Frequent Releases

Recent practice has moved toward very frequent build and release of code, even daily. In open source development each build of new code is generally available via CVS, with more stable releases tagged. In this scenario, effective testing is made possible by abundant hardware and automated scripts. A product that has been built and tested is a product whose status we understand in full. This fits in well with current programmer practices of test-driven development, although that is not necessary. As part of the practice of testing early and often, design should call for several versions to be released, as early as possible, and tested. To do this well, it is necessary to make an extra effort to find small systems that are useful in their own right and also as steps on the path to the larger system. For example, I worked on a reservation system whose final product allowed customers to book hotels, cars, and air travel over the Internet. The first interim release simply displayed air travel schedules, but this was useful by itself and could be distributed to users for testing.

Reporting accurately versus managing the plan is very important. Software development tends to slip, and it is more important to be aware of where we really are than to try to make our efforts look good. This is where common self-delusions and management dysfunction can affect our judgment. If we slip a date, we need to be really careful in two ways. First, we should take extra care to replace it with an accurate estimate, so we don't follow one bad date with another. Second, we need to review other estimates. If we slipped the first half from four weeks to five, it is not likely we will "make it up" by doing the second half in three: five if the correct new estimate.

The best way to do estimating is bottom-up. Those who will do the work should make the estimate. Generally, they will know better than managers, who usually do not have the time and current knowledge to make an accurate estimate. This is effective as motivation, since people are more committed to meet estimates that they made than to those imposed on them by others.

10.4.3   Support Elements

In order to control team-based application design and development, we must put a structure in place. All design work and code must be managed through source control. Application components must be put in a place where they can be reviewed and reused. Code must be consolidated onto a central server for integration testing. In order to tie the pieces together early and keep them working together, application components must be packaged and deployed to staging and production servers.

Code in all application tiers should be able to run in a debug mode, reporting everything we may need to know. We need facilities to run the application; monitor processing, performance, and results; and compare these to previous runs. We need the ability to find components that we can include in our solution—preferably open source but possibly in some cases not. In open source, source code management is generally done with CVS. There are alternatives; Subversion, which is an update to CVS by the original developers, is worth evaluating because it is easier to learn and use. Of course, if the organization is already using a particular source code management system, that could continue to be used. Projects can be found using SourceForge, the repository for most open source code, and Freshmeat, which serves as an index search for particular types of projects, such as an application or a solution implemented in a particular language.

10.4.4   Watching for Problems

Projects that are running into trouble can be measured technically, such as through bug reports or performance measures. They also reveal themselves in human factors. In team communications, there may be an increasing emphasis on secrecy or blame. Items may be piling up waiting for someone else, perhaps a new hire, to do them. The schedules of our team members may be expanding, leaving no time for other life activities such as shopping, so those get done during the day. Possibly the parking lot is full at midnight because there are heroes working away at all hours, but the schedule is still slipping. Unlike a technology concept, a product should have a clear focus on the customer and his or her needs. The product should be tending toward something. Its size and performance should be stabilizing.

10.5 Key Documents

Important documents include the project definition, functional, and technical specifications (specs).

10.5.1 Project Definition

Every project should have a definition. This begins with the vision phase and is carried through and updated at every phase, and finally evaluated at project completion. Table 10.3 shows the components of a project definition.

Table 10.3   *Project Definition*

Component	Description
Vision	Brief description of project and background
	Intended users and major scenarios
	Important goals, whether business or technical
Scope and constraints	Statement of boundaries and areas of impact, including time deadlines
	Constraints on technology choices, such as standards or interoperability
Risk	Prioritized dynamic list of risks with likelihood and severity
Costs and benefits	Hardware, software, manpower, whether one-time or continuing; expected returns
Schedule	Project plan with milestones
Team Structure	Full-time team members; virtual team members including partners and users (includes assumptions, skills, critical needs, dependencies)

10.5.2 Risk Management

The risk assessment document is created in the vision phase and then maintained up-to-date throughout the project. We will use the risk document to drive risk-driven scheduling. We identify the risky (hard) stuff and attack it first, even if that is not the most convenient approach. By attempting to remove risks early, we prepare ourselves for the likelihood that other problems will creep in later.

The purpose of the risk document is to identify risks that are of sufficient likelihood and severity to be a concern. This is typically a dozen or so; more than one or two, but less than a hundred. Severe risks should be addressed early, so that if things are going well the risk document may become smaller and less severe as the project progresses. For each risk, we create:

- Statement that captures the nature of the risk
- Probability that it will occur
- Severity of the problem that would be caused, described and given an impact number
- Mitigation plans that would prevent the risk from occurring
- Contingency plans that would minimize or cope with the problem if it occurs
- Ownership, or the party who will monitor the risk

A Risk Checklist

The following are all examples of common general risks for information technology projects. Listed first are external risks, which are related to areas outside the control of the project team, followed by internal risks, which are related to the project team and its members and structure.

- Is there sufficient commitment from senior management and users?
- What is the business impact on users, and how much change will they undergo?
- Do users understand the effects and limitations of the technology?
- How many outside bodies, such as regulatory boards, unions, or external partners, are involved?
- Are there multiple user branches or sites (or companies or countries) that may have different processes?
- Are the requirements expected to be detailed and stable?
- Are there immovable deadlines or time to market pressures?
- Was the team size and development schedule calculated from the requirements?
- Has the project manager done this sort of thing before?
- Does the team have sufficient relevant knowledge?
- Is there significant shipping experience among senior team members?

- Is there sufficient commitment from senior management or users?

- Has all the technology been seen working somewhere?

This list is worth reviewing, but it needs to be supplemented with more specific issues relating to the project technologies and specific goals.

10.5.3 Example of a Risk Assessment

Table 10.4 is a risk assessment from an actual project (names have been changed). Each risk is given an ID number and a description. Each is assigned a probability and severity. In this case, they were multiplied to generate a priority by which the table was sorted. Each risk has an owner and mitigation and/or contingency actions.

It is important to honestly identify risks in this shared document; but as this example shows, it may be necessary to be diplomatic.

Table 10.4 *Risk Assessment*

ID	Priority	Description	Probability	Severity	Owner	Mitigation Action(s)	Contingency Action(s)
1	4	Scalability and performance of several technologies, e.g., mobile device, and database connector are unknown. Consequently, presentation of product information may take too long or a caching scheme will need to be devised.	0.8	5	Carol	Work with DBA and architecture group to design queries. Run early performance tests to ensure system can meet spec.	Design a caching system and preload cache to isolate query time.
2	2.4	Team resources not completely identified or dedicated to the cause. Consequently, project deadline will be missed.	0.6	4	Mark	Commitment from team members' managers that they will are committed to the project.	Work overtime.

Table 10.4   *Risk Assessment (continued)*

ID	Priority	Description	Probability	Severity	Owner	Mitigation Action(s)	Contingency Action(s)
3	2	Store-only items do not have attributes defined in the database. These may not be entered in time for the pilot. Consequently, attribute data for many products may not be available. If these are important items, the pilot will not be accepted.	0.5	4	Susan	Determine source for missing information and arrange its entry.	Revise release plan or curtail pilot.
4	2	Editorial content to support the objective is incomplete. No editorial process currently exists. Consequently, there is a lack of compelling program information.	1.0	2	Carol	Meet with senior management to identify a process. RELEASE 2.	Deploy with limited functionality.
5	2	Physical issues (e.g., battery life of device) are currently unknown. Consequently, employees may find the devices inconvenient to use and abandon them.	0.5	4	Paul	Test to ensure acceptable battery life, comfort of straps and cases, etc.	Investigate options for devices as necessary during pilot.
6	1.6	Complete product comparison data not available. Consequently, comparison functionality will be available for a reduced number of products.	0.8	2	Susan	Work with data owners to locate/ create information.	Provide "not available" page.

Table 10.4 *Risk Assessment (continued)*

ID	Priority	Description	Probability	Severity	Owner	Mitigation Action(s)	Contingency Action(s)
7	1.2	Operational acceptance criteria may require more time than available to meet deadline. Consequently, missed deadline.	0.3	4	Paul	Meet early with operations team to gain acceptance for fast path.	Escalate issue.
8	1.2	Other applications on the hand-held must coexist with the portal. Web apps need to run on the device. Consequently, employee may need to perform a hard reset to access the other applications.	0.6	2	Paul	Meet with team responsible for local applications to coordinate. Run functional tests on device for all deployed apps.	Build portal to access only certified applications.
9	1.2	Enough people with appropriate store experience are not participating in the requirements. Consequently, functionality will not meet the needs of the employees.	0.3	4	Vera	Attempt to engage critical sales training resources and pilot stores early in process. RELEASE 2.	Reevaluate requirements at conclusion of pilot phase.

10.5.4 Functional Specification

A functional specification (spec) is a list of features to be included in the project, prioritized and spelled out in sufficient detail. The right level of detail is first a matter of trust and communication. Outsourced projects often have very detailed specifications. The ideal is just enough detail to enable a developer to build the system that is needed. Too much detail leads to time wasted on a paper process. Too little detail leads to coding in a vacuum.

The spec should break the product into features, explain the features, and indicate whether they are required or desirable. For most business systems, features will be broken into presentation, business, and data tiers.

Because it is repetitive, comprehensive, and subject to change, a spec should usually be maintained as a spreadsheet or in some database-driven format.

10.5.5 Technical Specification

The technical specification should indicate how the functional spec will be implemented. This includes the technical architecture and details of each of the included components. Many people would call this the technical architecture. It should be sufficiently detailed for skilled developers to build the system. It includes:

- Logical model of the system
- Physical model
- Key design points, technology choices, and proofs of concept
- Infrastructure for development, testing, and deployment
- Interoperability, including data flows and events
- Migration, including data conversion
- Security, including authentication/authorization and threat management
- Data stores, including schemata
- Management by operations, including logging and monitoring

10.6 Migration

In a migration, risks are higher than with a new system because expectations are higher and users have something to lose. If we have to replace an existing system with a new one, we need to take extra care to plan carefully, test everything thoroughly, and still be prepared for unexpected problems that require backing out changes. Problems may not be our fault now, but they will be after a migration. This work will increase the costs and the time to implement the system.

The same issues may not occur when implementing a new system, where a partial solution may be quite acceptable, at least for a first release.

10.6.1 Migration Approaches

In existing organizations, there generally is an existing system. There are several different approaches we can take for its disposition. We can:

- Keep the system, recognizing that the system is paid for and works, at least to a point. Abandon the system, outsourcing its function or doing it manually.

- Redeploy the system to another platform with minimal changes—for instance, from UNIX to Linux.

- Develop a replacement system with appropriate new tools and products. This may include redesigning the process more generally to streamline processes.

- Beautify it, leaving the core product but improving access, perhaps with a Web front end.

- Starve it, preventing further investment until we can cut it off.

In larger systems, we may combine these. We might leave part of a system and abandon the rest, build a new front end on a system while starving it, or redeploy a system to Linux and add a new GUI front end.

10.6.2 Assessing the Current System

To determine the right approach, we need to assess both the business and the technology situation. The business problem will be identified in the vision phase and built into the project definition, as described earlier in this chapter. The business situation has various opportunities and threats, including the actions of customers and competitors and new ideas in business organization.

Business opportunities are diverse. We might be able to target our existing customers with new products—for example, by accessing our information on them. We could compress the time to introduce a new product or to satisfy a customer requirement. We might access inventory or issue custom prices immediately, to support ideas such as real-time pricing or to sell our information as a product. We might develop ways to measure and improve our operating efficiency or product quality. Of course, we might develop new customers and/or products.

Business threats are also diverse. Our sales volume or margins might be down. Competitors might have a cost advantage from technology or labor cost. We might already be losing market share to competition or have competitors routinely beat us on price, speed of response, or product introduction. Expectations of customer service might be increasing, or demographic changes might be altering our customers or workforce. New or changing sales channels might need different support processes. Companies in our industry might be changing in size through mergers and acquisitions. A regulatory change may affect our business environment or our operations.

The technology situation includes an assessment of the current system and available replacement technologies and processes. It is difficult to assess an existing complex system. An assessment team needs to bring a variety of skills and points of view and be very open to working together. Nobody will understand the old and the new equally, so the whole must be greater than the parts.

Technologies change so fast that by the time a system is deployed the architecture is often obsolete. The team must understand the old system well enough without too much work. Maintainers of the old system will understand it, but may have an exaggerated sense of its complexity and value. A common problem is to end up writing the same system over. If important details are not specified sufficiently, the implementation team gets them from the system users and maintainers, although it was the potential offered by new technology that justified the migration cost.

It may be difficult to get good measurements on performance of the current system. People involved with existing systems generally do not report accurately on the customer satisfaction and reliability of the system. They measure what they do well, or what they can measure, not necessarily what matters.

The areas to assess for a system include:

- Size, performance, complexity, condition of applications
- Hardware and software infrastructure
- Current staffing, service requests, and workload
- Costs
- Problems that the current system cannot address

From this, we can tell if the application is a candidate for migration and start developing a project definition.

Issues we may find include data quality of the current system, its historical availability and cost of service, and security. Older systems often have issues with system availability, scheduled or unscheduled—for instance, they are not so likely to support Web or global 24/7 needs. There also may be difficulty in use, such as high training costs or data entry error rates.

A common strength of existing systems is that the system is paid for and the current staff is trained in its use. However, over time costs of security and maintenance may have crept up, and most systems have periodic maintenance and upgrades. Some companies outsource because these types of costs have gone out of control.

Development productivity is commonly an issue with older systems, making it difficult to respond to changes in the business or to access data in new ways. Development activities in old complex systems often have remarkably little connection with current customer priorities.

10.7 Interacting with the Open Source Community

We will interact with the open source community in several ways. We will have open source developers on staff, and need to consider how to hire and retain them. We will interface with open source products by using them, and may have opportunities to contribute to them with code, work, or finance.

10.7.1 Hiring from the Community

A few people in open source are famous in a general sense, but, much more importantly, at the level of code contribution to particular projects, many people have built reputations within a particular community. Open source is open and public, so you can see code, written postings, and so on that you would never see in a candidate from a closed code company. It may be a good idea to use those resources.

In some cases, you might want to hire the maintainer of a code project if it's important to you. Martin Fink of Hewlett-Packard cites a "two-hop" rule. If a project is important to his organization, he likes to know that he is two people away from a maintainer or key contributor to the project. Either someone on the project, or someone who is known and trusted by those on the project, should be known to him.

In any case, a maintainer from a successful open source project has a project management background. Maintainers have managed code contributions; motivated and given credit; attracted/retained developers and other resources, mostly without using money; and developed or adopted processes for code management and release. That is a good set of skills, even if the project they work on is directly relevant to you.

10.7.2   Employee Agreements

There are several issues where organizations generally do not have policies today, but may need to develop one. This may involve a review of relevant employment contracts. The following are some examples, but this is not an exhaustive list; there may be other issues.

Some employees will want to be allowed to work on open source projects while on organization projects—for instance, by sharing utility code or returning enhancements made to open source software. This is reasonable, but may conflict with current employment agreements. Others may wish to contribute to open source software on their own time. This is also reasonable, but many organizations have blanket policies prohibiting it. There is also the question of copyright ownership. Most open software projects, including Samba and Apache, do not allow retention of copyright by the contributing company. This again may conflict with current policies. Some employees may only be willing to work on open source, and your company will probably not be doing open source exclusively. This may require a special arrangement—for instance, they may have to work as contractors rather than employees.

10.7.3   Repaying the Community

Organizations that benefit from open source software often develop methods for repaying the community. The simplest can be allowing employees to work and contribute to the community, as well as serving as a reference and otherwise being a good citizen. There may be opportunities for sponsoring enhancements that are relevant to your organization's use. By directing investment toward enhancements your organization needs, you may gain leverage in the direction of the product.

In negotiating with open source developers, it may be helpful to bear in mind the motivation discussed in the previous chapter. Money is an element, but so is a measure of fame and an opportunity to work on something worthwhile. If your organization is able to offer a proposition that honestly meets those aspirations, it may be an attractive place for developers to spend their time.

It is often difficult to find people to work on less glamorous code, or on non-coding issues such as documentation. Documentation is an area where an organization using open source can contribute very naturally. This can be expanded to benchmarking and best practices.

Sometimes there may be an opportunity to release code to open source. For this to be successful there needs to be a community that can respond to it. This includes a market for use, plus people interested in developing, and a future. You should not do it because it is end of life or just a failure. But this type of move is not eccentric or noncommercial. Among organizations that have contributed in significant ways to the open source community are CERN (World Wide Web), IBM (Eclipse), Novell (iFolders), and Sun (OpenOffice).

10.8 Support

Support costs include software maintenance, internal resources, and contracted external resource. Software maintenance fees, typically annual charges of about 20 percent of the purchase price, are simply a cost of doing business when using many closed code program, which you will escape by using open source software.

The essential step in managing support is to analyze what we really need. One meaning of support is primarily hand-holding—helping people do something with the software—or training—teaching people features or how to use documentation and so on. Another meaning is developing code, fixing errors, or adding or extending features of the software to meet needs. These two different requirements interact. Often, reports on problems and missing features in software must be resolved into user or software error. Specifically, we can resolve support into three levels, as follows:

- Level 1: Report and identify issue, assign ID, triage and resolve if possible.

- Level 2: Get the issue to an expert in the problem area and resolve without development request.

- Level 3: A bug is filed, and a patch developed in the field and incorporated or the problem is worked on by a developer.

Level 1 support is usually managed internally (or outsourced directly). By definition, these issues are hand-holding or other trivial activities and need to be resolved inexpensively, not by calling a vendor. Level 2 support can be handled internally, through the software vendor, or through a third party or community process. Level 3 support requires developers with access to the source code. This is the bulk of what maintenance programmers do on custom code within organizations. It is a service that you must get from a closed code company for its software, since nobody else can perform it, so you must contract for it. For instance, look at support for Microsoft Office. Level 1 will be provided by an internal help desk. Level 2 will generally be routed to Microsoft Product Support Services, to a similar organization at IBM or HP, or could be handled internally by some large organizations. Level 3 must be handled by reporting a defect and allowing it to be handled by the Microsoft Office group. The correct reporting of a defect is potentially quite a lot of work in itself, and this will be handled by the level 2 support, which may be outsourced.

For open source, a lot of people worry that there is no place to turn for support. This is never true, since there is always the option of supporting yourself, as you do for custom software. It is certainly not true for the serious, commonly used products such as Linux and Apache. They are at least as responsive to level 3 defect reports as any commercial vendor; in my experience they are comparable to the best commercial support. There is an active community providing level 2 support; vendors will enter into commercial contracts to provide it with service-level agreements. The major difference with open source is that you don't have to buy support from the software vendor.

For smaller open source software products, the system is like the source code escrow you might use with a startup. There is a market risk that the product will not succeed, or will tail off before you are finished with it, and in that case you may have to take on the maintenance.

Some companies would like to buy warranties or other insurance-like arrangements. This is difficult to get in open source; if this is needed, you will probably need to deal with a large company such as IBM or HP.

In practice, when you have a problem it is always going to be your responsibility, legally and in practice. Software licenses always state that the software is not warranted for your particular purpose. Vendors will make their best efforts to work around problems, but if this involves purchasing additional hardware or rewriting your software to approach the problem differently, that will be your responsibility.

10.9 **Summary**

In this chapter, we reviewed how to manage a team, the process and roles, and the more important typical deliverable documents. There are some improvements to consider suggested by successful practices in the open source software community.

For most organizations, the new issues posed by open source software are less that they will be creating it than that they will be using the software, employing or otherwise interacting with authors, and integrating it with their own work. There may be opportunities to use open source methods within the organization. There may be a need to review policies that may be overly restrictive on copyright and work for hire in the light of open source possibilities.

The issue of support is critical for organizations adopting open source software. The organization needs a clear policy about what it expects in the way of support, what it is willing to provide, and what it wants to pay for. Given this, the resources are available to deliver this, generally at non reasonable prices and with more flexibility than from closed code vendors.

11

Application Architecture

In this chapter, we will look at different classes of applications, and then review some key design points for applications that will perform well. Then we will cover the methods for loosely coupled communication with other systems, which can include mainframes and Java application servers. Finally, we review the development platforms available and position the open source choices, which are LAMP and Tomcat/JBoss, against the major closed code products, which are server pages and application servers based on .Net and Java. The term LAMP refers to development with Linux, Apache, MySQL, and PHP. Less commonly, it might include the other open source languages Perl or Python or the open source database PostgreSQL.

11.1 Types of Systems

If an organization is planning to implement a complex enterprise application, the possibility of running it on an open source platform should be reviewed. At this time, it is usually possible to run the major enterprise applications, such as those from SAP, Oracle, and PeopleSoft, on Linux servers. There are fewer applications available that are open source from top to bottom, but there are some available and more can be built. This type of deployment has only been happening recently, yet already there are over 2,000 SAP deployments and over 500 Oracle deployments on Linux.

According to the Gartner report "Fear the Penguin" (January 2003), by 2005–2007 users will be commonly deploying complex tiered applications on Linux, using both clusters and "big iron" servers. It will typically take approximately two years to move from consideration through development or acquisition to deployment of the larger category of complex application, such as a substantial ERP deployment or a significant custom financial or manufacturing system. However, smaller systems of this type, such as a few ERP modules or a less comprehensive custom application, might be completed in a year or less. In either case, it is now time to plan in order to deploy in that time frame.

Since Apache is the most popular Web server and PHP the most popular Web development tool, it is not necessary to demonstrate that the majority of normal Web applications can be built this way. A cursory search of the Web reveals large numbers of attractive and reliable applications that have been built using the open source tools (LAMP) and that there is a large body of people available who can develop and maintain these applications.

Because of the fact that the Web is de facto an open source and LAMP playground, vendors of closed code systems usually focus on issues of scalability and enterprise integration to justify their products. This chapter will focus on those issues also. We will note that most needs fall comfortably in the range of performance of the open source products and that when necessary that performance can be increased through the appropriate techniques.

Systems vary by their customer types, their performance requirements, and the type of information they manage and display. Applications that serve external customers will usually handle large and unpredictable numbers of users. Of course, we have no control over their technology or behavior. Applications that service business to business (B2B) customers, such as channel, purchasing, or supply chain, can be as large in some cases as customer systems but should be more predictable, because we have a relationship with the customers that is more manageable. Internal sites should deal with predictable numbers of users, and quite often we can manage the technology platform for internal users if we want to. Call center sites are the most manageable, since they are internal and we generally control the platform, installed applications, and the manner of use.

11.1.1 Extreme Systems

The development tools discussed in this book will handle many complex distributed applications. However, many of the largest and best-known systems are really extreme cases that employ exceptional methods and are not typical of the way other business systems will be built. They are often the first application of their category, the largest company in their industry, or a unique organization such as a clearing-house. Examples include:

- Travel reservation systems, such as Sabre and Amadeus
- Banking clearing-house systems, such as SWIFT

- Exchange systems, such as the New York Stock Exchange (NYSE) and the Commodities Exchange (COMEX)
- Large organizations, such as Wal-Mart, Bank of America, and Citicorp
- Leading dot-com companies, such as Google and Amazon.com

These organizations have developed substantial innovative software systems using specialized transaction processors and low-level languages. Sabre and NYSE use Tandem (now HP NonStop) systems. Bank of America and Sabre use the custom mainframe IBM Transaction Processing Facility. The language used in these systems is C++ or older low-level languages, including PL/I and assembler. This behavior is really more like software product developers than typical business systems. In fact, several of these operations have spun off software product organizations.

When applications need the highest performance, the language to use is always C (or C++.) For example, Microsoft generally finds Web applications to be about twice as fast running benchmarks when written in (unmanaged) Visual C++ instead of VB and ASP. Other vendors just don't do database benchmarks except with Tuxedo and C++, because their application servers are even slower. This is surprising, since much of a Web application is a constant overhead, including the Web server, database, and network communication. It is not only the language performance, but more importantly the architecture it is deployed with, that determines the performance. C++ is used with ISAPI rather than ASP, direct database access rather than ADO, memory caching rather than simple database access, and so on.

If you are going to build a high-performance system in C, it will probably cost a few extra months to set up, take twice the development time, and you will have to pay higher rates for developers. For a small application, taking two developers three months, this could be a difference in development cost of $100,000 ($150K − $50K). Most applications will require much more than this effort level, and most organizations will have several such applications, so they could easily spend a half million. In order to make up these costs through better performance on servers, if the application is twice as fast, half a million would have to be saved. So the rule of thumb is that for systems with over a million dollars in deployed servers, we will consider building a complex custom-designed application; otherwise, we will use higher-level languages and build the system through integration.

Outside of benchmarks, most businesses don't need to complicate their development to achieve the highest possible performance. They can always approach the problem by buying some extra equipment. This is only a problem if the equipment becomes expensive. The cost saving from rapid development using developers with standard skill sets generally dwarfs the higher cost of extra servers.

11.1.2   Transactional Systems

Normal development in organizations is not the same as software product development or these extreme systems. Leaving aside these special cases, almost all transactional Web applications can be constructed with "server page technology," such as PHP, ASP, or JSP, with some sensible use of server-side components. In this way, systems can be quickly deployed by typical integration teams without special expertise.

Applications of this class that may run into performance limitations can follow standard risk management methods to mitigate the performance issue. We can develop a performance model early in the project and benchmark it. The following optimization techniques, which are described later, can give order of magnitude improvements in performance but must be designed into the application:

- Effective state management
- Queuing
- Good database design

If we have applications with unpredictable performance requirements, we should first attempt to gather some information on constraints, and then design for scalability. Applications designed in tiers can be scaled to support very high numbers of users, and database performance can reach very high numbers at some price.

11.1.3   Knowledge Management

Not all applications are transactional. Other applications typically have fewer users and offer a less directed and predictable set of interactions. This includes many kinds of information and support systems and forms of collaboration; we will put them all in the category of knowledge management. These applications usually interoperate with transactional systems indirectly. They may steer users to transactional applications, as portals do; allow analysis of data that ultimately is derived from those applications, such as business intelligence tools applied to data warehouses; or may add value to them, similar to custom shopping front ends, such as Amazon recommendations.

Knowledge management applications also commonly interact with infrastructure systems. They typically rely on the mail system to deliver messages, the directory for authentication, or the file system as a data store for documents. They commonly need programmatic access to these system interfaces. Transactional systems typically will not want to share resources with such systems, because they need to manage their scalability separately from the general organization.

11.2 Tiered Design

We will design applications as a number of logical components. This breaks down complex problems into smaller pieces and hides implementation details from calling components. Components for business applications generally have recognizable tiers for user interface, business rules, and data, although this does not have to be a hard and fast rule. Of course, applications may and commonly will use components from other developed applications. This has implications for documentation and testing of the original applications, and also on the need for multilanguage and cross-platform support, since applications developed at different times will often run on different platforms.

There is no strict general mapping between software tiers and hardware (logical and physical components). There is also no strict rule that there should be exactly three tiers, or any other exact number. As specific examples, business components can call business components, and database stored procedures can be nested. These are application architecture choices. In particular, there is no need for logical components to be implemented as physical components communicating via containers, as in the EJB and COM+ architectures. This is actually very expensive in terms of performance in many situations and should be discouraged. The usual design is to run application components on the Web server to avoid remote calls.

The partitioning design is about maintaining a balance between flexibility and control. A good design should also allow reuse of code between batch, Web, and GUI applications. Figure 11.1 shows the general mapping at a conceptual level. Clients can be a Web browser, an intelligent device such as a PC or a phone, or another system accessing through a Web service. Our application will consist of our business components interacting with framework components such as server pages and transac-

Figure 11.1
*Application
architecture.*

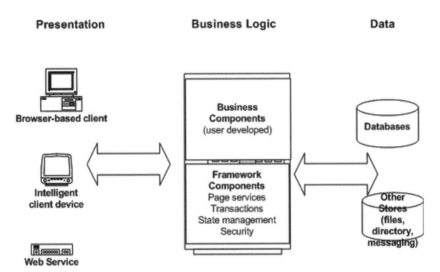

tion managers. While our back-end store will usually be a database, we may access other systems, such as a directory or email system, or access other applications.

In fully connected networks, business rules usually go into server-side components, to allow reuse and to avoid deployment problems. The trade-off here is possible duplication of code connected with validation. Because we can't usually trust client code and preparation such as data lookups performed at clients, it may be necessary to replicate tables to support this. In occasionally disconnected networks, business rules must be available where needed.

Different components can, in general, be written in different languages, subject to all sorts of real-world limitations. We may choose to do this to take advantage of the various strengths of different languages—for example, combining Java with PL-SQL or Python with C++. More commonly, we might be able to create a new application while reusing large sections of a legacy language.

Interlanguage calling conventions may not translate between platforms. It is usually possible to call anything from C and to call code written in C from anything; this is one of the reasons C is such a popular programming language.

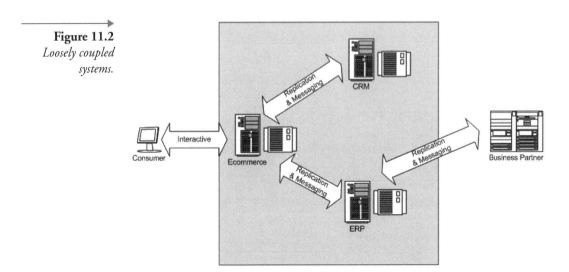

Figure 11.2
Loosely coupled systems.

11.3 Managing Performance and Scalability

What we want to achieve is loose coupling on commodity platforms. This provides scalability and is also best for costs, so the result is the best price/performance. Loose coupling combines queuing, to remove time dependencies with use of a non-application-specific data format to remove data dependencies. Figure 11.2 illustrates loosely coupled systems. A consumer is interacting with an ecommerce system. The ecommerce system has copies of elements of the product catalog and customer data. When a purchase is made, a message is sent to the ERP system for fulfillment. This system may, in turn, send a message to a business partner. These messages may be asynchronous, so that the customer interaction does not wait on the response from the back end.

11.3.1 State Management

The question of transient state management is where to keep data in the course of a long-running transaction. This could be a shopping cart in ecommerce, for example. We can choose to manage transient state at the customer, at the Web server, or at the database (see Figure 11.3).

We can maintain transient state at the Web server, and we will get good performance in the sense that we cut down on network traffic. However, we lose a great deal of function by giving up the database. We do not get transactions, which can give us a lot of extra work in the application or may expose us to corrupt data after a Web server failure. This model also

Figure 11.3
Transient state.

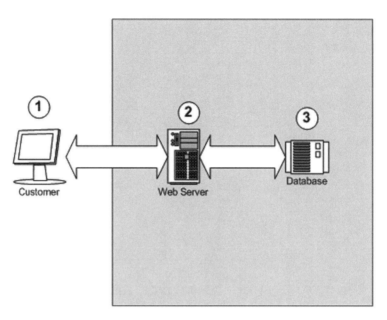

limits our ability to use distributed systems; for example, we must set Web server load balancing to "sticky," because customers must return to the same server. Finally, by holding server resources during a long-running transaction, we use them over much longer time frames because user time is orders of magnitude larger than machine time. Figure 11.4 shows the impact of holding resources at the Web server. If machine time is 100 times faster, a given server can serve 100 times more users if it can release all resources during user "think time." Resources could be many items, including allocated memory, entries in a shopping cart or cache table, or database connections. Database connections are such an important issue that they will usually be pooled.

We can maintain transient data in the database, either in regular database tables or special formats, such as temporary tables or dedicated dictionaries as in commerce products. If we manage state this way, we have transactions, and we have reliability against most kinds of failure. But we incur extra network communication and probably additional disk access, since databases are more general purpose than specialized stores.

If we manage state at the client, we will scale well, but we face issues of management, security (e.g., tampering with prices), privacy (cookies), and client identification (AOL caching issues).

We do not want to hold state in a transactional database over transaction boundaries or during user interaction. The general plan is to get in,

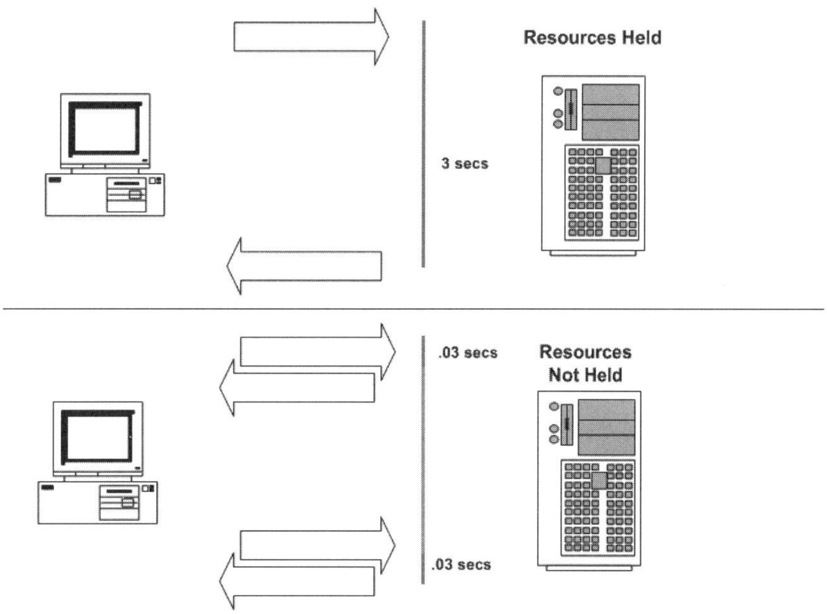

Figure 11.4
Effect of resources held at server.

do work, and get out. For transient state, we will normally store shared data in a database and keep nothing at the Web server. If we don't hold the state at the server we are also safe in the multiuser environment, safe against network failure, and safe against the user walking away. This was learned in the 1960s, using CICS instead of TSO; again in the 1990s, using COM or EJB; and it always applies. We can store client state on the client, most commonly a cookie that allows us to access other data but in some cases a disconnected set of data, if we combine this with an optimistic locking strategy.

Of course, the problem is that state needs to be saved somewhere. An important exception is data that is cached—in other words, it can be recovered from the database if lost. Caching data on the Web server can provide substantial performance gains, since typically a small set of data is used repetitively. A cached copy of data on the server is very useful. It is caching if, when you throw it away, you can get it back. This is fast, since as long as the server stays up, there may be no need to return to the database. It is robust, since data may be recovered from the database. And it secures client data from tampering, since it may be checked against the server. But a caching strategy has to be designed for a set of data to get these features, which are trade-offs.

11.3.2 **Queuing**

One of the most important elements of design for performance is to use asynchronous methods correctly to decouple components from each other—for instance, front end from back end. There are several names for this but I'll simply call it queuing. A correct use of queuing was behind many of the most successful transaction processing systems of the last 40 years. IBM IMS/DC and the Tandem (now HP) NonStop platform both used asynchronous design effectively within their products, which have been extensively used in the financial industry over the last 30+ years.

There are ways to achieve the design feature without using message queue products, such as by writing queues into the file system or database, and that is what most people do.

Queuing offers improvement to an application in reliability and throughput. The first advantage of queuing is that it increases reliability. Queuing decouples a business transaction from issues of server, client, or network availability—in other words, it can provide "success in the face of failure." Queuing also allows us to remove tight coupling from business partners, who may have different capacities or availability cycles. For example, our order processing may depend on a shipping component. But possibly shipping faces delays or is not in operation all the time. We can acknowledge orders now and then queue them for later processing and shipping.

The second advantage of queuing is that it allows us to economically manage large variations in demand. Businesses do not experience consistent demand for services, but have many cycles from hourly and daily to periodic, and also may experience heavy volumes caused by unusual events. Examples include workers logging in at the beginning of the day, "end of month" payroll processing, the impact of TV advertising on a home shopping channel, or the effect of the Superbowl on a sports site. It is common for peak events to be an order of magnitude over normal. For example, suppose we are building a system that we expect will do 1 million transactions a day. We will take orders around the clock, seven days a week. Peak orders might be in the morning from 9:00 A.M. to 12:00 noon and in the afternoon from 2:00 P.M. to 5:00 P.M. The average order rate for this system is around 50,000 an hour, but possibly a peak hour could be 500,000 orders. If ordering and shipping are tightly coupled, the shipping system will need to be sized for 500,000 orders per hour. If ordering is loosely coupled to shipping, so that it can pass off orders into a queue without waiting for fulfillment, a shipping system sized for 50,000 orders per hour could do the workload, although we would probably size it larger than that to pre-

Figure 11.5
Queuing improves reliability and throughput.

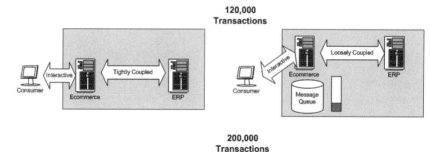

120,000
Transactions

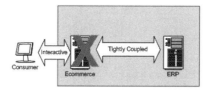
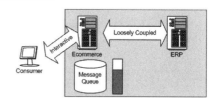

200,000
Transactions

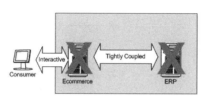
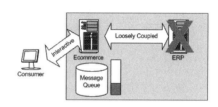

ERP Down

vent the queues from getting too large. See Figure 11.5, which sizes the back end around 100,000. The tightly coupled system would need more back-end servers and is still subject to failure. The loosely coupled system is good until the queue size is exceeded.

Queuing is not for every application, because of the extra work it introduces. This includes:

- Marshalling the data into and out of the queue format

- Handling business error situations, which can occur if, for instance, an order is not fulfilled

- Replication of data, such as catalogs

We must make sure that the extra work caused by queuing is not disproportionate to the benefits it brings the application. The error situations that can occur in a long-running transaction involving queuing can be complex to reverse.

Figure 11.6
Queuing in the database.

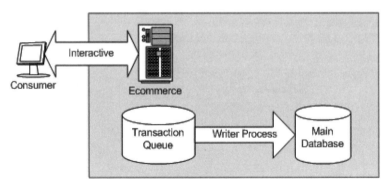

One form of queuing that is relatively easy to implement is to write changes into a staging table. This table is designed for fast writes; for instance, it may be a set of sequential rows with all transaction details in a row and no or only one index. The table could be in a separate database or on another machine. Then a writer program can apply the updates. A strategy like this is used by several enterprise applications, such as leading ERP products. By using the database for queuing, we do not need to acquire another piece of software and we can use a data format compatible with the final destination. The problem is latency, since the delay in the update might affect another transaction, and we need to take that into account in the design, possibly by checking the queued transactions when necessary. Figure 11.6 illustrates queuing in the database.

Queuing is a very good method for loosely coupled communication between applications. One obvious way to get queuing is to employ a "message queuing" product. While messaging can be implemented over a database, mail, HTTP POST, or FTP, message queue products can provide higher-level facilities including serialization, idempotency, and support for long-running transactions and transaction reversal. Proprietary products include IBM Message Queue Series, BEA, and Microsoft Message Queuing. There are several open source tools for messaging, including JBoss, and several Java Messaging Services (JMS) products, OSMQ and MOM4J are two open source products that implement JMS for open source languages in addition to Java.

11.3.3 Database Design

For large systems, we will need to optimize the database. I have spent several years in a consulting practice reviewing databases; our team was usually called in when the customer had decided to replace the database with another because of lack of performance. Our experience was that we could always get much more performance, often as much as an order of magnitude. The techniques to do this are as follows:

- Measure performance, isolate the problem areas to allow focus on the important areas, and use tools to see the actual database queries running.

- Review the application requirements and design against the database design. It is common for implementers of the application not to be aware of data volumes, and database administrators not to be familiar with application logic.

- Use database-specific optimizations, such as stored procedures, cursors, indexes, and prepared statements, correctly. In MySQL, this includes choosing the storage type.

- Find a clean way to pool database connections so that the pool is maintained, rather than continually connecting and dropping.

The next two figures show examples of high-performance database design. Figure 11.7, adapted from an account of the Travelocity system given at the MySQL conference, shows a travel reservation system that uses replication to uncouple pricing, which is higher in volume and lower in criticality, from ticketing. The system uses six HP NonStop 16-processor systems running Open System Services for ticketing and 45 HP 4-processor Itanium systems running Red Hat Enterprise Linux and MySQL for pricing. The application is written in C++ (GNU 3.2.3). Each MySQL system has a 50GB to 60GB database. The NonStop systems are the database master. Golden Gate Extractor is used to replicate data from the master to the pricing systems. This design allows complex processing to be performed on the more scalable systems.

Replication can be used to separate update transactions from read-only. Figure 11.8 shows a scheme modeled on Slashdot that works well for high-volume content management. Read access is a hundred to a thousand times the volume of write access, as on many Web sites. Updates are applied at one database and replicated to as many others as volume requires.

Storage Engines

MySQL offers several table types, which refer to different storage engines. The two most important are InnoDB and MyISAM. The MyISAM type has no transactions and is not good at handling mixed reads and writes, but

Figure 11.7
Travel reservation system.

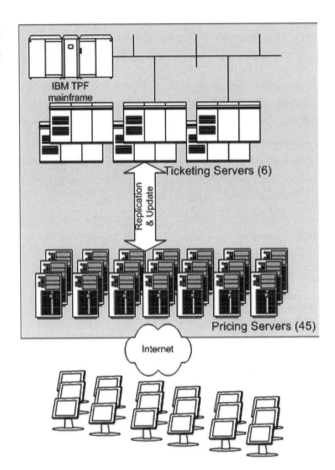

Figure 11.8
Replication with content management.

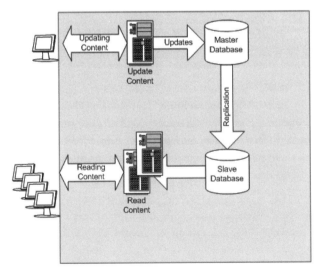

Figure 11.9
Combining MySQL storage engines.

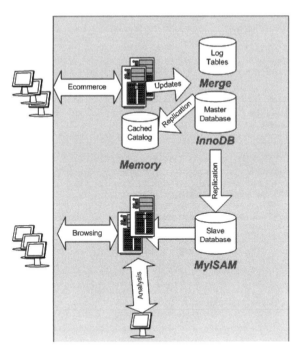

it is fast at writing or reading. The InnoDB type is best for normal mixed database activity. In Figure 11.8, we will most likely write to an InnoDB engine for transactions, and then replicate to MyISAM for text search and read speed.

Two other types are useful for specific purposes. The Memory type is fast but has no disk storage, so is appropriate for caching. We can copy translation tables, pricing, and other nonvolatile information into a cache to avoid database access. We can even cache transient state to allow quick access on subsequent visits in a session. The Merge type can be useful for logs, since it allows us to maintain a different physical file for each day or week of activity, yet combine them when needed. Figure 11.9 shows these four storage engines (table types) used together in a Web application.

11.3.4 Application Servers

Application servers provide a number of useful things. They provide transactions (this is the main point of EJB and COM+), including transaction composition, automatic failure handling, and two-phase commit. They allow us to split our application into parts, in some cases across languages and particularly across system boundaries. They perform the work of sharing some number of users across an arbitrary number of processes. They give us thread and process management in a language-independent manner while hiding the details. They manage resource pooling, such as database connections.

Remarkably, the best choice is often not to use these features. We should certainly not just assume that we are going to do it. If we stick to a single database, that will provide the transactions. For multiple databases, we will try to use a loosely coupled approach. We can use language-independent services on a single platform, but when operating over multiple platforms we will use shared database or Web services. Given a decision to build several loosely coupled connected systems, most applications should be developed in a single language.

The leading open source choice for an application server is JBoss. This is the most deployed Java application server among developers. At the time of writing, it rivals the closed code leaders in deployment. It was second in deployment to IBM WebSphere and ahead of BEA WebLogic.

11.4 Interoperability

A typical large organization has several distinct environments. Applications written to run on any of these platforms must be able to share information and interoperate with any of the others. So it is important to have a plan for interoperability between systems running different software on those different operating systems. These include:

- Microsoft Windows infrastructure with COM and/or .Net development
- IBM mainframes with COBOL, CICS, DB2, and possibly AS/400 systems, often with WebSphere
- Systems based on Java application servers, such as WebLogic or WebSphere, generally on UNIX or Linux
- Linux systems with LAMP applications

One would certainly expect that a system should be accessible to its owners, so that any information contained in it can be recovered with reasonable time and skills. In contrast, many companies feel that their data is "trapped inside" their legacy systems, unreachable except by an expensive project akin to archeology.

All of this, of course, can be greatly complicated by security issues. Obviously, applying security to a multivendor heterogeneous situation is very different from relying on a single vendor. So if you have the option of putting everything inside one vendor's protection, it can be considered. This is a very serious kind of lock-in because once all applications are in a common security perimeter, it will be hard to escape. Depending on the vendor, this could be very expensive and inflexible, and may not necessarily be very secure.

Strategies for interoperability can be placed under the broad headings of shared access to data, including file transfer and shared database, and process communication, including Web services. Whichever approach is chosen, if data formats are complex, as they generally are, there is a need for data sharing standards. These are usually structured around XML. The two preferred alternatives are shared database and Web services.

11.4.1 Shared Data

We can share data using a file system or a database. For knowledge management applications, we will often use file transfer or shared access to files. This can include FTP; network file sharing with Samba, NFS, or iFolders; or files sent as mail attachments. This is a good way to manage slowly changing data that is distributed from a central point. It can also be used to replicate databases in some circumstances. We can map a database into XML and send it as a file.

There are some basic problems of file sharing that must be addressed. Windows, Linux, and the Mac encode text files differently, and binary data is subject to platform variations. Network file shares are subject to more frequent and different types of error than local files.

This is a very difficult way to manage transactional data. If the data changes regularly, the file distribution becomes absurdly large and we must start looking at delta mechanisms. If the data is changed at multiple locations, we are managing multimaster replication, which is a hard problem. Even simple file drops need planning to deal with locking and event notification. Once we get past the simple cases, it becomes time for a database.

Shared Database

Shared database is the preferred way of doing cross-system interoperability. The database handles a range of data types, the network communication issues, and transactions and serialization.

Database replication is often a requirement. With homogeneous databases, this is commonly provided; MySQL and PostgreSQL both support replication as a database feature. We can also manage replication with scripting. For complex replication needs involving several heterogeneous databases, it is worth considering products such as Golden Gate.

11.4.2 Process Communication

Process communication generally involves development. It includes:

- TCP/IP socket programming
- Screen scraping
- Messaging
- Application integration engines
- Web services

Socket programming is a good mechanism for tightly coupled communication. It is not always as easy as one would wish, and there are data marshaling issues, but use of a high-level language such as Python and XML for encoding makes this reasonably simple. Network errors are difficult to handle.

Screen scraping is an unattractive technique that we fall back on if we have no access to an application. A variant of this is Web scraping. This is very vulnerable to changes in screen layouts. We would prefer to use Web services.

11.4.3 Application Integration Engines

The general-purpose integration engines such as WebMethods, BizTalk, and IBM WebSphere Integration Server can sound appealing. Integration engines offer an attractive interface, which demos well, and a long list of packages they can work with. But there are many issues with these packages that generally make them not worth the hassle. Several of these problems are similar to other "big picture" solutions, such as CASE tools and 4GLs, in the past.

The problems these tools address are more complex than they appear, so often the tool fails and has to be superseded with custom code for the harder problems. These tools are sold to bypass developers by using pretty GUIs and such, but they don't bypass developers (because the details really are complex). Developers don't like the pretty GUIs, because they lack support for versioning, backup, and often basics such as scalable diagrams. In any case, good developers like to work with a standard set of tools. This is a different tool, typically quite difficult to learn to use well, and since it is for a very specialized function most developers don't learn it well. Integration of this type of tool is, ironically, not particularly easy.

These tools are expensive, so there is often pressure to use them in several projects to amortize the cost. There may not always be a good fit. In practice, most people write their own solutions for application integration. At any time, most people have a point-to-point integration need, which can usually be addressed with a program in a scripting language such as Python.

Two cases from personal experience, one involving WebMethods, the other using BizTalk Server, illustrate problems with integration engines. One example is a hospitality organization hosting many different retailers within the resort. These stores needed to exchange transaction data with the resort. Originally we had planned to slightly extend a TCP/IP socket protocol that was in place. Bringing in an integration engine changed a two-month project into a six-month one, increasing costs proportionately; delayed the start by a further six months while waiting for the initial engine deployment; and worsened performance by a factor of ten.

The second example is a distribution company that used an integration engine to manage sales of product at many hundreds of "stores within stores" at dozens of retailers with different reporting formats. Unfortunately, performance was slow because of the large amount of reformatting needed by the engine, as things went in and out of XML. Customization was difficult; it turned out that requirements of the most important partners were too complex for the integration engine, and custom code was needed to manage many parts of the process. That code jumped through such hoops to work with the engine that it was more complex than if the problem had just been solved by custom code.

Once again, the most general solution to this problem is Web services.

11.4.4 Web Services

Web services offer a standard method of communication that is independent of language and platform. Using Web services, we can make a call to another system regardless of the platform on which it runs. The data is marshaled and tagged in XML, and the call is made across platform and operating system. As Figure 11.10 illustrates, we can use Web services to achieve interoperability between WebSphere, .Net, and LAMP applications. This

Figure 11.10
Web services.

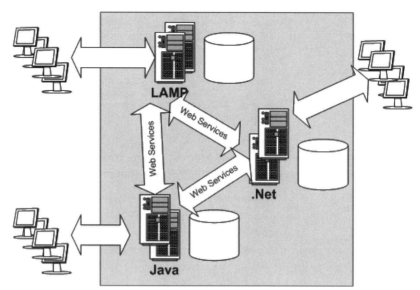

can be achieved at quite small levels of granularity, such as a function call, or large levels, such as a file of purchase orders.

Web services can be asynchronous or synchronous. Asynchronous calls allow for loosely coupled systems, particularly combined with document-style XML to allow transfer of large quantities of related data.

The simplest form of Web service is XML-RPC. XML-RPC may be the best choice for internal use and rapid development. SOAP is a more elaborate standard, with more features and choices. SOAP is more likely to be used for industry standards or interbusiness communication. All of the open source languages have good support for Web services.

For simple communication, replacing socket programming and screen scraping, particularly in internal applications, Web services work very well. It is still difficult to use them for interbusiness development. Many of the standards at higher levels are not really ready yet. Encryption, standards for interorganization communication, and security all have to be addressed.

To solve the integration engine scenarios using Web services, we develop our own code to address the specific problem or problems we are facing, using XML and queuing if appropriate. If the problem is somewhat generalized, such as many customers or vendors, we develop a general solution to the problem on a hub and spoke basis. It is very unusual for such a solution to be more expensive and difficult than using the integration engine, and, of course, it will use the standard development tools and database of our

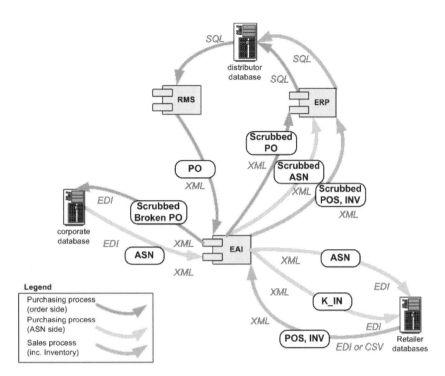

Figure 11.11
*Distribution
example.*

organization. Figure 11.11 shows the previous distribution company example. The relationship between the three entities (distributor, corporate, and retail) is loosely coupled using XML files passed variously by mail and file transfer (FTP). The XML schemata differ for different documents (purchase orders, invoices), as we might expect, and also, unfortunately, for different retailers. The largest challenge, as often in long-running transactional systems, is tying related documents together. We rely on lookup against the ERP system to do this.

11.4.5 Data Formats

The problem of data marshaling, which is an issue for most of the interoperability techniques, occurs at several levels. At the lowest level is the issue of character representation: encoding (such as Unicode), line endings (carriage return and/or line feed), and byte order (big endian or little endian). At the next level, we need a system for tagging field names, then for data typing, and then to manage linkages between fields to support hierarchical representations. Above this are semantic issues, such as agreement on the content and relationships of fields. Shared database solves many of these directly, but more complex relationships still need to be mapped to XML.

For loosely coupled interoperability, the minimum we need is self-describing data, which is typed and represents correctly on each platform. XML does this very well. For many purposes, we can use a simple one-level XML generated from flat files, which is easily done with a Python or Perl script and involves no overhead. In any case, the open source languages support powerful XML parsers. Different systems will use different schemata, but as long as we can identify fields, we can transform them from one XML schema to another.

There are excellent XML parsers and libraries available for all the open source languages—notably, Perl, Python, and Java.

11.5   Development Platform Choices

For corporate development today, the choice generally comes down to one of the following:

- Java, including Java Server Pages (JSP) and/or Java application servers such as WebSphere, WebLogic, and JBoss
- Microsoft .Net, including C# or Visual Basic with ASP and the CLR run-time environment
- LAMP (Linux-Apache-MySQL-PHP)

Any of these approaches can be used for rapid development of simple applications and then scaled up where necessary, at some trouble and cost, to produce large architected solutions that meet complex requirements with high performance. All of these can be developed to run on various servers, including Windows and Linux. All are cross-platform at the client if developed as Web applications and tested correctly, and all can create client/server cross-platform code under the right circumstances. We'll compare them in some detail.

11.5.1   Java

We can build simple applications with JSP (Java Server Pages), which is how most Java applications are done. We can build complex applications with a Java application server using a framework such as Struts.

The leading open source choice for Java Server Pages is Jakarta Tomcat. Application servers include JBoss, the leading open source application server, or one of the closed code application servers:

- IBM WebSphere
- BEA WebLogic
- Oracle Application Server
- SUN ONE

The products from IBM, BEA, and JBoss are the leading choices of large corporations. The closed code application server development environments are typically very expensive. JBoss apparently has about a 25 percent share of production systems, although closer to 50 percent share among developers (many of whom are individuals).

JSP and Java applications are cross-platform across Linux, Windows, UNIX, and other servers, as well as across clients, including Windows, Mac, Linux, and others, if developed and tested correctly.

Pure Java Server Page applications are pretty portable. Unfortunately, applications that use the vendor application server environments such as WebLogic and WebSphere are difficult to move between vendors, since these environments are integrated with proprietary vendor tools and services. My experience is that companies find this too difficult, and often finish up with more than one of these application servers supporting different applications. Roger Sessions, of the newsletter *ObjectWatch*, quotes the IBM publication "Migrating WebLogic Applications to WebSphere V5," available at www.redbooks.ibm.com, as taking 260 pages to describe how to do this move.

The main strength of the Java approach is its cross platform, which is excellent. These systems can be scaled for high performance, albeit at a high price. The weaknesses of the Java approach are cost and difficulty of development. While the majority of Java systems have been developed using JSP, and probably could have been done with open source approaches, most organizations have used expensive tools to do it.

The ability of large systems built as recommended using application servers to scale economically is very questionable. All the benchmark evidence is that large Java systems are significantly less efficient than alternatives developed in C++ or .Net. A few years ago, there was a year-long debate over a "Java Pet Shop," which Sun had published to show how to build a Java application. The story demonstrated, in a nutshell, that vendors are not recommending or selling the same architecture to the enterprise that they use themselves for performance or internal applications. In any case, at some point as the application scales, large vendors that support this option will predict failure unless you move to their closed code tool sets.

The best bet for this approach would be to use Java Server Pages and the open source product Tomcat. If an application server is needed, we can use JBoss.

11.5.2   .Net

With this approach, we can build simple applications with ASP.Net using C# or VB. We can build complex applications using tiers, with COM+ as the application server and SQL stored procedures.

Many dot-net development tools are available from Microsoft and third-party tool vendors for the Microsoft platform; of course, most developers will use Visual Studio.

Dot-net is noticeably less expensive than a full Enterprise Java solution. In fact, ASP.Net is arguably free with Windows 2003 Server if you can forgo the Visual Studio development environment and use a programming editor instead.

Dot-net applications are not necessarily confined to the Windows platform. They can be deployed cross-platform using Mono or DotGNU. The Mono project allows .Net applications written in C# to run on Linux systems, although typically Mono developers now recommend building on Visual Studio and porting to other platforms. The language and many classes have been submitted to a standards body. It is planned to extend this to VB as a source language and to OS X as a target platform. Mono is a project of the Novell division Ximian and has a heavy-duty development team behind it. They are motivated because they want to move their code base (e.g., Gnome) from C to an object-oriented type-safe language, so we can expect that this will happen. Since Mono can support the Gnome code, it should be robust and high-performance enough for just about anything. It still seems unlikely to me that in the next few years C# adoption will catch up to Java, let alone pass it, outside of the Windows closed code area. Mono is beta in at the time of writing, so it will be some time before it is in general production use.

The strengths of the .Net approach are scale, cost, and ease of development. The weakness of the .Net approach is that it is not cross-platform—at least until the Mono project is more widely used. It is true that development for the Web allows cross-platform applications, but even here there is a bias in the documentation toward closed systems, such as recommending use of client-side COM, Office, and IE-specific browser features.

The best bet for .Net is to use C#, but it is not an open source language and is not going to be chosen for cross-platform development yet.

11.5.3 LAMP

Using this approach, we can build simple applications with PHP, Perl, or Python. We can build complex applications in the traditional way for open source software, tiered with a scripting language in front and C/C++ server and library elements as necessary, or we can use the JBoss application server. All of these systems are cross-platform at the client if developed as Web applications and tested correctly.

LAMP applications are cross-platform across Linux, Windows, UNIX, and other servers, as well as across clients, including Windows, Mac, Linux, and others, if developed and tested correctly.

The strengths of the LAMP approach are cost, cross-platform capability, and ease of development. The potential weakness of the LAMP approach is complexity growing with scale.

Successful LAMP implementations include many small to medium systems, which have been developed simply, and some very large ones, including Amazon, Sabre, and Slashdot. As discussed earlier, some very large applications will need to have some seriously competent C++ programmers available.

Open source languages such as Python typically compile to an intermediate code, similar to VB and Java, and as a result Python code can be slower than C. When this matters, individual Python classes can be recoded in C without alteration in the calling code. The Python variant Jython runs on Java and is free to call Java classes directly. So just as VB programmers in Windows can call VC++ components, Python programmers using Jython can call Java components. This is a great cross-platform tool, and it also means that Python can access Java components such as Lucene and JBoss. Integration with Java applications can be done using Jython.

The best bet here is to deploy with LAMP as the default choice. For very large systems, we will architect carefully and be prepared to substitute components for the highest scale or to interoperate with other enterprise systems.

Migrating Microsoft Developers to Open Source

The majority of programmers today are not working in Java, .Net, or LAMP. Surveys of programmers on all platforms find that most people who identify themselves as programmers do most of their work in Visual BASIC (VB).

Microsoft documents of the last ten years, from the DNA era on, have generally advocated development through "components," which would be assembled through scripting into custom solutions for business. This has usually meant, in practice, VB. VB has been the most widely used language in the world practically since its introduction, when it supplanted plain old BASIC. It is easy to learn, supports interactive development, batch, and Web development, and has the support of a healthy market in third-party components. It has lagged in performance, but the components, usually written in C, could be as fast as necessary, and recent versions perform well.

For Web development, most Microsoft shops use Active Server Pages (ASP). ASP, as with JSP and PHP, is a mixture of HTML, with scripting for "quick and dirty" development. For batch development, most Windows organizations use Windows Scripting Host (WSH). ASP and WSH are used with VBScript. Data Transformation Services (DTS), a graphical scripting tool for data management, also employ VBScript. Most programmers in Windows are familiar with Visual BASIC, and most applications in the Microsoft environment involve a version of Visual BASIC. In the .Net component architecture, the language can as well be C# as Visual BASIC, and Microsoft would probably prefer that but my experience is that in corporate America, the migration, such as it is, is to VB.Net. VB is changed significantly by VB.Net and may change again in a few years when Longhorn is introduced. ASP.Net allows and encourages a strict separation between code and markup language, particularly using Visual Studio. ASP.Net supports the VB.Net and C# languages, with books and documentation providing examples in both. In the long run, .Net improves the story greatly for the Microsoft developer, but for now, the main effect is to add VB.Net to the several VB flavors that must be handled.

What Should Visual BASIC Programmers Do?

Visual BASIC runs only on the Microsoft Windows platform. The question for the majority of programmers in a world where open source plays a larger part is what language will play the role played by VB in Windows? There is no realistic chance of a cross-platform Visual BASIC. Other versions of BASIC exist, but are little used in comparison to Visual BASIC and are incompatible. The Mono project plans a port of VB.Net to Linux, but this is not yet available, applies only to VB.Net, and is unlikely to ever have much share on that platform. The Mono project's primary goal is the porting of C#, and programmers who are interested should learn C#. There is plenty of time to become proficient in C# before Mono is production ready.

How can a developer escape lock-in to the Windows platform while using a single language to develop applications that are graphical, batch, or Web based? The language should be relatively easy to learn and able to be extended to cover almost any type of development problem.

VB programmers or their managers (whoever makes the language decision) have already had the opportunity on Windows to consider C++, Java, and C#, and they have, for whatever reasons, chosen VB instead. Of course, given a stronger need for cross-platform development, they could revisit that choice. If they did not choose to be Visual C++ programmers, they are not particularly likely to become GNU C++ programmers either (although the free-structured nature of the open source community will make this choice possible for a few).

Java is a good choice—one that frees VB programmers from their single platform and limited engineering—but again it is not the only or even the most obvious choice, since they could have made it years ago (e.g., Visual J++.) If they are predominantly Web developers (ASP), they will probably be comfortable with JSP, and that is a possibility.

VB programmers should consider the open source languages PHP, Perl, and Python. Web developers should look first to PHP, which is the most used Web development language, doubling in use every 18 months. Perl is an interesting choice for individuals with an administrative bent, who may have used VB to manage Exchange or BizTalk or to perform database imports or WSH scripting (of course, they might have already used Perl on Windows).

The one language that is the most effective way to get an open source application shipped, whether it is Web, GUI, or script, is Python. I argue that for VB programmers the language of the next few years is Python. Python has the good features of Visual BASIC (and some of its own) without most of the drawbacks.

Python is an easy language to learn. It can be used for GUI, script, or Web-based development. Everyone comments on its one idiosyncratic point of syntax: the significance of white space; after that, it is pretty much common sense. The Python language is similar to VB in the availability of components (class libraries) that can do just about anything. They are generally written in C for best performance, and, unlike VB, they are almost all free (no charge and source code available). Many of the most useful come with the standard distribution. So, as with VB, Python is a language where the general developer starts by finding and using classes rather than by defining and building them.

Python runs on Windows, Linux, and the Mac; simple self-installing binary packages are available for these platforms. Most Linux distributions (e.g., Red Hat and SuSE) include Python installed, as does Mac OS X 10.3. It also runs on any UNIX system and some others; less common platforms may need a source code install.

The Windows version of Python is very powerful and a good place for a Windows professional to start. It is easily downloaded (e.g., from www.python.org); that download is self-installing and ready to go for most purposes. There has been serious thought given to cross-platform compatibility, and it is a simple matter to develop code on, for example, Windows that will run on Linux and the Mac (this book contains an example).

11.6   Summary

If we are interested in performance, the first rule is to get the basic architectural choices right, using multiple commodity systems for price/performance, loose coupling using queuing to control peaks and failures, managing resources carefully, and with database tuning using the specific features of the available engines.

We can build open source applications with the three major architectures, and many larger organizations will do this. If we want to choose .Net, we can set up a Visual Studio.Net development environment and a Mono (or DotGNU) development environment and build ASP.Net applications with C#. If we want to choose Java, we can set up Jakarta Tomcat with JDBC and our chosen database and build JSP applications. If we move to an application server, we can use the open source product JBoss.

LAMP is a good choice for many applications even if you plan to use Java or .Net for others. There are several ways to ensure interoperability, including shared databases and Web services. LAMP applications can be scaled and are inexpensive to deploy. The majority of business systems, with databases of tens of gigabytes and hundreds of requests per second, suit the LAMP approach very well, and the systems can be scaled up if necessary.

The development environments, debuggers, and tools are powerful. Apache is the most used Web server and PHP the most used Web development language, so you are not sticking your neck out.

12

The Cost of Open Source Systems

Of course, it is not difficult to price open source software products, since they are almost all free. The difficulty comes when we move past this to do these more difficult things:

- Price comparable closed code products.
- Price all associated costs, including hardware, staffing, and support costs, to derive a total cost of ownership (TCO).

In this chapter, we will compare open source software prices with similar closed code software. Of course, there are not always similar products and where there are, we may have a preference for one feature set over another. In this chapter, we will only compare costs.

Then we will examine the total cost of ownership of open source and closed code products and compare those. To do this, we will take some scenarios for businesses of different sizes. The estimates for hardware and staffing are kept very simple, and you are invited to substitute your own numbers.

Because so many factors differ, this is only a framework, which will need to be adjusted for a particular organization. The tables here are available at the Web site *www.kavana.org/opensource* for download if you would like to adjust them for your own situation. Figure 12.1 illustrates the major cost elements, which are staffing, hardware, and software, usually in that order.

We will review these costs by category, and then put the per unit prices into simple tables. We can use these tables as the cost basis for some typical scenarios. In all cases, we should substitute our local information into this table, since our prices may vary.

Figure 12.1
Cost elements.

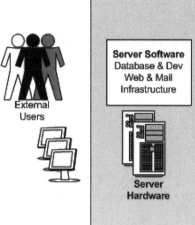
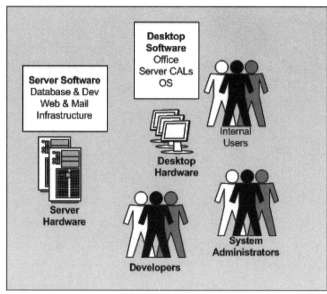

12.1   Total Cost of Ownership

There is a simple answer to the question of open source software costs, where open source solutions are comparable to closed code alternatives. When compared with similar closed code systems, open source systems as a general rule cost:

- Much less for software

- No more and often less for hardware

- If other things are equal, no more for anything else

As far as software costs are concerned, we will review tables with the prices for common open source and closed code products, and see that open source software costs much less.

As far as hardware is concerned, open source products are available for effectively all current hardware platforms, including the systems with the best price/performance. Open source performance on a platform is usually similar to closed code competitors, as already discussed throughout this book. So hardware for open source software generally costs the same as for the least expensive system for closed code. In most cases, we are comparing the same hardware running Windows or UNIX on the one hand versus Linux on the other.

Other things may not be equal and total cost of ownership (TCO) studies offer an opportunity to show that. There are many forms of these, and there is a small industry that compares and contrasts TCO versus ROI versus various other terms. Here, we will keep this simple and use TCO to include the other costs involved over a reasonable period of time when making a software decision.

The issue usually comes down to staffing costs. There are some published TCO studies that attempt to show that open source software costs more than you think, or that hardware costs more for Linux in some specific situation, but they are from obviously biased sources and are not really credible. The three big cost elements of TCO are staffing, hardware, and software. Of these, staffing dwarfs the others in all the scenarios we will look at. Because of the dominance of staffing costs, even where open source software saves millions, this will not represent a particularly large percentage difference in TCO. However, software may be the only controllable cost. In these cases, TCO can obscure the real savings by adding large costs, which are effectively fixed, such as system administration and support, to both sides of a comparison.

12.1.1 Staffing Costs

Personnel costs dominate software costs for infrastructure. Because of this, the savings from open source software such as Linux and MySQL will be small compared with the costs of personnel for development and management.

An IDC report on Windows and Linux infrastructure costs estimates the TCO cost breakdown for infrastructure, as shown in Figure 12.2.

This may understate software costs, but it is broadly consistent with work by Gartner on IT costs, which again shows staffing and downtime as the major costs for infrastructure. So for IT infrastructure systems, the impact of a system on system administration and end users can be ten times more important than its purchase cost. This indicates how inexpensive IT infrastructure is today measured at the server. Desktop costs alter this substantially, as we will see later.

Application solutions can be much more expensive. Large applications can incur millions of dollars in costs for software acquisition or development, as well as large server hardware costs, particularly for database sys-

Figure 12.2
TCO elements for infrastructure.

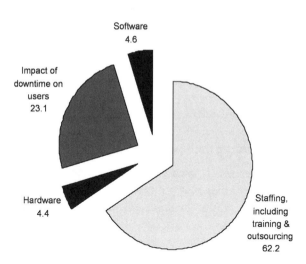

tems. Even for simple Web applications, hardware and software are higher than for infrastructure.

Table 12.1 has a simple estimate of resource prices for developers and system administrators. The costs are loaded, including salary, vacation, management overhead, general training, taxes, and benefits. They are averaged, with no effort to distinguish between skill levels. There is also an entry representing a week of training. Many projects require training of a week or two for developers and administrators.

Support costs are difficult to calculate, because there are so many different options. For mission-critical systems, an organization will want to contract with the system developers to ensure coverage whenever there is a system problem. For desktop systems and infrastructure, it is usually enough to maintain competent staff and solve the issues in house. A support contract with a software vendor such as Microsoft Product Support Services, providing a full-time equivalent, costs upward of $250,000. Contracts involving a named contact and some number of incidents might start

Table 12.1   *Staffing Costs*

Item	Cost	Per	Details/Comments
Developer	$95,000	Year	Loaded cost
Sysadmin	$75,000	Year	Loaded cost
Training	$10,000	Week	Including class, travel, and expenses

→
Table 12.2 *Hardware Costs*

Item	Cost	Per	Details/Comments
Big 4-processor box	$25,000	Server	HP DL745 4-processor 2gig RAM
Medium box	$12,000	Server	Dell 2650 2-processor
Small box	$4,000	Server	Dell 1750 2-processor
SAN, shared disks	$80,000	Project	Dell/EMC

at around $50,000 annually. Similar contracts can be struck for open source software products. They are likely to cost much less (a third or a quarter as much) and will be structured less formally.

12.1.2 Hardware Costs

Hardware costs include servers, clients, networking equipment, and other appliances such as firewalls. Hardware costs are generally about the same between Windows and Linux, unless there is some unusual performance issue causing a difference. Usually, the same hardware can be used at all levels. Before the recent releases of the Linux 2.6 kernel or some specialized late 2.4 kernels, such as Red Hat Enterprise Linux 3, Linux threading was slower than the hardware allowed, and this had a negative effect on database and application server measures.

Table 12.2 includes estimates for hardware. Most organizations will use a few standard boxes so that service parts can be stockpiled and one set of trained users can maintain all the systems. I have used commodity systems of the type commonly used for Windows and Linux. Most systems can be put together with these components. There are, of course, much more expensive servers available for specialized purposes.

12.1.3 Software Costs

The closed code comparative software prices that follow are given for Microsoft. The major vendors track each other's pricing and Microsoft's pricing is more transparent than other larger vendors. In my experience, Microsoft is very rarely more expensive for the same class of product than IBM or Oracle, and its pricing is relatively stable, easy to get, and easy to work with.

Microsoft server prices are discounted for volume purchasing. This can reduce prices by 25 percent for a large organization, more in some cases.

Microsoft server products are licensed by processor or by client access licenses (CALs). This is usually decided by the product, but SQL Server allows you to license either way. If you have a two-processor machine supporting 70 users, you could license per processor for $10,000 ($5,000 per processor) or per CAL for $10,110 ($1,500 plus $123 × 70). This is the practical cutoff; for more than 70 users, you would pick the unlimited per processor license. Considering that even a small two-processor system would be expected to support more than 70 users, and this method removes licensing hassles of the CAL mode, this will be the way most people will license.

Infrastructure Software

In this category, we will include the operating system and any essential tools for networking and system management. There is a variety of good open source administration tools available. Windows includes directory, file, and print services; simple routing; and a Web server, so we will count them in also. In Windows environments, firewall and proxy services (ISA) and mail (Exchange) are additional products, and we will factor that into the costs since organizations generally need those services. There is a simple mail server included with Windows Server, but this is not usually used for enterprise mail.

The majority of Windows customers do not use the more expensive server products such as BizTalk Server, Content Management Server, Sharepoint Portal Server, or Commerce Server. These products cost from $10,000 to $40,000 per processor. Competitors such as WebTrends, Vignette, Plumtree Portal, or Blue Martini are even more expensive. We will do one comparison using these types of products for completeness.

Open source software will generally be less expensive. In addition, license tracking is wholly or partially eliminated. For Windows, client access licenses (CALs) must be counted for all these, including directory access. Client access licenses are generally the largest software cost element.

Database and Development Software

In a Windows environment, this usually includes SQL Server and Visual Studio as items of additional cost. Other development tools, such as the IIS Web server, the .Net development framework, application server components, and Active Server Pages, are included with Windows Server.

In an open source environment, we will take this to include MySQL, Apache, and PHP, and in some cases JBoss and Tomcat. These products generally ship with and always install on popular enterprise Linux choices, such as Red Hat and SuSE. MySQL has a small license fee in a commercial environment, and JBoss has a support charge; we will include those where appropriate.

Many organizations will use Oracle or DB2 as the database. These typically cost as much or more than SQL Server.

12.1.4 Using Third-Party Application and Database Servers

In both the open source and Windows environments, there are many alternative choices of third-party tools and database servers. Popular choices include:

- Oracle or IBM DB2 database servers
- IBM WebSphere, BEA WebLogic, or Oracle application servers
- Tools for modeling, debugging, code management, and so on, such as Rational and ClearCase

These products have the same performance and functionality and are about the same price in either environment. People who choose these products generally choose them at least partly for this ability to offer the same experience across the Windows and Linux platforms; they do not see the Windows-only tools as equivalents.

These products are very expensive in comparison with open source software or Windows development software. In 2003, for example, IBM was listing the following prices:

WebSphere Advanced Server	$11,400 per processor
WebSphere MQ	$5,000 per processor
WebSphere Interchange Server	$123,000 per processor

Counting the necessary maintenance and support contract, the three-year price is twice that quoted. So the list price to put WebSphere on a couple of four-processor servers to perform a typical complex Web application with components and queuing will cost $32,800 × 8, which is $262,400, not including any database. There are several warnings to consider with this price; there are lighter, less expensive versions of WebSphere that will work for many situations, these prices are subject to discount, and may have changed since the time of writing.

The effect on cost calculations of including these products is to add a fixed (large) element to each side of the comparison, damping the overall difference. Of course, if you add these products to one side of the comparison only, their cost will determine the outcome, but your comparison will be of very limited value.

12.1.5   Pricing Open Source Software

Table 12.3 lists the prices of commonly used open source software products. Note that you can always distribute an open source software product, so you only need to buy a single copy to get documentation and CDs. The two exceptions here are MySQL, which is sold under a commercial license priced per server, and Red Hat Enterprise Linux, which is only sold including support, so that is also priced per server.

All prices for open source software are per system. Note that the Red Hat Linux product prices include support. The MySQL database is dual licensed, with a commercial license price of $500 per server, or is available as free software under the GPL; we included it as $500.

Table 12.3   *Open Source Software Prices*

Product	Price	Function
Server Software		
Fedora Core	$0	Server OS
Debian GNU/Linux	$0	Server OS
Red Hat WS Standard	$300	Server OS
SuSE Standard Server	$450	Server OS
Red Hat Enterprise Linux AS	$1,500	Server OS
SuSE Enterprise Server	$1,000	Server OS
Squid and iptables	$0	Proxy and caching
OpenLDAP	$0	Directory
Samba	$0	File and print sharing
MySQL Commercial	$500	Database

Table 12.3 *Open Source Software Prices (continued)*

Product	Price	Function
PostgreSQL	$0	Database
Postfix, Horde, Courier	$0	Mail server
JBoss	$0	Application server
Client Software		
Eclipse (or alternatives)	$0	IDE
OpenOffice.org	$0	Office suite
Dia	$0	Diagramming
GIMP	$0	Image editing
Fedora Core	$0	Desktop OS
SuSE Professional	$0	Desktop OS
Debian GNU/Linux	$0	Desktop OS

12.1.6 Pricing Closed Code Software

It is difficult to fully determine closed code software costs for several reasons. Not all systems have a published price list, and the lists that exist are incomplete. Products are often offered with very different prices to different customers, and even different pricing models. Most companies offer substantial discounts, which are not published, to large customers. Some products are only available through personal contact and quotation from a salesperson. Prices can change substantially overnight, such as Oracle database prices, which went down with the release of 10*g*. Complex products such as WebSphere have many components and several different pricing models. Deals can be made, particularly if vendors know they are in competition with lower-priced products.

Although it is not possible to predict the precise number that a vendor will quote to a particular customer, we can get a good estimate of the selling price for that class of customer. For example, I have quotes received in recent consulting engagements, or shared with me by customers, and all companies provide pricing examples for their published benchmarks and comparisons.

When we calculate prices in detail, many things can raise prices above the initial expectation. Two examples are add-on products and software maintenance. These costs are usually higher for closed code. Software maintenance is commonly 25 percent of the purchase price annually.

12.1.7 Pricing Windows Software

Microsoft has a published price list, so we can work with those numbers. Table 12.4 lists prices of Windows software. It is often a good practice to compare list prices, since discounts are unpublished and can vary considerably. Although list price comparison usually tends to be roughly fair, it is not fair when comparing open source with closed code. Closed code software has higher prices and is often discounted considerably, so ignoring discounts will tend to overcount the price of the closed code. I have used list prices in Table 12.4, because that is what is available publicly. Large organizations should often be able to get substantial discounts—for instance, 25 percent less than these prices.

Table 12.4 *Windows Software Prices*

Item	Cost	Per	CAL	Details/Comments
Server Software (unlimited clients)				
Windows Server Web	$400	Server	—	Windows maintenance 25% annual
ISA Standard	$1,500	Processor	—	—
SQL Server Standard	$5,000	Processor	—	Up to 4 processors, 2GB RAM
SQL Server Enterprise	$20,000	Processor	—	Clustering, 64GB RAM
BizTalk Server Enterprise	$25,000	Processor	—	BizTalk Standard is not practical
Server Software (per computer with CALs)				
Windows Server Standard	$800	Server	$25	Windows maintenance 25% annual
Windows Server Enterprise	$3,300	Server	$25	Windows maintenance 25% annual
Exchange Standard	$1,300	Server	$67	—
Exchange Enterprise	$7,000	Server	$67	—
SQL Standard	$1,500	Server	$123	SQL is licensed by CAL or processor

Table 12.4 *Windows Software Prices (continued)*

Item	Cost	Per	CAL	Details/Comments
SQL Enterprise	$11,000	Server	$123	—
Client Software				
Visual Studio Professional	$1,080	Desktop	—	$2,500 for MSDN Universal
Office Standard	$500	Desktop	—	$600 for Professional (Access, XML)
Visio Standard	$200	Desktop	—	—
Adobe PhotoShop	$600	Desktop	—	—
Windows XP Professional	$300	Desktop	—	—

The column titled Per in the table shows how the product is priced. Microsoft prices its products either per processor or per server with client access licenses (CALs). The CAL column shows the per user price for products priced in that manner. Other companies may have other licensing systems, but per processor licensing is the most common for large servers. Per user pricing is less common for servers but is often a way of offering low prices to small organizations.

This table only lists Microsoft prices, because they are more generally available. Commercial prices for comparable products from other vendors, such as IBM, Sun, and Oracle, are usually similar or more expensive. We can start from the spreadsheets here and feed in our own situation for quoted prices and numbers of systems and users.

12.2 Types of Costs

We must take into account several cost factors that weigh heavily, including fixed, off-budget, sunk, and switching costs. In a direct comparison of two new systems, where things are equal, open source software will be less expensive in almost every case. But often the comparison is in some sense a migration, where there will be a big advantage to the incumbent, most likely Windows today. This is what most TCO studies comparing proprietary software against open source actually do. In a migration, assumptions favoring the incumbent product will increase staffing costs and probably dominate the software savings. There are even some incumbent advantages to Windows in a new installation situation, at least perceived. Decision makers may be unfamiliar with open source and inclined to assign higher risks or expect to pay more for services.

12.2.1 Fixed Costs

IT and higher management costs above the level of project management are a given and will not vary based on project activities.

Network and desktop infrastructure, including firewalls, storage area networks, and personal computers, can be treated as a fixed cost when looking at applications in most contemporary organizations. If we are funding a project that brings technology to a new population, we will have to consider these costs in the project, but they will in any case be the same for open source or closed code.

12.2.2 Off-Budget Costs

End-user costs, including training, possible downtime or dissatisfaction, and self-supporting ("messing around"), can be important, and some cost models show these costs as the highest single cost component. However, they are not usually reported as costs by IT organizations, because they are not on the budget.

The effect on users may sometimes be reflected in penalties related to a service-level agreement, but more commonly as a constraint on the IT organization, which must maintain a particular level of service. The effect of off-budget costs, when included, is to make estimates of user downtime and dissatisfaction the largest elements of the cost models, although these are very difficult to measure objectively.

These elements are not included in the models here. Instead it is assumed that the systems being compared will offer equivalent availability and ease of use. This is very likely to be true for server systems, which run on the same hardware and are not directly visible to the end user. It is less easy to demonstrate for desktop systems, and may be a factor to consider. Presumably, organizations that do not find desktop systems equivalent in this regard will not deploy them regardless of cost savings.

12.2.3 Sunk Costs

Sunk costs are the costs already spent on existing systems and are not recoverable. It is difficult to get money for old systems, particularly after the dot-com bubble; many systems that are a couple of years old are only worth about ten cents on the dollar on the hardware, as a quick search on eBay will reveal. Software and support costs and other soft costs, such as training, can add up to much more than hardware and they will never be recovered.

The effect of sunk costs is to make it much more difficult to move to new technology, because the acquisition cost of the new system is compared with the residual value of the existing system, which is much less than it cost.

12.2.4 Switching Costs

Switching costs are the additional costs it will take to move from an existing system to a proposed new one, as opposed to keeping the existing one. The effect of switching costs is to make new technology harder to adopt. The first application with a new technology will cost more than subsequent ones, because of training of developers and administrators, who presumably know the old technology, and because of first purchase of servers, development tools, and other infrastructure that will be reused for future applications. If there were a single standard before, then adding the new technology also leads to having to support two technologies, which may lead to additional cost.

Sunk costs are similar to a switching cost in effect, since they make existing systems and skills appear less expensive than they would be if acquired now. However, existing systems still have costs, since equipment has to be maintained, software upgraded, and new staff trained. Often, after a period of time, an existing system must undergo a migration of its own, and this is the best time to consider a switch.

Staffing is usually the highest cost in a TCO calculation, and the effect on staffing costs of a migration will usually be to increase them. IT staff will need to be retrained or rehired, possibly with expensive training. If there are end users, they also need to be retrained. They also may have satisfaction or quality issues in the transition. Of course, these are generally off-budget costs, but they may need to be included as a one-time cost when part of a conversion project.

If we look each year at our existing system, the switching costs will always be there. Because they effectively raise the price of the alternative, they act as a premium to the vendor of the existing solution. Any charge less than the switching cost is not sufficient to cause the switch. Although a switching cost is a one-time charge, this "vendor premium," which the cost makes possible, can be applied every year, as shown in Figure 12.3. In this

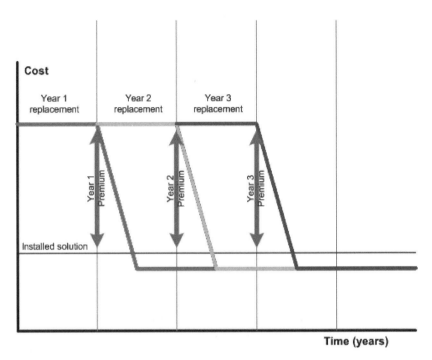

Figure 12.3
*Switching costs and
vendor premium.*

diagram, the cost of a replacement in year 1 is high because of switching costs; the replacement would be lower in subsequent years. If the migration is not done, the same situation recurs in year 2 and subsequent years.

Vendors are well aware of this situation, as evidenced in this quote from Aaron Contorer of Microsoft in an email to Bill Gates in 1997, quoted by the European Commission 2004:

> There is a huge switching cost to using a different operating system. . . . It is this switching cost that has given customers the patience to stick with Windows through all our mistakes, our buggy drivers, our high TCO, our lack of a sexy version at times. . . . It would be so much work to move over that they hope we just improve Windows rather than force them to move.

It is the nature of vendors to attempt to hold us captive, whether it is Microsoft, IBM, SAP, or Oracle. Our best defense is flexibility, avoiding lock-in by preserving our ability to choose. Flexibility manages risk, because it allows the possibility to use another technology or platform. Lock-in is also a cost now because of the vendor premium and later when we'll have to move anyway.

Of course, this premium is not literally charged but is an opportunity for additional costs or unsatisfactory quality or service to pass. Software maintenance charges are an example of this.

12.3 Scenarios

The following examples illustrate two companies with greatly varying numbers of internal desktops: 50 and 15,000. They have different scenarios of internal and external applications that represent different issues. We will calculate likely costs for infrastructure, development, and application products separately and then sum them. Costs will include hardware (expected to last three years), software purchase, software maintenance (typically 25 percent of the purchase cost per year), development (one-time), management (for the three years), and any switching costs (one-time).

Cost savings generally need to be produced in two years or less to justify the return on investment (ROI) of a project. Longer time frames are riskier because the project may outlast the personalities and circumstances that justified it and the technologies deployed may be surpassed. Small projects should probably produce payback in under a year. However, systems are deployed for longer than this. Hardware generally survives for three years, at which point it has little residual value. Benefits are harder to calculate than costs and many tend to be vague, such as "better communications" or "improved productivity." Some benefits of a project should be tangible; a rule of thumb is that if we take a real objective away, the project should differ in scope.

In these cases, we will use an assumed life of three years, include a one-time development cost in the first year, and ignore switching costs by assuming a new installation.

12.3.1 Small Organization: Web Site

Figure 12.4 is the first scenario for us to examine. This is a small company with an ecommerce server. The system has a small production database, a pair of Web/application servers, and a development box, all of which are small two-processor servers.

Table 12.5 compares the costs for this system with three development approaches: SQL Server with ASP.Net on Windows, MySQL with Apache/

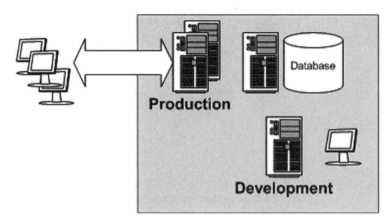

Figure 12.4
Small ecommerce system.

PHP on Linux, and WebSphere (or WebLogic) with Oracle or DB2 on Linux. The system uses four two-processor servers: two Web servers, a database server, and one system for development and testing. Application development is assumed to be four months using PHP or ASP, or six months using Enterprise Java, which can have a more substantial setup involved. System administration would be a quarter of a resource annually, priced over three years. Databases are priced with the unlimited user license, which is usually the best for Web systems.

The Linux system with open source software is less expensive than the Windows one. If you add Oracle and an application server, you get the results shown in the third column, where the Linux system is more expensive due to the cost of these two items.

Microsoft likes to compare the first and third columns, finding that .Net development on Windows is less expensive than proprietary Java development on Linux. Of course, if you want to use WebSphere and Oracle, you should add them to the Windows solution costs too, bringing the cost up considerably.

The cost differences here are small, really amounting to the cost of the database server and application server. An open source solution on Windows, such as LAMP or Jakarta/JBoss, would also be possible and cost little more than the Linux solution.

The largest variable in this model is the cost of staffing. If a good package can be found reducing development cost, if the available development resources skills favor a particular choice, or if one system is easier to manage because it is compatible with other systems in the data center, then that will change the equation. For example, I believe the Java/Oracle development

Table 12.5   *Small Web Site Costs*

Microsoft	Cost	LAMP	Cost	J2EE	Cost
Dell servers	$16,000	Dell servers	$16,000	Dell servers	$16,000
Windows Server	$1,200	Linux	$450	Linux	$450
SQL Server	$5,000	MySQL	$500	Oracle or DB2	$5,000
Visual Studio, Com+	$1,000	PHP/Apache	$0	WebLogic	$20,000
Develop application	$32,000	Develop application	$32,000	Develop application	$48,000
Management	$57,000	Management	$57,000	Management	$57,000
TOTALS	$112,200		$105,950		$146,450

choice will have somewhat higher development costs. Others may believe that one or another system is easier to manage or develop.

Small Organization: Internal Use

Of course, the small company in the previous example will have internal operations, too. We can add 50 desktops with an office suite, mail, and file and print services, and a couple of internal servers to support them with an intranet. Figure 12.5 illustrates this added to Figure 12.4. In this case, the third column might be IBM.

The costs for this are shown in Table 12.6. In this case, while staffing is still the highest cost, software prices are a higher percentage. This is usually

Figure 12.5
Added internal operations.

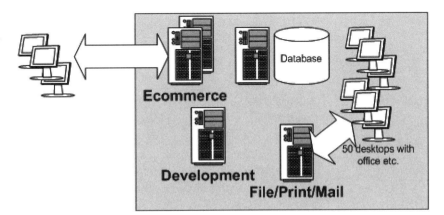

Ecommerce

Database

50 desktops with office etc.

Development

File/Print/Mail

Table 12.6   *Internal Costs*

Microsoft	Cost	LAMP	Cost	J2EE	Cost
Dell servers	$8,000	Dell servers	$8,000	Dell servers	$8,000
Windows Server	$2,800	Linux	$450	Linux	$450
Exchange	$4,700	Mail	$0	Notes	$5,000
Intranet	$0	Intranet	$0	Intranet	$4,250
Office	$25,000	Office	$0	Office	$25,000
Other	$2,600	Other	$0	Other	$2,500
Management	$57,000	Management	$57,000	Management	$57,000
TOTALS	$100,100		$65,450		$102,200

the case when desktops are included. Because of this, the open source solution is much cheaper than the proprietary ones.

This system will use two two-processor systems for Web, file, and print services. A quarter of a system administrator should suffice, priced over three years. Fifty client access licenses are needed for Windows ($40) and Exchange ($67). The intranet can be done with Microsoft Sharepoint Team Services and functions from the .Net community Web sites. An alternative would be the Microsoft portal and content management software, but that is much more expensive. An IBM solution would use the WebSphere portal. Open source choices include Plone among others. Office suite choices would include the Microsoft, Lotus, or OpenOffice suites. A couple of specialists might need Visio, PhotoShop, and Visual Studio.

If we sum Tables 12.5 and 12.6, we get these comparative totals:

Microsoft:	$212,300
Open Source:	$171,400
Java/IBM:	$248,650

Of course, each of these approaches can be varied, and would be for a cost-sensitive organization. In this example, IBM might recommend using the portal instead of its office suite for most users, saving over $20,000. Once again, there is room for opinions on the staffing costs. Many would argue that removing Office from the desktops and leaving them as browser-

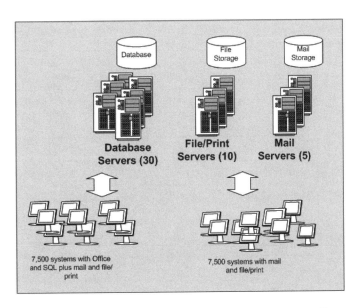

Figure 12.6
Large IT shop.

based could save significantly on management costs. Once again, we can adjust these numbers as we choose to reflect these opinions.

12.3.2 Large Organization: Internal Use

In Figure 12.6, we show a large company supporting its internal operations for 15,000 desktops. In this case, we assume that there is a custom application using a relational database supporting 7,500 desktops. There are 7,500 users running Office; from a cost point of view it does not matter if this is the same or another group. All users are supported with a mail server (Exchange in the Microsoft case) and file and print services.

We have not given Office licenses to all employees with desktops. This is realistic and holds down Microsoft costs compared with giving Office and SQL to everyone, which would cost another $5 million.

A large company such as this would probably save over $2 million through Select or Enterprise licensing. There are additional costs for Software Assurance if chosen.

Note that Advanced Server costs three times the standard server. This was priced to be broadly revenue neutral for Microsoft, so if you used standard servers you would probably purchase three times more of them. Table 12.7 lists the costs. Now the difference is very large, because in this situation desktop and client licenses are the dominant costs.

Table 12.7   *Large company IT Costs*

Functions	Microsoft Cost	Open Source Cost
Database servers	$750,000	$750,000
Other servers	$180,000	$180,000
Database licenses	$1,650,000	$15,000
File/print licenses	$630,000	$450
Mail licenses	$1,055,000	$0
Office licenses	$3,750,000	$0
Development	$285,000	$285,000
Sysadmin	$1,200,000	$1,200,000
TOTALS	$9,500,000	$2,430,450

Notes: Total

SQL Server for 7,500 users:

30 Enterprise Servers	$90,000	
30 SQL Enterprise	$330,000	
7,500 CALs	$1,230,000	
		$1,650,000

File/print for 15,000 users:

10 Advanced Servers	$30,000	
15,000 CALs	$600,000	
		$630,000

Mail for 15,000 users:

5 Advanced Servers	$15,000	
5 Exchange Enterprise	$35,000	
15,000 CALs	$1,005,000	
		$1,055,000

| **Office for 7,500 users:** | $3,750,000 | |
| Medium Servers | $12,000 | |

Staffing

| Development: 24 person-months, 6 months/yrs 2/3 | $285,000 | |
| Sysadmin: 4 resources, 3 years | $1,200,000 | |

12.4 Summary

These days, many CIOs want to commoditize core computing. By abstracting the applications they are running from the infrastructure layer, they can allow the business more flexibility. Systems that are more flexible can select solutions for their business impact without being constrained by the technology they have deployed. They can scale systems up or down on demand or distribute or outsource functions. They can share components and infrastructure between systems. This also lowers staffing costs by allowing a more consistent approach to infrastructure and sharing components and tools. Cost is also lowered by the ability to negotiate for components from multiple vendors and to escape the premium vendors obtain from lock-in.

Many organizations have a proliferation of staff doing infrastructure and desktop maintenance and want to get that under control. By stripping costs out of the infrastructure and desktop, the money will be there to support the business. The industry structure shown in Figure 12.7 indicates the direction we are going. The emphasis is shifting further"up the stack."

Systems employing open source software will usually be less expensive than alternatives. This is clear in any straightforward comparison. In some circumstances, such as infrastructure, where software costs are small compared with staffing, this difference may not be large in TCO measurements. In situations where there are many users running desktop software or server

Figure 12.7
Software industry structure.

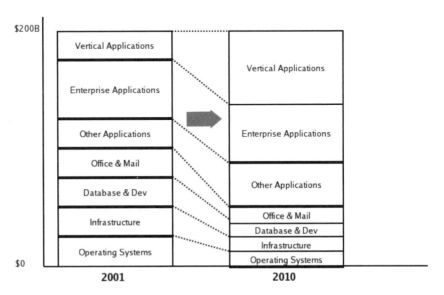

client access licenses, the software costs may be high. Client access licenses can be incurred for most internal desktop uses and some external: file sharing, mail, database access, and authentication to a directory.

At this time, switching and sunk costs and de facto industry standards are tending to delay adoption of open source, particularly at the desktop. As this situation changes over the next few years, the natural cost advantages of open source will apply in even more situations.

13

Licensing

Software licensing has always been a part of the process of managing systems. The issues around open source licensing are not really different from licensing in general, but they do seem to receive more attention at the moment.

Many professionals find legal issues and, in particular, licensing, one of their least favorite parts of the job. However, it is essential for all of us to know the basics of licensing. We will cover the basics in a simple way here. If your needs are more complex, you will require a lawyer.

If open source licensing documents seem long and difficult to read, you are probably just not used to reading legal documents. Typical closed code licensing agreements such as those from Microsoft or Oracle are no better. They are usually longer and more difficult, and very often more restrictive.

13.1 Types of Licenses

Open source licenses can be divided into two groups: the reciprocal or "free" licenses, of which the GNU General Public License (GPL) is best known, and the nonreciprocal or "open" licenses, such as the BSD and Apache licenses.

Reciprocal licenses contain a provision that requires that on relicensing the code must be open source. This is reciprocal in the sense that if a distributor receives the source code, then it passes it on to others. For example, Linux uses the GPL. If you choose to distribute an operating system based on Linux with some changes you have contributed, you must distribute the source code to that system.

Nonreciprocal licenses do not contain a relicensing provision, so they allow derivative works from open source code to revert to closed. This is nonreciprocal in the sense that a distributor can receive source code but may not necessarily pass it on. So, for example, Apple uses FreeBSD code as part of Mac OS X without needing to distribute the Mac OS X source code.

13.1.1 Relicensing Only Matters If You Distribute

Some people use the term *viral* for reciprocal. The implication is that handling viral licenses is dangerous, as Microsoft sometimes suggests. It is true that Microsoft needs to be careful using products licensed with the GPL. Microsoft is a distributor of products, such as compilers and operating systems, which could appear to be derivatives. This is a risk it can handle: Microsoft actually distributes a product (Microsoft Services for UNIX) that includes components licensed under the GPL. This risk only applies to organizations that are distributing software that extends the GPL-licensed product. Software companies that distribute code based partly on GPL-licensed products need to establish guidelines on their use.

13.1.2 Reciprocal Licenses Are Similar to Commercial Licenses

Reciprocal licenses are quite similar to commercial (closed source) licenses, which commonly contain terms that restrict relicensing and distribution of information. A common commercial restriction prevents you from relicensing the software or derivative works. The GPL has provisions that affect your subsequent licensing of derivative works, which is less restrictive than preventing relicensing. Commercial licenses normally require you to agree not to disclose proprietary information that you acquired under the license to others. This may include elements of source code (such as APIs) and other information such as performance data. The GPL requires that you agree to disclose the source code you acquired, and any you have added, to others.

13.2 Licenses in Use

There are many licenses in use today, but only a few that need to be considered by most organizations. The Freshmeat site lists about 50 categories of licenses, some of which are groups of licenses, but only about 20 are used by at least 100 projects. Figure 13.1 shows the distribution of licenses as reported on Freshmeat. Over two-thirds use the GPL, and about one-sixth use one of the LGPL, BSD, Apache, Mozilla, or MIT licenses. One of these five licenses should suffice for most purposes.

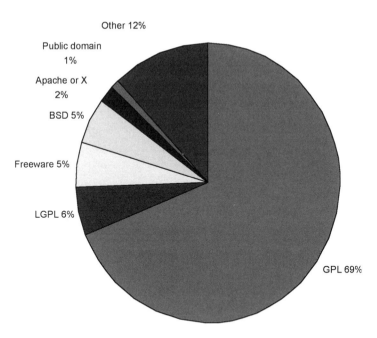

Figure 13.1
License use by project.

13.2.1 Reciprocal Licenses

The GPL is the original "free software" license. It is used by Linux and many other core tools and will be used by everyone at some time. The GPL is also an important piece of work in its own right, and a source of controversy in some quarters, so everyone should read it.

The Mozilla Public License is similar to the GPL but with clearer terms in requiring future free use.

13.2.2 Nonreciprocal Licenses

The other licenses (LGPL, BSD, Apache, and MIT) are nonreciprocal. The Lesser General Public License (LGPL) is a nonreciprocal version of the GPL intended for certain libraries. There are two forms of the BSD license. The new form omits an advertising clause in the license that was officially rescinded when the Director of the Office of Technology Licensing of the University of California stated on July 22, 1999 that clause 3 was "hereby deleted in its entirety." The new BSD license is thus equivalent to the MIT license, except for a no-endorsement final clause. The MIT license is best known for its use in the X Windows System. The Apache license is very similar.

The nonreciprocal licenses are less restrictive than the GPL on distributors. Subsequent users can use, modify, and redistribute the code without distributing their source code. This lack of restriction for the distributor removes the rights of users downstream from them to see that code. The restriction that the GPL places on distributors has the effect of later users retaining their rights to view and modify code.

Some companies take open source software, add little or nothing, and resell the result as a closed code solution, possibly for substantial prices. Reciprocal licenses address this by ensuring that companies cannot extend code without giving it back for others to offer also. Of course, these companies may add value by improving support, documentation, bundling the product for a particular market, or developing a complementary product. They just cannot gain a proprietary advantage from changes to the code, since those enhancements must go back to the community.

13.2.3   Which License to Use

It is strongly recommended that if you are distributing your own open source product you adopt one of these licenses without alteration:

- GNU General Public License
- Mozilla Public License
- BSD, Apache, or MIT license
- GNU Lesser General Public License

The alternative is to hire an attorney who specializes in these issues to develop a custom license, as large companies such as IBM do.

The GPL, Mozilla Public License, and BSD license are attached as Appendix D. Machine-readable copies of these and other licenses can be obtained at http://www.opensource.org/licenses.

13.3   Mixing Open and Closed Code

It is quite possible to use closed code and some open source software together. This is common today and is likely to be the way most systems are built in the future.

The majority of open source developers spend most of their time on closed code development. Most open source developers work primarily on internal or closed code development within companies, so they are quite familiar with closed code.

Most open source products above the operating system are offered on one or more closed platforms, generally Windows and UNIX. Products that use databases often support some closed code databases, most often Oracle.

Open source products are often sold as part of a bundled sale, which includes closed code products. Large organizations often purchase the top level of the software and service stack from a major closed code vendor. Their primary purchase might be outsourcing or other services from IBM Global Services, Accenture, or CSC; software from IBM, BEA, Oracle, or SAP; hardware from IBM, HP, or Dell, with Linux and other open source products included in the overall sale.

Table 13.1 shows examples of open source and closed code deployed together.

The most common hybrid case is simply organizations that obtain a variety of open source and closed code products, and then deploy them to meet

Table 13.1   *Using Open Source and Closed Code Together*

Product	Example
Compiere	An open source ERP system built on Java (closed code) and Oracle (closed code).
SAP	Closed code ERP system available on Linux and other operating systems. SAP converted its internal database, SAP DB, to open source and gave it to MySQL to manage (as Max DB).
Apple OS X	Closed code operating system (charging license fees) based in large part on the open source FreeBSD. Apple distributes an open source operating system called Darwin without the Apple GUI, as well as its own distribution of Xfree86.
Oracle	Closed code database (charging license fees) available on Linux (open source), as well as Windows, UNIX, and other systems.
DB2	Closed code database available on Linux, Windows, Solaris, and IBM operating systems.
WebSphere	IBM brand for a variety of middleware products. Includes many components, some of which are open source, such as Linux and Apache.

their own internal needs or their customers' needs. Google, for example, employs a great deal of open source software in systems development. Its own software is not open source, and there are license restrictions on access to most Google services to prevent others from getting a free ride—for instance, by republishing a Google search as their own.

As this example shows, a company can develop closed code software using open source tools and distribute it on open source systems, as long as it follows a few simple rules. Enhancements that an organization makes to the open source software it uses, however, MUST be contributed back.

It is common for companies to take open source projects, add a layer of additional functionality in closed code, offer support for both their enhancements and the open source base, and charge a fee. This describes IBM WebSphere, Red Hat, and some other distribution companies. It is a healthy part of the process, because customers have a choice of whether to choose the enhanced bundle or the open source system.

13.4   Dual Licensing

Some products are dual licensed. They are available with either an open source license or a commercial license. Examples of such products are:

- Qt, from TrollTech, the GUI toolkit used by KDE
- MySQL, from MySQL AB, the database server
- Berkeley DB, from SleepyCat Software, the embedded database program

The dual license allows these companies to offer open source products to those who are developing open source software, or to individual end users. Depending on their intentions or organization, others may be required to pay for a commercial license.

There are probably many ways to do this, but the path taken by these three companies is to license under the GPL, and then offer a commercial license to companies that would prefer not to meet the GPL terms. This exact strategy requires a development tool, such as a toolkit or database; it leverages the property of the GPL so that if you link to it you fall under its terms. Vendors of a pure application might need to write different licensing terms, but of course they could.

A dual license strategy relies on code ownership. It will be difficult in practice to get a large group of contributors to assign ownership to a commercial organization. In fact, the cases of dual licensing listed, and others I know of, have the look of a commercial company, where development is done in house and external contributions are signed over and compensated for.

13.5 Other Intellectual Property Issues

While the term *intellectual property* is a good description of this area, it includes the specific ideas of trademark, copyright, and patents, as well as contracts, including licensing agreements and employment contract terms such as *right for hire*. It is important not to confuse these, so it is always helpful when looking at a particular claim to see which of these it is based on rather than using loose terminology such as "intellectual property."

Open source licenses use intellectual property law in general, and copyright law in particular, to selectively distribute works for broad use while retaining ownership and restricting certain behavior that would have an adverse effect on others. These licenses are voluntary and gain their power from the ownership of the author.

Open source software should not be confused with public domain. Open source uses copyright and licensing law to enforce intellectual property rights, essentially like any other licensing agreement but with a particular purpose in mind. Including public domain as an option, then, our distribution choices come down to these:

- Closed code—you grant a license with restrictions that you specify, typically including relicensing and publication of proprietary information, and retain ownership.

- Open source (reciprocal, e.g., GPL)—you grant a license with restrictions on relicensing of derivatives and retain ownership.

- Open source (nonreciprocal)—you grant a broad license and retain ownership.

- Public domain—you relinquish ownership and all rights to it permanently.

13.5.1 Provenance

There is always risk in any business decision, including software licensing, and open source is generally similar. One area where some open source products may have more risk is provenance. Provenance is the issue of whether code that you have licensed from some party was actually its to offer. This is a concern with any type of licensing. Programmers working for a vendor might have copied code into the product from elsewhere. If this was proprietary, it would contaminate your system and your system would fall under restrictions imposed by that code's licensing terms. It might expose you to a license fee, for instance, or a requirement to share your source.

All projects need to maintain records of where any contributed code was obtained. Because some open source projects receive code from many contributors, it may be more onerous for them. For others, it is no different from any other project. When acquiring a product, we need to make sure this provenance work was done.

There are occasionally specific allegations that a piece of open source software is stolen "intellectual property" from private companies. This may happen on occasion, but it is not common. It is illegal to appropriate copyrighted code, to use others' trademarks, or to obtain others' trade secrets. There is nothing unusual about open source in this regard. The laws against these activities have been used often and still apply. However, it is the nature of open source that all the code is available for inspection, so any wrongdoing is far more likely to be caught than with closed code. Although open source software has been around for 30 years, nothing has yet been found. There has been no lawsuit that has succeeded in proving that any significant amount of closed code has been incorporated into open source. If such a lawsuit were won, that offending code would need to be replaced, but the status of open source in general would not be different.

The same laws also apply if a closed code developer appropriates copyrighted or trademarked material or wrongly uses trade secrets. There have been several such lawsuits in the private sector. There may be issues where closed code developers wrongly appropriate open source code, which is easy to get. The company Black Duck was founded to address this problem. Organizations with a concern that open source code has made its way into their products can use the Black Duck product to search online open source libraries for code that looks like code in their products.

Of course, it is fine if an open source product is functionally equivalent to closed code software, was built cleanly without access to that code and does not copy the expression closely, and has no copyright or trademark infringements. There were major lawsuits over "look and feel" between Apple and Microsoft over Windows' similarity to the Macintosh, and between Borland and Lotus over Quattro Pro's similarity to Lotus 1-2-3, but they were resolved.

The software patent issue is another area, and there may be grounds for long-term concern here. Bill Gates has said that patents are being interpreted now in ways that would have made software development as we know it practically impossible in the past. In addition, legislation such as the Digital Millennium Copyright Act (DMCA) and proposals regarding Digital Rights Management (DRM) threaten to extend restrictions further. These issues are complex and cannot be covered usefully here. I suggest referring to Lawrence Lessig's books, particularly *Free Culture* and *The Future of Ideas*; searching the Electronic Freedom Foundation, Free Software, and Open Source sites for the terms software patent and DMCA; and visiting the Creative Commons site for other information and activities.

13.6 Summary

There are legal issues with open source software, as there are with closed code. There are risks, as there are with all business decisions. Companies can breach contracts, go bankrupt, and so on, as they always could. Support arrangements need to be specified and contracted for, as they always do.

There is little in open source that is different in principle from closed code. For example, a company such as MySQL will offer either a commercial license or a GPL license for the same code. Clearly, support arrangements, concerns about provenance, and many other issues are the same whichever license you choose.

Open source software is always voluntary. Developers of software can choose the licensing model for their work, and adopters of software can choose products from the many licensing models available. It is one more choice we can consider in either case.

Resources

A.1   Managing an Open Source Lab

An open source software lab will serve as a resource for:

- Selling the advantages of open source software to executives who want to understand what it is all about.

- Demonstrating relevant products and practices, and their operation and features, for users and professionals who want to see the software before using it.

- Identifying internal systems and people who already have been successful.

- Developing solutions to problems in the organization that can be assembled from these products and practices.

- Training professionals, developers, and system administrators, who want to evaluate open source software and learn to use it.

- Testing system operation—for instance, to check vendor claims, make sure elements work together, and practice migrations.

- Benchmarking capacity and performance—for instance, database performance in requests/seconds, or the number of users supported by a directory.

This is such a useful list of activities, and a simple lab is so easy to get started, that this is the first thing we should do in the course of investigating and/or introducing open source software.

We can set up an adequate lab with two or three machines as Linux servers. They will support file and print services, directory, Web server, database, and other applications. We will also set up several clients running whatever we are likely to work with in our organization. This might be, for instance, Mac OS X, Windows XP, and whichever Linux flavors we want to examine (e.g., SuSE Linux 9, Debian GNU Linux, or RHEL 3). To test Web systems, we may want to run several browsers. Many of the systems can be older, particularly for clients, perhaps adopted from other lab functions, or second-hand systems after a desktop refresh. Many Linux functions run well on older systems. However, the latest desktop applications running on KDE and Gnome with "eye candy" turned on usually require a new system.

If the lab is used for training in a regular way, or for short-notice demonstrations, it will need to be reasonably permanent with dedicated systems. In other circumstances, the systems don't need to be completely dedicated and we can set systems up as dual boot or multiple boot. We should keep some machines running all the time for demonstrations, education, and to prove reliability, but let others be brought up and down and reconfigured by staff who are learning to use the systems. As a general rule, clients can be dual boot but servers should usually be dedicated, because we may want to access files, printers, or databases at any time without having to reboot.

If finances allow, we can expand on the adequate lab by using better equipment and facilities. With better funding, the lab can be more of a sales tool. We could use the same equipment we normally order for new locations, which will be faster and better looking than used stuff and will allow benchmarks to be more realistic (and faster). If we are looking for large systems, perhaps a cooperative vendor can loan us equipment. For a real impression, we could pay someone to design the layout. If executives are going to see the demonstrations, it can be worth making them look fancy. This may work for a consulting or training organization that would see many customers over a period.

We won't forget to allow vendors to see our open source lab. When a closed code company is made aware that we are seriously considering open source, this can have a very significant effect on its pricing and support offers. There are companies that have told their sales force that they must never lose to Linux (or other such products) and must "do whatever it takes" to win.

If finances are an issue, we can create a technical lab as long as we have a computer. We can get an available laptop or desktop with a 10GB hard drive running Windows XP or Windows 2000 Professional. Then we can set it up as dual boot so it can be started as either a Windows or a Linux system. We do this by partitioning the hard drive as half Windows, half Linux using Partition Manager, and then installing from a CD-based copy of Linux with all software. On such a system we can learn and test all software mentioned in this book, and yet continue to run Windows and any software we need that requires it.

Many organizations already have some equipment and space set aside for this type of activity, and the only cost involved will be the time to set up the systems and evaluate them. Such a project involves a few days to a few weeks of staffing, and could well be encompassed during downtime from other projects. If space and equipment are dedicated over some months, and training is conducted and analysis work performed to support migrations, then we will need to budget for a significant project.

A.2   Installing an Evaluation Linux System

Most people evaluating Linux will want to put their hands on a Linux system and get a feel for how it compares to what they are used to. As with any system, it is more difficult to install a system correctly than to use it. Installation is a place where potential users can get frustrated or even give up before even getting a system to work. The following text will try to steer you to the right machine and Linux distribution to make installation go well.

The installation problem occurs with Windows; when I worked for Microsoft, I would go into retail stores on special occasions such as Christmas and Windows launches to meet the public. My least favorite part of this was meeting people who had attempted to install a new version of Windows for themselves and got stuck. However, with Windows you can always choose to buy a new computer that is set up correctly, and that option is still an issue with Linux.

If you don't feel that you have the time to install Linux, you can just run it from a live CD using Knoppix or another distribution that loads that way. This is a great method for initial evaluation and is also useful for experienced users who are borrowing or repairing a machine.

Most systems can run Linux, but not all systems will be easy to install. It is common for a new Linux user to spend a few days scraping up information to solve problems such as those listed in Table A.1. If our goal is to spend a week learning how to manage Apache and Samba and review the operation of OpenOffice, Evolution, and KDE, it is worth thinking about

Table A.1 → *Possible Problems with Linux Install on Windows Machine*

Problem	Comment	Workaround
Hardware supported by Windows but not Linux	Particularly older systems. More likely with Windows 98/ME, which supports more old hardware than NT/2000. Component problems include large disk drives in old machines, 3D graphics cards (e.g., nVidia), sound cards, and modems.	Select the machine carefully before installing. Some machines may not ever work well or will need difficult activities (such as kernel patches) to get going.
Notebook and laptop computers	More likely to have unusual cards and drivers that might not be supported. Quite likely not to have full support for all power management features without manual installation. If used, more likely to have weird defects.	Decide if you must use a notebook. Check sites such as Linux on Laptops, http://www.linux-laptop.net/, to see that your notebook and graphics card are specifically supported.
Disk partitioning	If a machine has Windows installed, you probably need to shrink the Windows partition to get space to install Linux, not an easy task.	Most Linux installs will let you delete the entire Windows partition, but that's probably not what you want. See dual boot.
Graphical (X Windows) install hangs or fails	This is pretty common and is why most systems offer a text-mode install. Installers can usually detect the graphics adapter but often don't detect the monitor sync rates.	Use text-mode install and then do X after. Note the monitor sync data from Windows before you start and enter it manually. If you can choose, get an ATI (e.g., Radeon) adapter rather than nVidia, since the nVidia driver may need tricky installation.
System does not use entire screen for display	System did not detect the monitor and is using VESA, or did not detect adapter memory.	Note monitor and adapter information from Windows before starting.

Table A.1   *Possible Problems with Linux Install on Windows Machine (continued)*

Problem	Comment	Workaround
Dual boot	You may want to keep your Windows system and add Linux so you can choose which operating system to bring up: a dual-boot system. Dual boot adds risks; it is harder to set up, and a severe failure could knock out both setups. It can be annoying to use if you need to switch back and forth.	Use a Windows-based disk partitioning tool, such as Partition Magic, to shrink the Windows partition before installing Linux. Most computer techs have a disk partitioning tool. Most Linux versions support dual boot (using LILO or GRUB). A second system or a swappable boot drive is preferable. Don't dual boot unless you have a spare system or are completely backed up.
Reading from the Windows partition	When in Linux, you may want to read files from your Windows file system (which is presumably where any files you've created, such as Mail, are today).	Linux can mount FAT32 or NTFS file systems: FAT32 read/write, NTFS generally read-only. See Chapter 11.
Accessing files and printers on the Windows network	There will be some setup needed to do this, possibly scripting. In some security configurations, it may not be possible.	See Chapter 11. Work in a lab setting where the Windows security can be simplified.
Wireless and PCMCIA cards	Current Red Hat and SuSE Linux should set up automatically (you'll need to enter the ESSID). Older and unusual cards may not work. Very new cards may not work (today, 802.11g fast wireless is very hard to set up).	Older Linux versions (e.g., Red Hat, SuSE 7) are less likely to work without manual intervention.
You run into a problem that needs Internet access to solve	Many possible problems could leave you with a machine that does not work or does not connect to the Internet.	Have a spare machine available.

whether we want to begin with installation. We could spend the week setting up DNS and IP addresses and searching the Internet for the scripts that can make particular devices work correctly. If you know an experienced Linux user, this is a good point at which to ask for help.

Alternatively, if money is not an issue, the easiest course may be to buy a new system set up for the version of Linux you want to use, or pay someone to install it. The major manufacturers (Dell, IBM, HP, etc.) don't sell these systems retail as I write but will do it as a custom service. This is changing very rapidly, with IBM and HP committing to offering installed Linux systems. Already, many smaller companies will be happy to sell a machine set up with a Linux system or to install the operating system on your machine (stand-alone or dual-boot) for a fee. I do recommend getting the system you want to evaluate, so it is not worth popping into Wal-Mart and buying a Lindows system, since that probably won't be what your organization will select.

At a later point, you may want to put in the effort to configure a Linux system exactly as you want it. If you have the disk space available, it may be better to just load up everything.

A.2.1 Setting up Interoperability

We will need to establish interoperability between Linux systems and our existing systems. There are several ways to do this, starting with those that work on a single machine. Options include a dual-boot system, running Linux on Windows, and running Windows on Linux. Of these, the most generally useful is to create a dual-boot system.

A.2.2 Dual Boot

A dual-boot machine can start in either Windows or Linux, for example, but we must choose. If we need an application from the "other side," we must stop and restart, and that is inconvenient. If a machine is dual boot, you can see exactly how it compares on the same hardware—for instance, speed, graphics. Second, if you have difficulty with something in the course of testing (which might be a seldom used Windows program or a logon via modem you only use on the road), you preserve the ability to boot in Windows to do that. Finally, you can later take off whichever operating system you don't need.

To set up a dual-boot system, which leaves your Windows install intact and allows testing of a full version of Linux, you will need a disk drive with a minimum size of about 10GB (5GB for each system). The dual boot is a little harder to set up in the first place, and there is a slight risk that a failure setting up the dual boot will disable the Windows system. Any data should be backed up before trying this, and you may need some expert help for this if a problem occurs. If you have a new system, you can install Windows using half the drive, and then install Linux on the unused space.

Since I often find systems with Windows installed and data on them, if only from the manufacturer, I usually use the program Partition Magic, which runs from Windows and allows resizing of existing partitions. This is not open source but is fairly inexpensive for workstations, and it is likely that administrative staff in a Windows-based organization have this already. One alternative if your partition(s) is FAT32 is the Linux program "parted," but this does not work to resize NTFS partitions.

Once the dual-boot system is working, you will want to set up file access from the Linux system to the Windows partition. Windows systems cannot read Linux partitions. Linux systems as a rule can read and write FAT and FAT32 and can read from but not write to NTFS partitions. For two-way communication, it is better if the Windows system has at least some space partitioned as FAT32. Some Linux systems will mount the Windows partition automatically. If they do not, it is necessary to edit the /etc/fstab file with something like this, and then ensure that appropriate permissions are granted:

```
//dev/hda1          /mnt/xp          ntfs
```

A.2.3 **Running Linux on Windows**

Instead of booting one of Linux or Windows as needed, it is possible to run the one under the other. To run Linux (or at least UNIX) under Windows, we can use emulation or a virtual machine. Emulations include:

- Cygwin (open source)
- Microsoft Services for UNIX (SFU)
- Commercial packages such as MKS

Cygwin is the open source package that provides a UNIX-like set of utilities and APIs under Windows. This allows a program such as PostgreSQL to run under Windows. It is also popular with technical staff who are used to the UNIX command line and would like the same features under Windows. SFU, which is functionally similar to Cygwin, is available as a no-charge download from Microsoft.

People who need to switch often between operating systems will use a virtual machine system, which allows the systems to run simultaneously without need for reboot. The leading such system is VMware. The workstation product is reasonably priced and very powerful, and I use it. It is an excellent tool for developers testing different versions of their products, for example. VMware is available for Windows or Linux as the underlying operating system, and will then run the other as a guest (as well as other systems such as Novell). Microsoft also offers a similar product, Virtual PC.

Some people are tempted to try VMware on Windows to support their first Linux installation. I do not recommend that. VMware supports specific operating system versions; as I write, it does not support the latest Fedora or SuSE workstation versions. Setting up VMware is an art in itself. When completed, your system networks from the Linux or Windows side, can read files across both, and operates quickly in a full graphical environment. However, setup issues may occur that will leave you in an incomplete situation, and debugging will involve learning and getting support from VMware (not Linux). VMware is an excellent choice for a lab environment once the first couple of Linux systems are set up.

A.2.4 Running Windows on Linux

In this direction, the choice is also emulation or a virtual machine. In addition to running Linux on Windows, VMware can be used to run Windows on Linux. For example, we could set up Windows XP, Windows NT4, and Windows ME systems on a single Linux box and test an application on them. The Windows systems will access installed printers, network cards, and so on.

A common problem with Linux systems is the need to run some Windows applications that are not available on Linux—for example, Microsoft Office, the MacroMedia Director plug-in, and many games. To support this, emulation is required. Crossover Office, from CodeWeavers, lets you run Office, PhotoShop, Lotus Notes, Visio, and browser plug-ins on Windows (e.g., QuickTime, Microsoft Office Viewers, and Macromedia Director). You do need to get specific versions of Crossover Office for the programs you want to run, and you also need to license the programs themselves.

Wine (short for WINdows Emulation) is the open source product that underlies Crossover Office (and is sponsored by it). Wine exposes the Windows APIs so that a program written for Microsoft Windows can run on Linux. This is mostly aimed at developers.

It is possible to run Microsoft Windows drivers under Linux in order to access hardware that has only been released with Windows drivers, using drivers from Linuxant.

Another alternative to achieve the need of running Windows programs is using Citrix clients to access Windows programs on servers.

A.3   Next Steps

Develop personal skills. Install Linux on a system; the easiest way is to use Knoppix, so if nothing else do that. Get your hands on open source software that meets your needs.

Join a local user group. There is no substitute for personal meetings. I would be much worse off without user groups, and I am convinced everyone needs user group involvement. This is important in any software, but more so with open source, because some of the other communication channels are less effective. Open source user groups are also more likely to contain deep technical resources. I believe it is because of access to the source code, so that people can help themselves; the opportunity to contribute, which motivates; and the absence of dominant vendors that tend to turn their user groups into marketing events. Sign in to open source communities such as Slashdot and Freshmeat.

Develop an open source strategy. Always include open source software in the alternatives for evaluation when buying products. Prepare for the open source sales model, the absence of sales representation and freebies, and the low-key branding and press coverage. For complex deployments, plan measures now to set up for migration later.

Consider open source now if you need to:

- Buy or replace infrastructure products.

- Select standards, particularly for interoperability and integration.

- Build, buy, or rewrite applications.

- Deploy solutions in new areas, such as suppliers, channel, customer access, community access, call centers, and retail stores.

A.4   Top Ten Reasons to Use Open Source Software

1. The open source development model has worked for over 25 years for highly complex and secure systems.

2. Open source is the international solution because of the cost model, ability to employ local talent, and capacity for localization.

3. You can access a growing pool of skilled professionals who share with and learn from each other.

4.   The Internet runs on and empowers open source software.

5.   You can see and fix the code that your system runs on, or your representatives can.

6.   There are no proprietary information formats unless you choose to employ them.

7.   There is no licensing to manage, no piracy, and you can upgrade your systems as you choose.

8.   You are free to change and mix products from different platforms, vendors, and service providers.

9.   You can do your own integration and customization.

10.   It costs less money for licenses and less for hardware, and no more for staffing, support, or anything else.

A.5   Web Links

This set of technologies and practices is large enough and new enough that we all need a variety of resources to learn about them and stay on top of them. Fortunately, the Internet comes to our aid here. Some useful URLs are included in Table A.2. There is a tremendous amount of literature, including system documentation, on the Internet and this should usually be the first place to look. The user manuals for GIMP and MySQL are just two examples of really high-quality, online documentation. The Web links in Table A.2 are a small sample of the resources available.

Table A.2   *Web Links*

URL	Description	Comment
linuxshop.ru/linuxbegin/win-lin-soft-en/table.shtml	Table of Linux equivalents for Windows	Lists all of the open source Linux equivalents for programs on Windows
freshmeat.net	Freshmeat	Index of available open source projects
sourceforge.net	SourceForge	Repository of open source code and center of open source software development

Table A.2   *Web Links (continued)*

URL	Description	Comment
www.apache.org	Apache Foundation	Manages the Apache Web browser development team, and also related products including Jakarta.
www.dwheeler.com/oss_fs_why.html	Why OSS/FSS?	Essential resources if compiling data on open source market share or performance
www.fedstats.gov	FedStats	Useful site of information on U.S. statistics
www.freebsd.org	Free BSD	The "other" free operating system.
www.fsf.org/philosophy/free-sw.html	Free software and GPL	Essential philosophy
www.gnome.org	Gnome Foundation	Manage development of Gnome desktop and tools, including Evolution.
www.gnu.org	Home of GNU and FSF	
www.ibm.com/developerworks/linux	IBM Developer Works Linux page	Often a good resource for non-proprietary tools, in addition of course to the IBM tools.
www.kbst.bund.de	German federal government site	search the English documents
www.kuro5hin.org	Kuro5hin	Discussion site on technology and culture
www.linux.org	Linux	Linux
www.linuxjournal.com	Linux Journal	Monthly magazine
www.linux-laptop.net	Linux on Laptops	Information on installing Linux on laptops
www.linux-mag.com	Linux Magazine	Another Linux magazine
www.mozilla.org	Mozilla	Home site for Mozilla browser and other software

Table A.2   *Web Links (continued)*

URL	Description	Comment
www.newsforge.com	NewsForge	Online daily newspaper for Linux and open source
www.netcraft.com	NetCraft	Reports on Web software usage
www.objectwatch.com	Object Watch	Roger Session's developer site. Good pricing spreadsheet. Great on WebSphere versus .Net.
www.opengroup.org	Open Group	Manages open standards, including the UNIX APIs
www.opensource.org	Open Source Initiative	Manages the Open Source Definition and keeps list of approved software licenses.
www.python.org	Python	Main Python site
www.redbooks.ibm.com	IBM RedBooks	Practical books on software issues
www.securityspace.com	Security Space	Research reports on e.g. Apache module usage
www.slashdot.org	Slashdot	Essential reading on technology-related subjects every day
www.ssc.com/glue/groups	Groups of Linux users everywhere	Big list of user groups
www.stanford.edu/class/cs240/readings	Readings in computer history	This directory contains many useful papers including Richard Gabriel's paper on the UNIX design philosophy, The Rise of "Worse is Better"
www.tldp.org	The Linux Documentation Project	Great resource for Linux documentation
www.tpc.org	TPC	Database benchmarks

Table A.2   *Web Links (continued)*

URL	Description	Comment
www.w3.org	W3C	World Wide Web Consortium; the major standards body of the Web.
www.xfree.org	XFree86	The open source Intel implementation of the X Windows System.
http:www.opensource.org/licenses	Repository for all open source licenses	Essential resource.

B

The Open Source Definition

Introduction

Open source doesn't just mean access to the source code. The distribution terms of open-source software must comply with the following criteria:

1. Free Redistribution

The license shall not restrict any party from selling or giving away the software as a component of an aggregate software distribution containing programs from several different sources. The license shall not require a royalty or other fee for such sale.

2. Source Code

The program must include source code, and must allow distribution in source code as well as compiled form. Where some form of a product is not distributed with source code, there must be a well-publicized means of obtaining the source code for no more than a reasonable reproduction cost preferably, downloading via the Internet without charge. The source code must be the preferred form in which a programmer would modify the program. Deliberately obfuscated source code is not allowed. Intermediate forms such as the output of a preprocessor or translator are not allowed.

3. Derived Works

The license must allow modifications and derived works, and must allow them to be distributed under the same terms as the license of the original software.

4. Integrity of The Author's Source Code

The license may restrict source-code from being distributed in modified form only if the license allows the distribution of "patch files" with the source code for the purpose of modifying the program at build time. The license must explicitly permit distribution of software built from modified source code. The license may require derived works to carry a different name or version number from the original software.

5. No Discrimination Against Persons or Groups

The license must not discriminate against any person or group of persons.

6. No Discrimination Against Fields of Endeavor

The license must not restrict anyone from making use of the program in a specific field of endeavor. For example, it may not restrict the program from being used in a business, or from being used for genetic research.

7. Distribution of License

The rights attached to the program must apply to all to whom the program is redistributed without the need for execution of an additional license by those parties.

8. License Must Not Be Specific to a Product

The rights attached to the program must not depend on the program's being part of a particular software distribution. If the program is extracted from that distribution and used or distributed within the terms of the program's license, all parties to whom the program is redistributed should have the same rights as those that are granted in conjunction with the original software distribution.

9. License Must Not Restrict Other Software

The license must not place restrictions on other software that is distributed along with the licensed software. For example, the license must not insist that all other programs distributed on the same medium must be open-source software.

10. License Must Be Technology-Neutral

No provision of the license may be predicated on any individual technology or style of interface.

Copyright © 2004 by the Open Source Initiative

*This is available on the Web at http://www.opensource.org/docs/definition_plain.php. An annotated version, which explains the purpose of each paragraph and is probably to be preferred, is also available at http://www.opensource.org/docs/definition.php.

C

Examples of Open Source Licenses

C.1 GPL

GNU GENERAL PUBLIC LICENSE

Version 2, June 1991

Copyright (C) 1989, 1991 Free Software Foundation, Inc.

59 Temple Place, Suite 330, Boston, MA 02111-1307 USA

Everyone is permitted to copy and distribute verbatim copies of this license document, but changing it is not allowed.

Preamble

The licenses for most software are designed to take away your freedom to share and change it. By contrast, the GNU General Public License is intended to guarantee your freedom to share and change free software--to make sure the software is free for all its users. This General Public License applies to most of the Free Software Foundation's software and to any other program whose authors commit to using it. (Some other Free Software Foundation software is covered by the GNU Library General Public License instead.) You can apply it to your programs, too.

When we speak of free software, we are referring to freedom, not price. Our General Public Licenses are designed to make sure that you have the freedom to distribute copies of free software (and charge for this service if you wish), that you receive source code or can get it if you want it, that you can change the software or use pieces of it in new free programs; and that you know you can do these things.

To protect your rights, we need to make restrictions that forbid anyone to deny you these rights or to ask you to surrender the rights. These restrictions translate to certain responsibilities for you if you distribute copies of the software, or if you modify it.

For example, if you distribute copies of such a program, whether gratis or for a fee, you must give the recipients all the rights that you have. You must make sure that they, too, receive or can get the source code. And you must show them these terms so they know their rights.

We protect your rights with two steps: (1) copyright the software, and (2) offer you this license which gives you legal permission to copy, distribute and/or modify the software.

Also, for each author's protection and ours, we want to make certain that everyone understands that there is no warranty for this free software. If the software is modified by someone else and passed on, we want its recipients to know that what they have is not the original, so that any problems introduced by others will not reflect on the original authors' reputations.

Finally, any free program is threatened constantly by software patents. We wish to avoid the danger that redistributors of a free program will individually obtain patent licenses, in effect making the program closed code. To prevent this, we have made it clear that any patent must be licensed for everyone's free use or not licensed at all.

The precise terms and conditions for copying, distribution and modification follow.

GNU GENERAL PUBLIC LICENSE

TERMS AND CONDITIONS FOR COPYING, DISTRIBUTION AND MODIFICATION

0. This License applies to any program or other work which contains a notice placed by the copyright holder saying it may be distributed under the terms of this General Public License. The "Program", below, refers to any such program or work, and a "work based on the Program" means either the Program or any derivative work under copyright law:

that is to say, a work containing the Program or a portion of it, either verbatim or with modifications and/or translated into another language. (Hereinafter, translation is included without limitation in the term "modification".) Each licensee is addressed as "you".

Activities other than copying, distribution and modification are not covered by this License; they are outside its scope. The act of running the Program is not restricted, and the output from the Program is covered only if its contents constitute a work based on the Program (independent of having been made by running the Program). Whether that is true depends on what the Program does.

1. You may copy and distribute verbatim copies of the Program's source code as you receive it, in any medium, provided that you conspicuously and appropriately publish on each copy an appropriate copyright notice and disclaimer of warranty; keep intact all the notices that refer to this License and to the absence of any warranty; and give any other recipients of the Program a copy of this License along with the Program.

You may charge a fee for the physical act of transferring a copy, and you may at your option offer warranty protection in exchange for a fee.

2. You may modify your copy or copies of the Program or any portion of it, thus forming a work based on the Program, and copy and distribute such modifications or work under the terms of Section 1 above, provided that you also meet all of these conditions:

a) You must cause the modified files to carry prominent notices stating that you changed the files and the date of any change.

b) You must cause any work that you distribute or publish, that in whole or in part contains or is derived from the Program or any part thereof, to be licensed as a whole at no charge to all third parties under the terms of this License.

c) If the modified program normally reads commands interactively when run, you must cause it, when started running for such interactive use in the most ordinary way, to print or display an announcement including an appropriate copyright notice and a notice that there is no warranty (or else, saying that you provide a warranty) and that users may redistribute the program under these conditions, and telling the user how to view a copy of this License. (Exception: if the Program itself is interactive but does not normally print such an announcement, your work based on the Program is not required to print an announcement.)

These requirements apply to the modified work as a whole. If identifiable sections of that work are not derived from the Program, and can be reasonably considered independent and separate works in themselves, then this License, and its terms, do not apply to those sections when you distribute them as separate works. But when you

distribute the same sections as part of a whole which is a work based on the Program, the distribution of the whole must be on the terms of this License, whose permissions for other licensees extend to the entire whole, and thus to each and every part regardless of who wrote it.

Thus, it is not the intent of this section to claim rights or contest your rights to work written entirely by you; rather, the intent is to exercise the right to control the distribution of derivative or collective works based on the Program.

In addition, mere aggregation of another work not based on the Program with the Program (or with a work based on the Program) on a volume of a storage or distribution medium does not bring the other work under the scope of this License.

3. You may copy and distribute the Program (or a work based on it, under Section 2) in object code or executable form under the terms of Sections 1 and 2 above provided that you also do one of the following:

a) Accompany it with the complete corresponding machine-readable source code, which must be distributed under the terms of Sections 1 and 2 above on a medium customarily used for software interchange; or,

b) Accompany it with a written offer, valid for at least three years, to give any third party, for a charge no more than your cost of physically performing source distribution, a complete machine-readable copy of the corresponding source code, to be distributed under the terms of Sections 1 and 2 above on a medium customarily used for software interchange; or,

c) Accompany it with the information you received as to the offer to distribute corresponding source code. (This alternative is allowed only for noncommercial distribution and only if you received the program in object code or executable form with such an offer, in accord with Subsection b above.)

The source code for a work means the preferred form of the work for making modifications to it. For an executable work, complete source code means all the source code for all modules it contains, plus any associated interface definition files, plus the scripts used to control compilation and installation of the executable. However, as a

special exception, the source code distributed need not include anything that is normally distributed (in either source or binary form) with the major components (compiler, kernel, and so on) of the operating system on which the executable runs, unless that component itself accompanies the executable.

If distribution of executable or object code is made by offering access to copy from a designated place, then offering equivalent access to copy the source code from the same place counts as distribution of the source code, even though third parties are not compelled to copy the source along with the object code.

4. You may not copy, modify, sublicense, or distribute the Program except as expressly provided under this License. Any attempt otherwise to copy, modify, sublicense or distribute the Program is void, and will automatically terminate your rights under this License. However, parties who have received copies, or rights, from you under this License will not have their licenses terminated so long as such parties remain in full compliance.

5. You are not required to accept this License, since you have not signed it. However, nothing else grants you permission to modify or distribute the Program or its derivative works. These actions are prohibited by law if you do not accept this License. Therefore, by modifying or distributing the

Program (or any work based on the Program), you indicate your acceptance of this License to do so, and all its terms and conditions for copying, distributing or modifying the Program or works based on it.

6. Each time you redistribute the Program (or any work based on the Program), the recipient automatically receives a license from the original licensor to copy, distribute or modify the Program subject to these terms and conditions. You may not impose any further restrictions on the recipients' exercise of the rights granted herein. You are not responsible for enforcing compliance by third parties to this License.

7. If, as a consequence of a court judgment or allegation of patent infringement or for any other reason (not limited to patent issues), conditions are imposed on you (whether by court order, agreement or otherwise) that contradict the conditions of this License, they do not excuse you from the conditions of this License. If you cannot distribute so as to satisfy simultaneously your obligations under this License and any other pertinent obligations, then as a consequence you may not distribute the Program at all. For example, if a patent license would not permit royalty-free redistribution of the Program by all those who receive copies directly or indirectly through you, then the only way you could satisfy both it and this License would be to refrain entirely from distribution of the Program.

If any portion of this section is held invalid or unenforceable under any particular circumstance, the balance of the section is intended to apply and the section as a whole is intended to apply in other circumstances.

It is not the purpose of this section to induce you to infringe any patents or other property right claims or to contest validity of any such claims; this section has the sole purpose of protecting the integrity of the free software distribution system, which is implemented by public license practices. Many people have made generous contributions to the wide range of software distributed through that system in reliance on consistent application of that system; it is up to the author/donor to decide if he or she is willing to distribute software through any other system and a licensee cannot impose that choice.

This section is intended to make thoroughly clear what is believed to be a consequence of the rest of this License.

8. If the distribution and/or use of the Program is restricted in certain countries either by patents or by copyrighted interfaces, the original copyright holder who places the Program under this License may add an explicit geographical distribution limitation excluding those countries, so that distribution is permitted only in or among countries not thus excluded. In such case, this License incorporates the limitation as if written in the body of this License.

9. The Free Software Foundation may publish revised and/or new versions of the General Public License from time to time. Such new versions will be similar in spirit to the present version, but may differ in detail to address new problems or concerns.

Each version is given a distinguishing version number. If the Program specifies a version number of this License which applies to it and "any later version", you have the option of following the terms and conditions either of that version or of any later version published by the Free Software Foundation. If the Program does not specify a version number of this License, you may choose any version ever published by the Free Software Foundation.

10. If you wish to incorporate parts of the Program into other free programs whose distribution conditions are different, write to the author to ask for permission. For software which is copyrighted by the Free Software Foundation, write to the Free Software Foundation; we sometimes make exceptions for this. Our decision will be guided by the two goals of preserving the free status of all derivatives of our free software and of promoting the sharing and reuse of software generally.

NO WARRANTY

11. BECAUSE THE PROGRAM IS LICENSED FREE OF CHARGE, THERE IS NO WARRANTY FOR THE PROGRAM, TO THE EXTENT PERMITTED BY APPLICABLE LAW. EXCEPT WHEN OTHERWISE STATED IN WRITING THE COPYRIGHT HOLDERS AND/OR OTHER PARTIES PROVIDE THE PROGRAM "AS IS" WITHOUT WARRANTY OF ANY KIND, EITHER EXPRESSED OR IMPLIED, INCLUDING, BUT NOT LIMITED TO, THE IMPLIED WARRANTIES OF MERCHANTABILITY AND FITNESS FOR A

PARTICULAR PURPOSE. THE ENTIRE RISK AS TO THE QUAL-
ITY AND PERFORMANCE OF THE PROGRAM IS WITH YOU.
SHOULD THE PROGRAM PROVE DEFECTIVE, YOU ASSUME
THE COST OF ALL NECESSARY SERVICING, REPAIR OR COR-
RECTION.

12. IN NO EVENT UNLESS REQUIRED BY APPLICABLE LAW OR
AGREED TO IN WRITING WILL ANY COPYRIGHT HOLDER, OR
ANY OTHER PARTY WHO MAY MODIFY AND/OR REDISTRIB-
UTE THE PROGRAM AS PERMITTED ABOVE, BE LIABLE TO
YOU FOR DAMAGES, INCLUDING ANY GENERAL, SPECIAL,
INCIDENTAL OR CONSEQUENTIAL DAMAGES ARISING OUT
OF THE USE OR INABILITY TO USE THE PROGRAM (INCLUD-
ING BUT NOT LIMITED TO LOSS OF DATA OR DATA BEING
RENDERED INACCURATE OR LOSSES SUSTAINED BY YOU OR
THIRD PARTIES OR A FAILURE OF THE PROGRAM TO OPER-
ATE WITH ANY OTHER PROGRAMS),EVEN IF SUCH HOLDER
OR OTHER PARTY HAS BEEN ADVISED OF THE POSSIBILITY
OF SUCH DAMAGES.

END OF TERMS AND CONDITIONS

How to Apply These Terms to Your New Programs

If you develop a new program, and you want it to be of the greatest
possible use to the public, the best way to achieve this is to make it
free software which everyone can redistribute and change under these
terms.

To do so, attach the following notices to the program. It is safest
to attach them to the start of each source file to most effectively
convey the exclusion of warranty; and each file should have at least
the "copyright" line and a pointer to where the full notice is found.

<one line to give the program's name and a brief idea of what it does.>
Copyright (C) <year> <name of author>
This program is free software; you can redistribute it and/or modify

it under the terms of the GNU General Public License as published by the Free Software Foundation; either version 2 of the License, or (at your option) any later version.

This program is distributed in the hope that it will be useful, but WITH-OUT ANY WARRANTY; without even the implied warranty of MER-CHANTABILITY or FITNESS FOR A PARTICULAR PURPOSE. See the GNU General Public License for more details.

You should have received a copy of the GNU General Public License along with this program; if not, write to the Free Software Foundation, Inc., 59 Temple Place, Suite 330, Boston, MA 02111-1307 USA. Also add information on how to contact you by electronic and paper mail.

If the program is interactive, make it output a short notice like this when it starts in an interactive mode:

Gnomovision version 69, Copyright (C) year name of author

Gnomovision comes with ABSOLUTELY NO WARRANTY; for details type `show w'.

This is free software, and you are welcome to redistribute it under certain conditions; type `show c' for details.

The hypothetical commands `show w' and `show c' should show the appropriate parts of the General Public License. Of course, the commands you use may be called something other than `show w' and `show c'; they could even be mouse-clicks or menu items--whatever suits your program.

You should also get your employer (if you work as a programmer) or your school, if any, to sign a "copyright disclaimer" for the program, if necessary. Here is a sample; alter the names:

Yoyodyne, Inc., hereby disclaims all copyright interest in the program

`Gnomovision' (which makes passes at compilers) written by James Hacker.

<signature of Ty Coon>, 1 April 1989

Ty Coon, President of Vice

This General Public License does not permit incorporating your program into proprietary programs. If your program is a subroutine library, you may consider it more useful to permit linking proprietary applications with the library. If this is what you want to do, use the GNU Library General Public License instead of this License.

C.2   Mozilla Public License

Version 1.1

1. Definitions.

1.0.1. "Commercial Use" means distribution or otherwise making the Covered Code available to a third party.

1.1. "Contributor" means each entity that creates or contributes to the creation of Modifications.

1.2. "Contributor Version" means the combination of the Original Code, prior Modifications used by a Contributor, and the Modifications made by that particular Contributor.

1.3. "Covered Code" means the Original Code or Modifications or the combination of the Original Code and Modifications, in each case including portions thereof.

1.4. "Electronic Distribution Mechanism" means a mechanism generally accepted in the software development community for the electronic transfer of data.

1.5. "Executable" means Covered Code in any form other than Source Code.

1.6. "Initial Developer" means the individual or entity identified as the Initial Developer in the Source Code notice required by **Exhibit A**.

1.7. "Larger Work" means a work which combines Covered Code or portions thereof with code not governed by the terms of this License.

1.8. "License" means this document.

1.8.1. "Licensable" means having the right to grant, to the maximum extent possible, whether at the time of the initial grant or subsequently acquired, any and all of the rights conveyed herein.

1.9. "Modifications" means any addition to or deletion from the substance or structure of either the Original Code or any previous Modifications. When Covered Code is released as a series of files, a Modification is:

A. Any addition to or deletion from the contents of a file containing Original Code or previous Modifications.

B. Any new file that contains any part of the Original Code or previous Modifications.

1.10. "Original Code" means Source Code of computer software code which is described in the Source Code notice required by **Exhibit A** as Original Code, and which, at the time of its release under this License is not already Covered Code governed by this License.

1.10.1. "Patent Claims" means any patent claim(s), now owned or hereafter acquired, including without limitation, method, process, and apparatus claims, in any patent Licensable by grantor.

1.11. "Source Code" means the preferred form of the Covered Code for making modifications to it, including all modules it contains, plus any associated interface definition files, scripts used to control compilation and installation of an Executable, or source code differential comparisons against either the Original Code or another well known, available Covered Code of the Contributor's choice. The Source Code can be in a compressed or archival form, provided the appropriate decompression or de-archiving software is widely available for no charge.

1.12. "You" (or "Your") means an individual or a legal entity exercising rights under, and complying with all of the terms of, this License or a future version of this License issued under Section 6.1. For legal entities, "You" includes any entity which controls, is controlled by, or is under common control with You. For purposes of this definition, "control" means (a) the power, direct or indirect, to cause the direction or management of such entity, whether by contract or otherwise, or (b) ownership of more than fifty percent (50%) of the outstanding shares or beneficial ownership of such entity.

2. Source Code License.

2.1. The Initial Developer Grant.
The Initial Developer hereby grants You a world-wide, royalty-free, non-exclusive license, subject to third party intellectual property claims:

(a) under intellectual property rights (other than patent or trademark) Licensable by Initial Developer to use, reproduce, modify, display, perform, sublicense and distribute the Original Code (or portions thereof) with or without Modifications, and/or as part of a Larger Work; and

(b) under Patents Claims infringed by the making, using or selling of Original Code, to make, have made, use, practice, sell, and offer for sale, and/or otherwise dispose of the Original Code (or portions thereof).

(c) the licenses granted in this Section 2.1(a) and (b) are effective on the date Initial Developer first distributes Original Code under the terms of this License.

(d) Notwithstanding Section 2.1(b) above, no patent license is granted: 1) for code that You delete from the Original Code; 2) separate from the Original Code; or 3) for infringements caused by: i) the modification of the Original Code or ii) the combination of the Original Code with other software or devices.

2.2. Contributor Grant.

Subject to third party intellectual property claims, each Contributor hereby grants You a world-wide, royalty-free, non-exclusive license

(a) under intellectual property rights (other than patent or trademark) Licensable by Contributor, to use, reproduce, modify, display, perform, sublicense and distribute the Modifications created by such Contributor (or portions thereof) either on an unmodified basis, with other Modifications, as Covered Code and/or as part of a Larger Work; and

(b) under Patent Claims infringed by the making, using, or selling of Modifications made by that Contributor either alone and/or in combination with its Contributor Version (or portions of such combination), to make, use, sell, offer for sale, have made, and/or otherwise dispose of: 1) Modifications made by that Contributor (or portions thereof); and 2) the combination of Modifications made by that Contributor with its Contributor Version (or portions of such combination).

(c) the licenses granted in Sections 2.2(a) and 2.2(b) are effective on the date Contributor first makes Commercial Use of the Covered Code.

(d) Notwithstanding Section 2.2(b) above, no patent license is granted: 1) for any code that Contributor has deleted from the Contributor Version; 2) separate from the Contributor Version; 3) for infringements caused by: i) third party modifications of Contributor Version or ii) the combination of Modifications made by that Contributor with other software (except as part of the Contributor Version) or other devices; or 4) under Patent Claims infringed by Covered Code in the absence of Modifications made by that Contributor.

3. Distribution Obligations.

3.1. Application of License.

The Modifications which You create or to which You contribute are governed by the terms of this License, including without limitation Section **2.2**. The Source Code version of Covered Code may be distributed only under the terms of this License or a future version of this License released under Section **6.1**, and You must include a copy of this License with every copy of the Source Code You distribute. You may not offer or impose any terms on any Source Code version that alters or restricts the applicable version of this License or the recipients' rights hereunder. However, You may include an additional document offering the additional rights described in Section **3.5**.

3.2. Availability of Source Code.

Any Modification which You create or to which You contribute must be made available in Source Code form under the terms of this License either on the same media as an Executable version or via an accepted Electronic Distribution Mechanism to anyone to whom you made an Executable version available; and if made available via Electronic Distribution Mechanism, must remain available for at least twelve (12) months after the date it initially became available, or at least six (6) months after a subsequent version of that particular Modification has been made available to such recipients. You are responsible for ensuring that the Source Code version remains available even if the Electronic Distribution Mechanism is maintained by a third party.

3.3. Description of Modifications.

You must cause all Covered Code to which You contribute to contain a file documenting the changes You made to create that Covered Code and the date of any change. You must include a prominent statement that the Modification is derived, directly or indirectly, from Original Code provided by the Initial Developer and including the name of the Initial Developer in (a) the Source Code, and (b) in any notice in an Executable version or related documentation in which You describe the origin or ownership of the Covered Code.

3.4. Intellectual Property Matters

(a) Third Party Claims.

If Contributor has knowledge that a license under a third party's intellectual property rights is required to exercise the rights granted by such Contributor under Sections 2.1 or 2.2, Contributor must include a text file with the Source Code distribution titled "LEGAL" which describes the claim and the party making the claim in sufficient detail that a recipient will know whom to contact. If Contributor obtains such knowledge after the Modification is made available as described in Section 3.2, Contributor shall promptly modify the LEGAL file in all copies Contributor makes available thereafter and shall take other steps (such as notifying appropriate mailing lists or newsgroups) reasonably calculated to inform those who received the Covered Code that new knowledge has been obtained.

(b) Contributor APIs.

If Contributor's Modifications include an application programming interface and Contributor has knowledge of patent licenses which are reasonably necessary to implement that API, Contributor must also include this information in the LEGAL file.

(c) Representations.

Contributor represents that, except as disclosed pursuant to Section 3.4(a) above, Contributor believes that Contributor's Modifications are Contributor's original creation(s) and/or Contributor has sufficient rights to grant the rights conveyed by this License.

3.5. Required Notices.

You must duplicate the notice in **Exhibit A** in each file of the Source Code. If it is not possible to put such notice in a particular Source Code file due to its structure, then You must include such notice in a location (such as a relevant directory) where a user would be likely to look for such a notice. If You created one or more Modification(s) You may add your name as a Contributor to the notice described in **Exhibit A**. You must also duplicate this License in any documentation for the Source Code where You describe recipients' rights or ownership rights relating to Covered Code. You may choose to offer, and to charge a fee for, warranty, support, indemnity or liability obligations to one or more recipients of Covered Code. However, You may do so only on Your own behalf, and not on behalf of the Initial Developer or any Contributor. You must make it absolutely clear than any such warranty, support, indemnity or liability obligation is offered by You alone, and You hereby agree to indemnify the Initial Developer and every Contributor for any liability incurred by the Initial Developer or such Contributor as a result of warranty, support, indemnity or liability terms You offer.

3.6. Distribution of Executable Versions.
You may distribute Covered Code in Executable form only if the requirements of Section **3.1-3.5** have been met for that Covered Code, and if You include a notice stating that the Source Code version of the Covered Code is available under the terms of this License, including a description of how and where You have fulfilled the obligations of Section **3.2**. The notice must be conspicuously included in any notice in an Executable version,

related documentation or collateral in which You describe recipients' rights relating to the Covered Code. You may distribute the Executable version of Covered Code or ownership rights under a license of Your choice, which may contain terms different from this License, provided that You are in compliance with the terms of this License and that the license for the Executable version does not attempt to limit or alter the recipient's rights in the Source Code version from the rights set forth in this License. If You distribute the Executable version under a different license You must make it absolutely clear that any terms which differ from this License are offered by You alone, not by the Initial Developer or any Contributor. You hereby agree to indemnify the Initial Developer and every Contributor for any liability incurred by the Initial Developer or such Contributor as a result of any such terms You offer.

3.7. Larger Works.
You may create a Larger Work by combining Covered Code with other code not governed by the terms of this License and distribute the Larger Work as a single product. In such a case, You must make sure the requirements of this License are fulfilled for the Covered Code.

4. Inability to Comply Due to Statute or Regulation.

If it is impossible for You to comply with any of the terms of this License with respect to some or all of the Covered Code due to statute, judicial order, or regulation then You must: (a) comply with the terms of this License to the maximum extent possible; and (b) describe the limitations and the code they affect. Such description must be included in the LEGAL file described in Section **3.4** and must be included with all distributions of the Source Code. Except to the extent prohibited by statute or regulation, such description must be sufficiently detailed for a recipient of ordinary skill to be able to understand it.

5. Application of this License.

This License applies to code to which the Initial Developer has attached the notice in **Exhibit A** and to related Covered Code.

6. Versions of the License.

6.1. New Versions.
Netscape Communications Corporation ("Netscape") may publish revised and/or new versions of the License from time to time. Each version will be given a distinguishing version number.

6.2. Effect of New Versions.
Once Covered Code has been published under a particular version of the

License, You may always continue to use it under the terms of that version. You may also choose to use such Covered Code under the terms of any subsequent version of the License published by Netscape. No one other than Netscape has the right to modify the terms applicable to Covered Code created under this License.

6.3. Derivative Works.

If You create or use a modified version of this License (which you may only do in order to apply it to code which is not already Covered Code governed by this License), You must (a) rename Your license so that the phrases "Mozilla", "MOZILLAPL", "MOZPL", "Netscape", "MPL", "NPL" or any confusingly similar phrase do not appear in your license (except to note that your license differs from this License) and (b) otherwise make it clear that Your version of the license contains terms which differ from the Mozilla Public License and Netscape Public License. (Filling in the name of the Initial Developer, Original Code or Contributor in the notice described in **Exhibit A** shall not of themselves be deemed to be modifications of this License.)

7. DISCLAIMER OF WARRANTY.

COVERED CODE IS PROVIDED UNDER THIS LICENSE ON AN "AS IS" BASIS, WITHOUT WARRANTY OF ANY KIND, EITHER EXPRESSED OR IMPLIED, INCLUDING, WITHOUT LIMITATION, WARRANTIES THAT THE COVERED CODE IS FREE OF DEFECTS, MERCHANTABLE, FIT FOR A PARTICULAR PURPOSE OR NON-INFRINGING. THE ENTIRE RISK AS TO THE QUALITY AND PERFORMANCE OF THE COVERED CODE IS WITH YOU. SHOULD ANY COVERED CODE PROVE DEFECTIVE IN ANY RESPECT, YOU (NOT THE INITIAL DEVELOPER OR ANY OTHER CONTRIBUTOR) ASSUME THE COST OF ANY NECESSARY SERVICING, REPAIR OR CORRECTION. THIS DISCLAIMER OF WARRANTY CONSTITUTES AN ESSENTIAL PART OF THIS LICENSE. NO USE OF ANY COVERED CODE IS AUTHORIZED HEREUNDER EXCEPT UNDER THIS DISCLAIMER.

8. TERMINATION.

8.1. This License and the rights granted hereunder will terminate automatically if You fail to comply with terms herein and fail to cure such breach within 30 days of becoming aware of the breach. All sublicenses to the Covered Code which are properly granted shall survive any termination of this License. Provisions which, by their nature, must remain in effect beyond the termination of this License shall survive.

8.2. If You initiate litigation by asserting a patent infringement claim (excluding declatory judgment actions) against Initial Developer or a Contributor (the Initial Developer or Contributor against whom You file such action is referred to as "Participant") alleging that:

(a) such Participant's Contributor Version directly or indirectly infringes any patent, then any and all rights granted by such Participant to You under Sections 2.1 and/or 2.2 of this License shall, upon 60 days notice from Participant terminate prospectively, unless if within 60 days after receipt of notice You either: (i) agree in writing to pay Participant a mutually agreeable reasonable royalty for Your past and future use of Modifications made by such Participant, or (ii) withdraw Your litigation claim with respect to the Contributor Version against such Participant. If within 60 days of notice, a reasonable royalty and payment arrangement are not mutually agreed upon in writing by the parties or the litigation claim is not withdrawn, the rights granted by Participant to You under Sections 2.1 and/or 2.2 automatically terminate at the expiration of the 60 day notice period specified above.

(b) any software, hardware, or device, other than such Participant's Contributor Version, directly or indirectly infringes any patent, then any rights granted to You by such Participant under Sections 2.1(b) and 2.2(b) are revoked effective as of the date You first made, used, sold, distributed, or had made, Modifications made by that Participant.

8.3. If You assert a patent infringement claim against Participant alleging that such Participant's Contributor Version directly or indirectly infringes any patent where such claim is resolved (such as by license or settlement) prior to the initiation of patent infringement litigation, then the reasonable value of the licenses granted by such Participant under Sections 2.1 or 2.2 shall be taken into account in determining the amount or value of any payment or license.

8.4. In the event of termination under Sections 8.1 or 8.2 above, all end user license agreements (excluding distributors and resellers) which have been validly granted by You or any distributor hereunder prior to termination shall survive termination.

9. LIMITATION OF LIABILITY.

UNDER NO CIRCUMSTANCES AND UNDER NO LEGAL THEORY, WHETHER TORT (INCLUDING NEGLIGENCE), CONTRACT, OR OTHERWISE, SHALL YOU, THE INITIAL DEVELOPER, ANY OTHER CONTRIBUTOR, OR ANY DISTRIBUTOR OF COVERED CODE, OR ANY SUPPLIER OF ANY OF SUCH

PARTIES, BE LIABLE TO ANY PERSON FOR ANY INDIRECT, SPE-CIAL, INCIDENTAL, OR CONSEQUENTIAL DAMAGES OF ANY CHARACTER INCLUDING, WITHOUT LIMITATION, DAMAGES FOR LOSS OF GOODWILL, WORK STOPPAGE, COMPUTER FAILURE OR MALFUNCTION, OR ANY AND ALL OTHER COM-MERCIAL DAMAGES OR LOSSES, EVEN IF SUCH PARTY SHALL HAVE BEEN INFORMED OF THE POSSIBILITY OF SUCH DAM-AGES. THIS LIMITATION OF LIABILITY SHALL NOT APPLY TO LIABILITY FOR DEATH OR PERSONAL INJURY RESULTING FROM SUCH PARTY'S NEGLIGENCE TO THE EXTENT APPLICA-BLE LAW PROHIBITS SUCH LIMITATION. SOME JURISDIC-TIONS DO NOT ALLOW THE EXCLUSION OR LIMITATION OF INCIDENTAL OR CONSEQUENTIAL DAMAGES, SO THIS EXCLUSION AND LIMITATION MAY NOT APPLY TO YOU.

10. U.S. GOVERNMENT END USERS.

The Covered Code is a "commercial item," as that term is defined in 48 C.F.R. 2.101 (Oct. 1995), consisting of "commercial computer software" and "commercial computer software documentation," as such terms are used in 48 C.F.R. 12.212 (Sept. 1995). Consistent with 48 C.F.R. 12.212 and 48 C.F.R. 227.7202-1 through 227.7202-4 (June 1995), all U.S. Government End Users acquire Covered Code with only those rights set forth herein.

11. MISCELLANEOUS.

This License represents the complete agreement concerning subject matter hereof. If any provision of this License is held to be unenforceable, such provision shall be reformed only to the extent necessary to make it enforceable. This License shall be governed by California law provisions (except to the extent applicable law, if any, provides otherwise), excluding its conflict-of-law provisions. With respect to disputes in which at least one party is a citizen of, or an entity chartered or registered to do business in the United States of America, any litigation relating to this License shall be subject to the jurisdiction of the Federal Courts of the Northern District of California, with venue lying in Santa Clara County, California, with the losing party responsible for costs, including without limitation, court costs and reasonable attorneys' fees and expenses. The application of the United Nations Convention on Contracts for the International Sale of Goods is expressly excluded. Any law or regulation which provides that the language of a contract shall be construed against the drafter shall not apply to this License.

12. RESPONSIBILITY FOR CLAIMS.

As between Initial Developer and the Contributors, each party is responsible for claims and damages arising, directly or indirectly, out of its utilization of rights under this License and You agree to work with Initial Developer and Contributors to distribute such responsibility on an equitable basis. Nothing herein is intended or shall be deemed to constitute any admission of liability.

13. MULTIPLE-LICENSED CODE.

Initial Developer may designate portions of the Covered Code as "Multiple-Licensed." "Multiple-Licensed" means that the Initial Developer permits you to utilize portions of the Covered Code under Your choice of the MPL or the alternative licenses, if any, specified by the Initial Developer in the file described in Exhibit A.

EXHIBIT A -Mozilla Public License.

``The contents of this file are subject to the Mozilla Public License Version 1.1 (the "License"); you may not use this file except in compliance with the License. You may obtain a copy of the License at
http://www.mozilla.org/MPL/

Software distributed under the License is distributed on an "AS IS" basis, WITHOUT WARRANTY OF
ANY KIND, either express or implied. See the License for the specific language governing rights and
limitations under the License.

The Original Code is _____.

The Initial Developer of the Original Code is _____.

Portions created by _____ are Copyright (C) _____
_____. All Rights Reserved.

Contributor(s): _____.

Alternatively, the contents of this file may be used under the terms of the _____ license (the "[___] License"), in which case the provisions of [_____] License are applicable instead of those above. If you wish to allow use of your version of this file only under the terms of the [____] License and not to allow others to use your version of this file under the MPL, indicate your decision by deleting the provisions above and replace them with the notice and other provisions required by the [___] License. If you do not delete the provisions above, a recipient may use your version of this file under either the MPL or the [___] License."

[NOTE: The text of this Exhibit A may differ slightly from the text of the notices in the Source Code files of the Original Code. You should use the text of this Exhibit A rather than the text found in the Original Code Source Code for Your Modifications.]

C.3   The BSD License

The following is a BSD license template. To generate your own license, change the values of OWNER, ORGANIZATION and YEAR from their original values as given here, and substitute your own.

<OWNER> = Regents of the University of California

<ORGANIZATION> = University of California, Berkeley

<YEAR> = 1998

License Template

Copyright (c) <YEAR>, <OWNER> All rights reserved.

Redistribution and use in source and binary forms, with or without modification, are permitted provided that the following conditions are met:

Redistributions of source code must retain the above copyright notice, this list of conditions and the following disclaimer.

Redistributions in binary form must reproduce the above copyright notice, this list of conditions and the following disclaimer in the documentation and/or other materials provided with the distribution.

Neither the name of the <ORGANIZATION> nor the names of its contributors may be used to endorse or promote products derived from this software without specific prior written permission.

THIS SOFTWARE IS PROVIDED BY THE COPYRIGHT HOLDERS AND CONTRIBUTORS "AS IS" AND ANY EXPRESS OR IMPLIED WARRANTIES, INCLUDING, BUT NOT LIMITED TO, THE IMPLIED WARRANTIES OF MERCHANTABILITY AND FITNESS FOR A PARTICULAR PURPOSE ARE DISCLAIMED. IN NO EVENT SHALL THE COPYRIGHT OWNER OR CONTRIBUTORS BE LIABLE FOR ANY DIRECT, INDIRECT, INCIDENTAL, SPECIAL, EXEMPLARY, OR CONSEQUENTIAL DAMAGES (INCLUDING, BUT NOT LIMITED TO, PROCUREMENT OF SUBSTITUTE GOODS OR SERVICES; LOSS OF USE, DATA, OR PROFITS; OR BUSINESS INTERRUPTION) HOWEVER CAUSED AND ON ANY THEORY OF LIABILITY, WHETHER IN CONTRACT, STRICT LIABILITY, OR TORT (INCLUDING NEGLIGENCE OR OTHERWISE) ARISING IN ANY WAY OUT OF THE USE OF THIS SOFTWARE, EVEN IF ADVISED OF THE POSSIBILITY OF SUCH DAMAGE.

Bibliography

I have occasionally heard complaints that open source software is not well documented, but that is not my experience. What I find is that there is an overwhelming amount of information available for the major software products. This information is available in several forms. This bibliography lists published hardcover books, but some software is extensively documented with online tutorials or HOWTOs which are freely available. The tutorials for MySQL and the GIMP, for example, or the German guide to open source migration are of excellent quality but not to my knowledge available as bound books. There are also many books from several publishers covering the major products, including Linux, Apache, and the development tools. In general, the web site of a product will refer to the available documentation. Some of these web sites are listed in this book; others can be found through a web search engine such as Google.

The books below were all used by me in the last year while planning or working on this book. The selection is pretty arbitrary, except that I selected them at the time as being the most current and having the best coverage, and found them useful and interesting. I've separated them into three categories; books on general issues, on system administration, and on software development including databases.

Software History and Philosophy, Business Principles, and Open Source

Title	Author	Publisher	Description
Open Sources	DiBona et al (ed)	O'Reilly	A collection of essays from the leaders of the open source movement (Stallman, Torvalds, Wall, Perens, etc.) at a critical time in its development.
From Airline Reservations to Sonic the Hedgehog	Martin Campbell-Kelly	MIT Press	A great book on software history with particularly good coverage of areas that get insufficient attention, including mainframe software and custom corporate development.
The Future of Ideas	Lawrence Lessig	Vintage Books	An essential book on the balance of rights that impact intellectual property and on the developing threats to that balance.
Linux and the Unix Philosophy	Mike Gancarz	Digital Press	This is an economically written introduction to the key points of the Unix philosophy of system development, which is important to understand. The book is a classic text that was recently updated for Linux.
The Business and Economics of Linux and Open Source	Martin Fink	Prentice Hall	A good management overview of open source issues by a manager who has been influential in its adoption. The book covers many general issues, but is particularly focused for managers at software and systems integration companies.
Loosely Coupled: The Missing Pieces of Web Services	Doug Kaye	RDS Press	A high-level view from a successful software business manager of how to achieve business integration using web services. It has an honest treatment of what works now and what is still to be developed.
Understanding Open Source Software Development	Feller & Fitzgerald	Addison-Wesley	An academic analysis of the impact of open source development methods on the software industry.

Software History and Philosophy, Business Principles, and Open Source (continued)

Title	Author	Publisher	Description
The Innovator's Dilemma	Clayton Christensen	HarperBusiness Essentials	The best-selling, highly influential book on disruptive technologies and their impact on established industries. The follow up, "The Innovator's Solution," develops the theory further.
Technological Revolutions and Financial Capital	Carlota Perez	Edward Elgar	A good analysis of how new technology is financed and sold, which provides useful analogies to use in analyzing software introduction.
Crossing the Chasm	Geoffrey Moore	HarperBusiness Essentials	The famous summary of principles for the successful marketing of high technology products beyond their initial niches.

System Administration

Title	Author	Publisher	Description
Fedora for Dummies	Jon "maddog" Hall	Wiley	A good starter book on Linux from a veteran industry evangelist. The book includes a full copy of Fedora Core Linux on DVD.
Moving to Linux	Marcel Gagne	Addison-Wesley	A simple book appropriate for end-users currently using Windows. The book is well-illustrated and includes a Knoppix live CD so the reader can evaluate Linux immediately..
Red Hat Linux and Fedora Unleashed	Ball & Duff	Sams	This immense manual is the latest in a series that has been released to cover every Red Hat version for years. It includes Fedora Core Linux on DVD
Unix System Administration Handbook, 2nd Edition	Nemeth et al	Prentice Hall	A long-established classic on Unix systems administration.

System Administration (continued)

Title	Author	Publisher	Description
Migration Guide: A guide to migrating the basic software components on server and workstation computers		KBSt Publication Service	This is an indispensable guide with great practical detail for anyone migrating to open source software from a Windows environment. This book comes out of the German government and Munich migration projects. It is well translated from German.
The Official SAMBA-3 HOWTO and Reference Guide	Terpstra and Vernooij (ed)	Prentice-Hall	An indispensable guide to interconnection with Samba. There are several books on this subject; this one has full coverage of Samba 3 and is written specifically for Windows administrators.
LDAP System Administration	Gerald Carter	O'Reilly	A practical manual on administration of LDAP. All examples refer to the OpenLDAP open source product.
Open Source Network Administration	Kretchmar	Prentice Hall	A "from the trenches" look at practical open source tools for network management. Kretchmar is a systems administrator at a large university.
Linux Security for Large-Scale Enterprise Networks	Becker	Digital Press	A book on the larger scale issues of Linux security.
Securing Linux	Koconis et al	SANS Press	A short book with practical scripts for securing Linux in detail.

Software Development

Title	Author	Publisher	Description
Microsoft Secrets	Cusumano & Selby	Simon & Schuster	There have been many books published on the theme of secrets at Microsoft. Despite the title, this book is the best reference on how development was done at Microsoft.
Dynamics of Software Development	Jim McCarthy	Addison-Wesley	This book has a powerful set of principles enriched by great stories on development from a successful manager of complex development tools including Visual C++.
JBOSS Administration and Development	Stark & Fleury	Sams	An overview of the JBOSS open source J2EE application server. Fleury is the product architect.
MySQL	Paul DuBois	Sams	A large, comprehensive book on MySQL, covering administration and development with examples in C, Perl, and PHP. The 2nd Edition covers MySQL 4.
Python Essential Reference	David Beazley	New Riders	In my view, this is the best reference book on Python.
PHP and MySQL Web Development	Welling & Thomson	Sams	A definitive book on PHP development by professional instructors.
PostgreSQL Developers Handbook	Geschwinde & Schonig	Sams	An extensive, comprehensive book with chapters on development from different languages.
Programming with GNU Software	Loukides & Oram	O'Reilly	Basic reference on using Emacs, the GNU C/C++ compiler, make, and revision control, which are the essential tools for maintaining most open source software.
The Wiki Way	Leuf & Cunningham	Addison-Wesley	Cunningham invented the Wiki idea. The book is illustrated with code examples in Perl and includes a CD-ROM with wiki software and Perl and Apache for Windows or Linux.

Software Development (continued)

Title	Author	Publisher	Description
Programming Web Services with XML-RPC	St Laurent, Johnston, & Dumbill	O'Reilly	Simple explanation of a key integration technology. The book contains examples in Java, ASP, PHP, Perl, and Python.

About the Author

I have been a corporate developer and consultant for over 20 years in London, New York, Chicago, and the southeastern United States. I started on IBM mainframes, was an early PC enthusiast, and had some Digital VAX experience, but I really fell in love with UNIX when I first saw networked Sun workstations. After that, I had a UNIX consulting business for several years. IBM was a major client, so the flavor of UNIX we used was mostly AIX. I had the opportunity to conduct training for thousands of IBM system engineers on TCP/IP and the Internet at a time when it was new to most of them. I was the subject matter consultant on a couple of books about AIX system administration.

In 1993, I wrote a book on the development strategies and methods of that time, generally called client/server computing. Research for that book convinced me that what was then called Windows NT was the best upcoming opportunity, so from 1994 to 2002, I worked for Microsoft on server adoption and enterprise consulting. This was mostly Microsoft Consulting, but included two years managing regional product sales for development tools and database. This included the introduction of SQL Server 7.0, which altered price/performance in the database market five years ago in rather the way open source database products are doing today. At one time I was a Microsoft Certified Systems Engineer, Solution Developer, and Trainer (MCP #22989), but most of my MCP qualifications have now expired.

In my last job with Microsoft as a .Net architect, my team was often called upon to debate with or otherwise compete with, and also to interoperate with, open source systems. In the course of those activities, I was surprised and impressed by the quality of the open source products, and I resolved to switch to them.

Since 2002, I have been developing and consulting on open source software, particularly migration from and interoperability with Microsoft

Windows systems. I have contributed to a couple of small open source projects, but I consider my role to be more a consultant than an open source developer.

I have done a lot of training, in technologies from OLTP to UNIX and TCP/IP to Microsoft .Net, and in how to build high-performance online systems, complex distributed software, and reliable server farms. Although the details differ, many of the important issues in developing systems are the same, and this book will emphasize those similarities as well as the differences.

Writing Environment

This book was developed, written, and tested from September 2003 to March 2004 using the following systems, which all share files and printers using Samba:

- ASUS dual-processor server running Red Hat Enterprise Linux 3.
- LinuxCertified notebook running SuSE Professional Linux 9.
- Dell Latitude L400 running Fedora Core 1. This old lightweight system has a 1,024 × 768 screen, which makes a good screenshot.
- Dell Inspiron 4100 running Windows 2003 Server for interoperability and cross-platform testing.
- Toshiba R100 notebook running SuSE Standard Server 8 under VMWare on Windows XP.
- Apple Powerbook G4 running Mac OS X 10.3 for interoperability and cross-platform testing.

All of the systems run MySQL, Apache, Python, PHP, and OpenOffice. Text was written with OpenOffice Writer, spreadsheets with OpenOffice Calc. Screenshots and other bit maps were edited with GIMP. Line art was done with Dia and Microsoft Visio.

Final files were assembled using a Mac platform (Apple PowerMac G4 dual-processor and PowerBook G4) and Adobe software (FrameMaker 7, Distiller, Acrobat, and PhotoShop). The final file for printing was delivered in PDF format.

Index